HINDUISM

The Anthropology of a Civilization

French Studies in South Asian Culture and Society

The aim of the series is to provide the English-speaking reader with a relevant selection of contemporary French works in the field of Human Sciences dealing with South Asia. It is widely recognized that French scholarship has produced distinctive theoretical perspectives which differ in many respects from the established Indian and Anglo-Saxon scholarly traditions. Significant studies ranging from Classical Indology to most social science disciplines are thus proposed for inclusion.

With this objective in view, the Maison des Sciences de l'Homme in collaboration with the Oxford University Press in India has sponsored the present series under the editorial direction of a joint committee of French and Indian scholars representing the major social science disciplines.

Editorial Committee

Jean-Claude Galey
Rajni Kothari
Triloki Nath Madan
Charles Malamoud
Jacques Pouchepadass
Romila Thapar

French Studies in South Asian Culture and Society III

HINDUISM

The Anthropology of a Civilization

MADELEINE BIARDEAU

Translated from the French
by
RICHARD NICE

DELHI
OXFORD UNIVERSITY PRESS
CALCUTTA CHENNAI MUMBAI

Oxford University Press, Great Clarendon Street, Oxford OX2 6DP

Oxford New York
Athens Auckland Bangkok Calcutta
Cape Town Chennai Dar es Salaam Delhi
Florence Hong Kong Istanbul Karachi
Kuala Lumpur Madrid Melbourne Mexico City
Mumbai Nairobi Paris Singapore
Taipei Tokyo Toronto

and associates in
Berlin Ibadan

Original edition © Flammarion, Paris, 1981
Published as L'Hindouisme: Anthropologie d'une Civilization
English edition © Oxford University Press, 1989
Oxford India Paperbacks 1994
Fifth impression 1997

The Publisher acknowledges with thanks the support given by the Maison des Sciences de I'Homme, Paris

ISBN 0 19 563389 X

Printed at Rekha Printers Pvt. Ltd., New Delhi 110 020
and published by Manzar Khan, Oxford University Press
YMCA Library Building, Jai Singh Road, New Delhi 110 001

Contents

Introduction

To aim to present a unified account of a culture and a history as vast as that of India, explicitly linking each part to a single totality, is no doubt a somewhat reckless undertaking. Would anyone dare to define a unit of the same kind within Western civilization, still less presume to embrace the whole of Western history in a single synthesis governed by a few simple norms that can be traced everywhere?

India is, however, a particularly favourable case for an undertaking of this sort. The texts and archaeological remains which it offers extend over a period of at least three millenia; and yet, in spite of a sizeable collection of inscriptions on stone or on copper plates, which have by no means all been studied or even published, this evidence scarcely enables us to reconstruct what one would call a history. It is true that we possess a few chronological references—partly hypothetical and still disputed—but these rare dates are not always particularly significant. In contrast to what has occurred with some other civilizations, we do not, for example, possess any ancient royal chronicle: even the *Rājataraṅgiṇī* of Kashmir (twelfth century) cannot be regarded as an exception, composed as it was in that eternal marchland, in contact with the 'Turks' and in an atmosphere in which Hindu norms were constantly flouted. The occasional Greek or Chinese visitors and later Muslim observers provide a few precious landmarks, but these too must be handled with care since they are based as much on hearsay as on direct information.

The paucity of strictly historical data might, on the contrary, serve as a challenge to scholars and exercise their sagacity; this it has indeed done, but on the basis of essentially a-historical material, since the enormous Sanskrit literature which extends through the ages up to the present day operates in the realm of the normative or the mythical or in their service.[1] The *Arthaśāstra*, a treatise on the art of royal governance that is almost unique in its own genre, is attributed to Kauṭilya, who is thought to have been a minister of the emperor Candragupta Maurya (fourth century BC). But who would be so bold as to date the text in that period? Estimates range between the fourth century BC and the fourth century AD. The famous Treatise on Love, the *Kāma Sūtra*, is equally ill-dated. As for that vast narrative and didactic summum, the epic of the *Mahābhārata*, it is thought to have been composed over a period of eight or ten centuries straddling the beginning of our era, but one would be hard put to find indisputable arguments to support this. Yet we know that the kings had their bards and their panegyrists, but these streams of eloquence have mostly come down to posterity only in mythic form, the person of the king being itself stereotyped or even reabsorbed into the divine model, as the *avatāra* of Viṣṇu. The other epic, the *Rāmāyaṇa*, more modest in scale, is not even classified by the Hindu tradition in the same literary genre as the *Mahābhārata*, although it too is a royal saga: it is a 'poem' and not a history; it was probably composed over a long period, and the arguments in favour of its being earlier than its literary twin are counterbalanced by evidence of later composition. Only when one comes to recent centuries do dates become more precise, attached to works by definite authors for which at least a relative chronology becomes possible.[2] But by then, the major mental and social frameworks of Hinduism had already been established. Buddhism had been expelled or absorbed, Jainism had withdrawn into itself to resist Hindu cultural pressure, and the tribes had been driven into the least habitable parts of the territory although they too were not allowed to ignore the powerful society which contained them on all sides.

Kingdoms great and small, longlasting or ephemeral, even empires, succeeded one another, but brahmanic India continued to adhere to its own norms; its thinkers and authors—all Brahmans—have given her a fundamentally timeless image, intended in their minds to live eternally, since she was the centre of the world, the measure of salvation, and spoke the language of the gods. That is indeed the main justification for an attempt at a systematic presentation. This endeavour consists in taking literally the desire of a whole society, as expressed by its scribes but also no doubt with a very broad consensus, to present itself as a well-ordered whole, as the realization of a socio-cosmic order which promises it eternity or an everlasting renewal. This amounts to saying that change, when it does appear, is only superficial and always refers back to a normative foundation, the one source from which spring the most transient phenomena. It is then a question of adopting this language as far as one can, of entering into this world view, forgetting one's own categories so as to discover those of the Other, accepting that its lines of cleavage are not ours, that its values are distributed in a way that for us is unexpected. Such a perspective in fact does no more than reconnect with the very modern and very Western preoccupations of the historians of 'mentalities'. There is simply a change of scale when dealing with India, because one cannot 'periodize' its history as one does for other areas, or divide it into territories as restricted as those of European countries. The documentation available does not lend itself to this either in quantity or, above all, in content, since it speaks of something other than 'history'. The psychological, the individual, the momentary collective movement escape us—or are they simply absent? A rigorous study of mentalities must in fact take care not to see these lacunae as something negative, as a limit on investigation. On the contrary, they have a heuristic value if they are regarded as indices of what the Hindu will or can say of himself. I do not deny that this is a risky undertaking: how can one be sure that the reduction of the fact to the norm does not conceal the intrusion of a historical contingency the data of which elude us? One cannot hope to make a system of Hindu culture as a whole, *without any remainder*. In particular, this would be to make light of the centuries of rationalizations which the Brahmans have accumulated in all good faith, deceiving themselves before catching us in their trap. More modestly, therefore, I shall endeavour to show the probability of an interpretation by examining it from several angles, not forgetting that the most solid pieces of evidence may themselves prove to be deceptive, that the insignificant anecdote takes on the air of a myth the better to charge itself with meaning. In short, I shall place a wager on meaningfulness, while remaining aware that meaninglessness also exists.

The twofold demand for an overall system and for a meaning immanent in each of its partial manifestations runs counter to an Indological tradition which has been firmly rooted in the West for decades and which has even caught on among contemporary Indian intellectuals. The vast sub-continent of India and its millenia of history do indeed at first sight give the impression of an irreducible diversity, an incoherent proliferation, even on the socio-religious plane where the inviolable norm ought to prevail: an innumerable pantheon, local caste systems, variations in marriage rules or diet, etc. The habit has developed of presenting Indian culture as a mosaic from which the unifying pattern seems to be excluded; some writers assert that one would be hard put to find a single belief valid over the whole Indian territory to provide cultural unity. What is offered here is, by contrast, a sketch of the main articulations of a single organization of the pantheon, whatever the multiplicity of divine names and cultural forms; of the central features of *a* caste system underlying the regional or local diversities; and of the principles which govern socio-religious relations. Unity is sought not so much in a synthesis whose harmony derives from the scholar's 'idea', but rather at a deeper level of the analysis of the data, on the basis of the explicit or implicit norms which every Hindu carries in his head.

But mosaic-style construction has been only one of the temptations of the Indologists, the one which has furnished so many manuals, especially catalogues and indexes which are of great value as exhaustive information. The most profound work, however, that of scrupulous philologists with well-kept files, has gone on according to quite different principles, in which specialists of classical antiquity would quickly recognize the skeletons in their own cupboards. Meticulous and extraordinarily erudite monographs have been published over the last century, and some of them are rightly still regarded as authoritative. Their central concern has been with Vedic literature, in which one might hope to get a grip on things *in statu nascendi*, or in their relationship to a more distant past, common to the Indo-European peoples who are fast becoming one of the myths of our century. It is in itself an enormous corpus in which the various states of the language betray an evident temporal thickness, even if relative dating remains problematic. The mosaic effect is then avoided by means of a distribution of supposedly incoherent facts along the course of a development in which history is seen at work, entirely reconstructed according to plausible lines of evolution whose logic is no doubt essentially that of the scholar's mind.

This staggering in time has also been assumed in order to account, firstly, for the break in continuity presented by the so-called revealed texts—the Veda as a whole—and the later tradition; then, even within classical or more recent Hinduism, temporal evolution seemed the only mental tool capable of bringing order to the proliferation of myths and the multiplicity of apparently irreconcilable versions, as well as the often contradictory diversity of the normative texts. Where cleavages were clearly visible, history came in to shed its own light on the problem. It would be pointless to deny that history had its reasons and that they are irrefutable: the 'Aryan' entry into India took place from the north-east, along the very route which was that of all the subsequent invasions. But the 'Aryan' tribes—nomadic and pastoral, as they used to be described—did not take possession of a land empty of men. Whatever the ethnic and cultural identity of the so-called Indus civilization (two to three millenia BC), it seems that largely Dravidian populations occupied the northern plain as well as the peninsula. So one can be sure that the invaders encountered organized societies, with their own beliefs and norms, in a word, their own culture; and since the 'Aryan' advance seems to have progressed towards the east and south, it is also safe to assume that the newcomers were able to conquer the previous occupants. We thus have here a clear principle which will serve to organize the fragmentary information given by the texts: if the Veda oppose noble, pure peoples to human groups whom they cast into outer darkness, this is no doubt because the victors had subjugated the vanquished. But if a god, a notion or a word appear in the texts at a given moment, this is, on the contrary, because the presence of the newly subordinated populations is making itself felt in the mental universe of the victors and symbiosis is producing effects that one would expect.

However, it is when one moves from the Vedic corpus to the enormous mass of archaeological and textual documents of Hinduism that this explanatory principle proves most effective. The break in level between the two sets of data is such, without it being possible to situate clearly a transitional phase or intermediate states, that the philologist-historian has no words strong enough to characterize this shift: intrusion, irruption, pressure from the base etc., at the origin of which some even go so far as to imagine a misfortune of the times, one—or several—crises. In short, the religion of devotion—*bhakti*—with the sudden promotion of the Vedic gods Viṣṇu and Śiva, sees the light of day because the vanquished have demanded their place in the sun, the silent ones of the Vedas have at last managed to make themselves heard. If the Goddess—of whom the Vedic texts provide only pale sketches—takes on such importance, it is because 'aboriginal', 'Dravidian' cults centred on her, force their way through and win for themselves a place in the most official Hinduism. But the old cleavages are still intact and serve to structure Hindu society: what is 'Aryan' is pure and is the norm, what is not is impure. A social hierarchy based on the sacred integrates the vanquished—the outsiders—at the bottom. Local folk beliefs are irreconcilably opposed to the pan-Indian beliefs advocated by the Brahmans, the cream of 'Aryan' civilization.

So is there a history, at least in very ancient times (second millenium BC) in which people speaking the Indo-European form of languages penetrate into India and, through their Brahmans, draw up the religious texts which will constitute the Veda? Maybe. But what if this seemingly historical structuring only existed in our minds; and perhaps even implicitly took its model from our most recent history? Between the assertion that ethnically and culturally different peoples must have learnt over the centuries to coexist, and the assertion that their cohabitation explains the present-day socio-religious structure of Hindu India, there is a gulf which cannot be crossed without examination. The point has already been made: the most ancient Tamil literature was already aware of Sanskrit literature, and its formal and linguistic properties do not suffice to reconstruct a Dravidian civilization which will therefore remain for us an unknown (as is the idea of *an* Indo-European civilization pre-existing all the realizations of it that can be identified in time and space).[3] Moreover, recent studies of the oral literatures have shown clearly that the history of their monuments cannot be reconstructed in terms of interpolations or successive layers.[4]

But the greatest problem that arises nowadays from the ambition of presenting an India in which the permanent has the upper hand over the changing lies in the progress made over the last few decades first by Western and then Indian archaeologists. Great hopes were built up on the excavations of pre-historic or proto-historic sites, some of which were known as early as the Vedas or in the epics and even today have the same names. For the Vedic period, the archaeologists are modest: there is a lack of remains, or of possibilities of carbon-14 dating. But even supposing we had a clear idea of the approximate dates of the Vedic corpus, no significant correlations have yet been found between the two orders of data. Animals, plants, or traces of human occupation of the soil are not sufficient to indicate the presence of populations who only left a religious corpus and whose cultural practices entailed no durable building.

It is true that the archaeologists attribute their meagre results to the excessively small number of sites catalogued and the difficulty of detecting relationships between excavations which are too sporadic. One may think, however, that there is a more fundamental difficulty, as would be shown by exploration of the epic sites. There is all the more reason to relate the search for a hypothetical Vedic archaeology to the excavations inspired by the epics, inasmuch as the two presumed states of culture must have partially overlapped in time, to judge from the texts alone. On the other hand, there is no reason to think that the material culture of the Vedic authors and the epic authors evolved significantly: iron, horses, cereals, etc. figure in both sets of texts. But what is currently yielded by an exploration of the sites? In the case of the *Rāmāyaṇa*, we have a seemingly firm starting-point, since the capitals of Ayodhyā and Mithilā, north-east of the Ganges valley, are still major centres of population. In the case of the *Mahābhārata*, Indian scholars have absolutely no qualms about identifying the present-day sites of Hāstinapura and Indraprastha (modern Delhi) with their epic counterparts. Kurukṣetra, the site of the great battle itself, is a place of pilgrimage; even so, Indians are bewildered by the present insignificance of the site. At Ayodhyā and Mithilā the existence of modern cities has greatly impeded progress in archaeological surveying of the areas. It is known that the land has been occupied for a very long time, but we are at a loss to say much more. As for the *Mahābhārata* capitals, the problems here are very similar to those which were faced by the first archaeologists at the site of Troy, archaeologists who had read Homer. A large number of strata, indicative of human occupation and distinguished by datable pottery sherds and tools or weapons, allow us to go far enough in India's proto-history to offer hope of yielding evidence about the period corresponding to the epic. But the fact has to be faced: no dwelling of any but the village type has ever been found at any level: no palaces, no cities, and certainly no battlefield. It would seem, then, that there is nothing to be gained by holding to the theory that the events related in the *Mahābhārata* are contemporary with such and such a pottery type found at a given level at Hāstinapura. There is no proof whatever to support such a correlation, and even if there were, it would tell us but little about the characters who figure in the epic.

But these are not the most difficult of our problems. The great Indian pre-historian, H. D. Sankalia, carefully sifted through the *Rāmāyaṇa* and then not only denounced the improbable and clearly imaginary scenes (our 'mirabilia') contained in it, but also condemned what he considered to be the ancient authors' ignorance of Indian geography. He therefore hypothesizes that behind a late, erroneous *Rāmāyaṇa* lies an original *Rāmāyaṇa*, characterized, in particular, by a coherent geography, i.e. one recognizable to a modern reader. For him, Lanka is not Sri Lanka, the sea is only a lake, and the bridge slung by the monkey Hanumān between dry land and the island merely a commonplace walkway built between the edge of the lake and an islet, by an aboriginal population represented, of course, by the monkeys. One of the main props of the demonstration and of the definite location of the *Ur-Rāmāyaṇa* is that *sāl* trees abound in the forests where the monkeys fight and that *sāl* only grow in a quite determinate region of India, in the northern part of the Deccan, a long way from Sri Lanka. As for the later narrators, they were simply talking about things they knew nothing about. The same argument could of course be applied to the *Mahābhārata*: the conventional descriptions take liberties with geography—one need only try to trace the course of the Sarasvatī river to understand this—and whereas the palmyra tree, *borassus flabellifer*, does not particularly flourish in the northern plains of India where the action is set, this tall, straight-trunked palm-tree is constantly evoked in varying contexts. Should one therefore construct an *Ur-Mahābhārata*, in which the scholar of today takes the place of yesterday's bard in order to rediscover the original bard?

It is no doubt more appropriate—and it is the position I have adopted in this book—to follow the hypothesis put forward some time ago by Georges Dumézil, if not with exactly the same terminology: whatever the advances of archaeological research in India, one will never find sufficient traces of the epic events or their cultural context, simply because these are mythical events without even the most elementary historical basis. Without a doubt, a certain relationship obtains between the imaginary and the real, but it is with archaeology in the strict sense of the word, with its buildings and its sculptural representations, that the greatest potential lies for delineating such a relationship. But by the time that any archaeological data appear for us to contribute to our analysis, the principal themes of the epics have already been fixed. One then has to reverse the perspective: when a *sāl* tree or a wine palm is mentioned, this is not necessarily because it is part of the everyday surroundings of the poet—quite certainly an educated man, a Brahman rather than a bard—but rather, perhaps, because it belongs to his mental landscape by virtue of the symbolic meaning or meanings that are attached to it. More generally, the regions referred to are not evoked for the sake of their real position on the map (*sic*), but on account of the positive or negative values with which they are charged. What is true of the epic is no doubt even more valid for even the most explicit Vedic texts, those which abound in the proper names of persons and places; if these had any historical foundation, we can be sure that it has long since been lost when the epic narratives re-use them to say something else. So whatever the specific history of these texts, one can argue that it is forever impossible to reconstitute it, and that in any case this is not the most important task. In one way or another, by a more or less distant reference and through endless re-interpretations (including, therefore, those of Indian archaeologists, historians or anthropologists), these texts live on in the Indian collective consciousness. What do they have to say? We seek safety in sense, in spite of the moments of apparent non-sense.

The epic and Vedic authors have moreover provided the means of access, if not to their system of problems—that would be an excessive ambition—then at least to a way of looking at things that is closer to their own. When they use the word *ārya*—from which we have coined 'Aryan'—what are they referring to? The answer is not simple, because there is no single answer, but the most fundamental texts are nonetheless very clear: to be ārya is first of all to behave in a particular way, governed by precise rules that are taught on the one hand by Revelation (the Vedas), and on the other by all the commentaries and the practice of those who have closely studied that Revelation and been guided by it—the tradition, therefore, conceived initially as an oral, lived tradition. By implication, to be ārya one has to be a member of the three higher 'classes' who are duty-bound to study the Vedas and to use the services of a Brahman master or priest. In the epic, the epithet is most often applied to the warrior prince, since he is the central figure. But it cannot be exclusive, for the warrior prince could not be ārya if he did not live in the company of learned and pious Brahmans, or if he were not surrounded by subjects who supply him with the wealth he needs in livestock, cereals and precious metals. We shall see that one has to go further.

But the term ārya also has a possible geographical connotation, although this is less firmly fixed and ultimately non-essential. The maximum extent of ārya country is that given to it by the *Laws of Manu*, i.e. the whole of the Indus-Ganges plain from one ocean to the other between the Himālayas and the Vindhya mountains which mark the northern limit of the Deccan plateau. But, within this zone, there are distinctions to be made which imply a hierarchy of the ārya themselves; it is well known that the requirements of purity and of ritual practices are such that the various degrees of shortcoming also determine degrees of 'āryan-ness'. Women's morals are an important element in this evaluation: they must be faithful and chaste. The most āryan of lands would thus be the area encompassed by the Ganges and the Yamunā. It is so difficult to be ārya that it gives a fragile status that is easier to lose than to regain. Although birth guarantees, in principle, the possibility of brahmanic or *Kṣatriya* or *vaiśya* status, it is not sufficient to preserve it. Hence the interest of this shifting notion of ārya, which designates not so much a given human group as a life style which is essential to it and which requires a certain natural environment; in particular, one has to be able to offer sacrifices, and the region in which sacrifices are offered is the land 'where the black antelope roams free'—apparently the dry northern plains. The black antelope is indeed linked symbolically to sacrifice, as certain myths and ritual practices indicate, although it is not possible to explain this in any definite way. The symbolic aspects are too striking for one to be satisfied with a purely ecological origin.

Opposed to the ārya are all those who are not ārya: first, the *śūdras*, the 'class' which groups together the servant castes, in particular the crafts, and then the *dāsas* who would later become the 'household slaves', but who, in the Vedic texts, are no doubt first and foremost the non-āryas, the barbarians, those who have no place in the brahmanic religion, the enemies. However, since wars are waged among āryas as well as between āryas and dāsas, we cannot place āryas and dāsas in opposition to one another as enemies pure and simple; nor can we simply refer to the latter as potential victims of battle. The *Mahābhārata* multiplies peoples in all directions of space, and at the same time the notion of ārya is diluted in an infinite gradation: the clearly non-ārya peoples leave between themselves and the āryas a host of peoples of uncertain status, which the lists classify sometimes on one side and sometimes on the other. Thus we learn that, setting aside the inhabitants of the northern plain, who are distinctly valorized, there is scant respect for those who live in the mountains—hunters—or those who live near the sea or in marshy regions, and those who come from the south. In the hierarchy of peoples (tribes? kingdoms?—we do not know what social realities all these names refer to) there is a centre, an ill-defined periphery, and then the outer darkness. But perhaps the most important thing is that the epic recounts a war between ārya enemy-brothers who fight each other for sovereignty over the earth. Incarnated in one camp are demons, enemies of the gods, in the other, gods; and victory must go to the gods' camp in order for the socio-cosmic order to be upheld. But each camp contains a fine mixture of ārya and non-ārya and every possible intermediate status. The camp of the gods includes many kings from south India, and the camp of the demons has as its war-lords some very pure āryas (who are also gods), one of whom, on his death-bed, even instructs the king of the camp of the gods in the duties of the ārya king. In a fine speech, a demon incarnate who secretly supports the camp of the gods (which includes his sister's sons) explains that everywhere there are āryas and non-āryas and that there is no territory or kingdom which bears the stamp of pure Aryan-ness.

The picture painted by the *Mahābhārata* is, of course, in no way historical. It is not easy to locate most of the peoples mentioned, including those who seem to have entered recorded history. But there is perhaps a deeper truth, not least in this extreme political fragmentation, since each 'people' is provided with a 'king', with the infinite gradation of statuses which has always characterized the real India. Moreover, even when one is classified as inferior or superior, one may be led to collaborate, each in his own place, in the overall destiny of the earth; and this is true of either camp. This is an invitation to re-read the *Rāmāyaṇa*. Although the location of the kingdom here is distinctly shifted towards the east of the Ganges plain (a fact which some have seen as a sign that the Indo-European invasions had continued their eastward advance), one could nonetheless carry out a fairly similar analysis. Rāma, the pure king exiled from his kingdom by a step-mother, has to fight to win back his wife Sītā (i.e. the Earth over which he reigns) against a king of the cannibal demons called *rāksasas*, whose capital is in Lanka on the top of a mountain. The same criteria come into play, and Rāvaṇa, the king of the demons, is clearly placed at a level inferior to Rāma's, but modern Indian scholars are mistaken in seeing Rāvaṇa as representing low-status tribes, since he has Brahman status and is therefore ārya, but an ārya who must be defeated because he wants to destroy the socio-cosmic order. The same argument applies to the monkeys who provide the bulk of Rāma's armies against him: how can they be seen as aboriginal tribes (the very notion is a modern one) when the gods Sūrya, Indra, king of the gods, and Vāyu, are incarnate among them?

Thus the dichotomy which, in each epic, opposes one party to another, when it is a question of ensuring the triumph of 'good' over 'evil' (quotation marks are called for when the notions are so different from our own), is at the same time a total refusal of an Iranian or Manichean type of dualism. In each party, the pure and the impure coexist, and the aim of the struggle is to bring about the triumph of an order which is objectively definable in ethico-religious terms in which everyone has his place. It is here that one is sure of finding something of the Hindu mental universe: there is no notion of specifically ethnic oppositions, and in particular none that can be based on the dichotomy Aryan-Dravidian. The Drāviḍas figure in the epic as one people among others, associated with the south, but nothing distinguishes them apart from this original fault.

Moreover, the Śūdras, who are not ārya, form the fourth 'class'—*varṇa*—of brahmanic society, which would not be complete, or even viable, without them. Has the question ever been asked as to what a society based on very exacting norms of ritual purity would be like if a part of itself were not devoted to the reputedly impure tasks, thus enabling the others to remain pure? No normative Indian text tries to base the inferiority of the Śūdras on any foreign origin, a defeat of ancient times recorded in legendary history. It is above all a matter of status, for all eternity. High-born children are Śūdra until they have received the complete sequence of sacramental rites. For women, it is marriage that enables them to cease to be regarded as Śūdra, whatever the rank of their family of origin. As for the lowest, most impure castes—those whom Europeans have named 'untouchables' (it is not an Indian term)—they are usually said to derive from forbidden unions between castes, particularly marriages in which the wife's status is higher than the husband's.

Beneath the surface dichotomy, the epic offers a vision of an extremely cohesive society, despite the apparent looseness of its political organization. One is all the more inclined to take seriously this classical image since one still finds it today when one observes what remains of traditional India. In each kingdom of the land of India, however small its surface, the king appears as the centre around which everything revolves. The king himself, moreover, is nothing more than the representative, the counterpart, the earthly incarnation of the god who rules his territory and whose temple is also the centre of the world. The fact that the palace and the temple constitute two faces of the same centre serves to remind us that the king, taken in isolation, is nothing. But his people would be incapable of structuring themselves other than around this dual centre, theoretically occupied by the Kṣatriya king and the Brahman priests. Social organization is governed by stable principles, and the separation of the pure and the impure is chiefly visible at the two extremes of the social ladder, leaving in the centre a vaguer region in which precedence is more contested. But the opposition high:low, pure:impure, which is essential to this hierarchical vision of society, has to be conceived above all as a close complementarity, even when it implies separations in space. To put it yet another way, in each territorial 'unit'—which can be as small as a village with its chief—one finds, theoretically at least, the totality of the Hindu socio-religious structure and its values. Each person knows the other and where he belongs: the patron and his clientele, the king and his subjects, the household priest and the families he serves, are bound together in a 'face-to-face' relationship which in our eyes would seem to rule out awareness of the extreme distance between the high and the low. Whatever the quarrels, and the more or less endemic factions, each person knows he is caught in a complex of vertical and horizontal relationships, more or less distant but nowhere really interrupted. As for the king, he is responsible for order in his kingdom, and through this for the whole socio-cosmic order, for solidarity does not end on earth but encompasses the three worlds of the gods, men and demons. This does not prevent him from organizing his defence either on his frontiers or through diplomacy. Ideally, and according to the very image that the *Mahābhārata* gives of him, the perfect king is he who must reign over the whole world by subordinating the other kings in a subtle pyramid in which economic and military power vies with status. It is also this image that is put forward by the great rituals of royal consecration and horse sacrifice. The totality, thus experienced and understood, is what has to be explained.

That is why we must eschew the historical overview; that is, any approach that would attempt to hypothetically reconstruct historical pedigrees—first on a Hindu, then on a Vedic level—as a means to re-establishing a linear continuity that is visibly lacking. Rather than concerning ourselves with their dating or origins, we prefer to recover these elements such as they were organized and hierarchized according to that value system which exists within the broader context of the atemporal vision that the Hindu has of his universe. If he mentions the Vedas—of which he generally knows nothing, and whose ultimate authority his particular group may well deny—it is not as a corpus of very ancient texts, but above all as a universal reference. Venerable age is, as it were, derived from the inviolability of the norm rather than the other way round. Therefore we will approach Vedic Revelation through the eyes of Hindus, taking care to avoid the misconception that all Hindus have the same monolithic view of it. But it is around the Revelation that we shall see taking shape a Hinduism which draws from it different readings and, within certain limits, readings that shift in the course of the centuries. The term 'Hinduism'—which is, of course, of

Persian and not Indian origin—is a convenient label to designate this set of readings *and* their structural organization. Orthodox Brahmanism, which is closer to the Revelation, is not the ancestor of modern Hinduism; it is its permanent heart, the implicit model for or/and against which *bhakti*, tantrism and all their sects have been constituted. It has moreover persisted to the present day, changing as little as possible to respond to the needs of the hour, living in castes of Brahmans of whom it is the *raison d'être*. It is not so much the evolution of Hinduism over the centuries as the very recent impact of western values that has caused it to lose its implicit normative function. So, without denying change over the centuries, one is nonetheless sent back to the complex, stable system of values, beliefs and practices that still underlines the surface variations and which alone makes them comprehensible.

The calculated risk taken in this method of presentation entitles me to an additional audacity—which might also help to prove its validity. In the last few years I have become convinced that what now remains of traditional India, and is observed by ethnologists and social anthropologists, is greatly clarified by reference to what I shall call the classical tradition, and that it is absolutely essential to move beyond the epistemological duality which, up to now, has opposed 'armchair' Indologists to 'field-workers'. Conversely, when the most venerable and most abstract texts start to come to life in conversation with learned Brahmans capable of commenting on them, one realizes that they literally take on flesh and blood when juxtaposed with contemporary observation. And so I shall not hesitate to telescope the centuries and to move from a text to a concrete experience of India whenever the same principle of understanding seems to be involved. The very accumulation of such connections is what will make the validity of the procedure increasingly probable.

CHAPTER 1

Man and the Absolute

When I was at school, one of my teachers once pointed out to us the breadth and depth that a line of French poetry took on as soon as it contained the word 'God' ('Dieu'). Whatever its etymological origins or its use in Greek and Latin for beings of lesser value, the name 'God' retains for us the absolute transcendence and holiness of the Biblical Yahweh. It can only be a proper noun, a name, because in our civilization it is unambiguously applied to the Absolute, who can only be unique. The attempts occasionally made to flaunt unbelief by writing 'God' without a capital letter—and without an article!—seem somewhat ridiculous. Even if believers have historically compromised themselves in many ways, the consequences fall on themselves and more especially on the Church which represents God on earth but is not God, and perhaps also on belief in the existence of God; but the name of the Absolute remains intact.

The situation is much less simple in India. One reason for this is that there have been not one but at least two terms to designate the Absolute, neither term being superior to the other. Secondly, and more importantly, these two terms, which originated within Indian culture, retain connotations and uses which inform us about the men who adopted them as names for the Absolute. We therefore have two reasons, rather than one, for taking the Absolute as our starting point when we consider Indian thought. As we know, this Absolute has, to a certain degree, captured the imagination of the West, and this with the approval of the Hindus; on the other hand, this Absolute is integrally connected, by the very terms used to describe it, to the society which upholds it. In particular, we shall see its relationship with the Brahmans, and therefore with a whole social structure, a relationship which is part of its very definition and cannot be ignored. To speak in such terms implies, of course, that for the moment, we shall set aside the very real concerns of the Hindu theologians who, as much as our own, have sought to express the ineffable and the non-relational in terms intelligible to man.

The Absolute and the Brahmans

The name of the Hindu Absolute that is best-known in the West is *Brahman*. *Brahman* (neuter substantive) is pure Being, pure Consciousness, the Unlimited, or, according to another triad, pure Being, pure Consciousness and Beatitude. This teaching is found in the earliest *Upaniṣads* (*c.* seventh century BC?). Rather than gloss these characteristics of *Brahman*, which have nothing disconcerting or even really new about them for us at first sight (if only because all translation is betrayal, presuming on equivalences that cannot be made), let us immediately turn to the 'human' correlate of the Absolute, *ātman* (literally, 'self'), i.e. the immortal principle which, in man, is destined to be released from the body, from all embodiment, and at last attains perfect identity with *Brahman*. This ātman is altogether human inasmuch as it must first dwell in a human body in order for liberation to be possible. But if, instead of fusing with the *Brahman*, it condemns itself by its deeds to be reborn in the body of an animal, lower down the ladder of Being, the ātman is no way changed, so that in this sense it is not specifically human. When, after having again dwelt in a human body and performed the necessary deeds, it is granted liberation, this ātman will, like the *Brahman* it always was, be pure Being, pure Consciousness, Beatitude. What will have changed in the meantime is not its ātman 'nature' but the relationships it maintained with the lower world through its actions—*karman*. People often speak of Hindu pantheism, because of this identification of ātman and *Brahman* in liberation; but there could not be a more total misunderstanding. Countless texts, revealed or not, warn against this interpretation. The most beautiful formulation, because it is the most dense, is the following: '*Brahman* is all, but all is not *Brahman*' (Maṇḍana Miśra, *Brahmasiddhi*, seventh century?). A misreading of this passage serves to reveal, in itself, a certain manner by which units of meaning may be delineated with but little concern for their real context. If, for example, we contrast the liberation of the ātman (*mokṣa*) with its transmigration from rebirth to rebirth (*saṃsāra*), it is self-evident that all cannot be *Brahman*, and that 'communion' with the universe, through some vaguely religious or aesthetic contemplation, is out of the question. The break which marks the passage to a liberated state ought to imply a radical change of perspective with regard to this world. So it is that only a consciousness that primordially differentiates itself from the world (from human society? from nature?) is capable of conceptualizing liberation in pantheistic terms, as a communion with the All. One who is liberated is indeed reunited with the All since *Brahman* is the All; but this All cannot be the object of a unanimist or aesthetic perception.

We have by no means fully explored all that the name *Brahman* can give us by way of knowledge of the Absolute. Its etymological meaning is of little consequence for our purposes. Nor is it of great relevance whether it has changed its meaning in the course of a historical evolution (which in any case we cannot reconstruct) or whether one meaning immediately called forth the complementary meaning. But the fact is that the same name has been applied over the centuries to two opposing and complementary orders of reality, as if there were two faces or two levels of the Absolute, a fact which is not without significance for the very conception of the Absolute and of what is not the Absolute (since 'all is not *Brahman*').

According to Indian tradition, the *Upaniṣads*, which speak of the *Brahman* as Absolute and which present themselves as the culmination of the Veda—*vedānta*—are the continuation of a group of texts: the *Saṃhitās*, or collections of hymns, and the *Brāhmaṇas*, ritual texts in prose, which describe the major Vedic sacrifices often in obscure terms and with heavy reliance on myth as an explanatory apparatus. These texts are undoubtedly very ancient but, to judge from their content, it would be very difficult, though perhaps not philologically impossible, to establish an indisputable order of succession among them. The most fertile approach, in any case, if one wants to understand what they represent for the Hindu consciousness, is to take them in the order in which they are traditionally given and recited for reasons which probably owe little to history. For, arranged in the order, *Saṃhitās-Brāhmaṇas-Upaniṣads* (together with a fourth group of texts which is inserted between the *Brāhmaṇas* and the *Upaniṣads* and to which we shall turn in a moment, the *Āraṇyakas*), they constitute the brahmanic Revelation, *Veda* in the widest sense (literally, 'knowledge') or *Śruti* (literally, 'hearing'), in other words the set of absolutely inviolable, irrefutable texts to which Brahmanism, and Hinduism in general, make reference. These texts, which are very difficult to understand for most Hindus and even for the majority of Brahmans now as in the past, were composed in very specialized Brahman circles, devoted both to sacerdotal practice and to theological reflexion around Vedic sacrifice. The data they provide, which are regarded as timeless (and even, in some schools of thought, as self-revealed), have been amplified and reworked by a mass of other texts of lesser authority, which constitute the tradition—*smṛti*. For the moment we shall only deal with what may help us to understand how the Revelation is organized: rules concerning the solemn brahmanic rites (those mentioned in the Śruti), domestic ritual, and the codes of socio-religious laws which complete the edifice of the ideal brahmanic society and its religion.

The revealed texts which deal with so-called 'brahmanic' ritual use the term *brahman* to designate several things. In the neuter, *brahman* can be the name of the ritual formula; in the masculine it is the name of one of the priests of the solemn Vedic sacrifice, who has a quite distinct place in the group of priests required by the sacrifice since he says nothing, handles nothing, does nothing, but bears within him perfect knowledge of the rite, sacrificial science, and silently oversees the co-ordinated unfolding of an extremely complex sequence of rites and recitations. Thus it is not surprising that *Brahman* (neuter) should also mean the totality of Vedic knowledge, a notion which may be understood in several ways: knowledge of the revealed texts, so that they can be recited by rote—this is one of the daily obligations of the orthodox Brahman, known significantly as *brahmayajña*, 'sacrifice to brahman'—or knowledge of the content of these texts, of the duties they impose and the rituals they describe. *Brahman* is ultimately synonymous with *Veda* in the Tradition, or with that which, in some circumstances, symbolizes the whole *Veda*, namely the syllable *Oṃ* which opens and closes every recitation of a Vedic text.

The term *brāhmaṇa*, which we have already encountered (in the neuter form) as the name of the revealed texts of ritual, is a derivative of *Brahman*. It also provides (in the masculine form) the Sanskrit name of the sacerdotal 'class', that of the 'Brahmans' (as they are known in English). The same revealed texts and their extensions in the Tradition indicate to us the place of these Brahmans in society: priests and scholars by right of birth (if not always in reality), they are at the top of the social hierarchy. In second place come the Kṣatriyas, who are both princes and warriors, followed by the Vaiśyas, farmers or merchants; finally, the Śūdras are defined as the servants of the other three 'classes', to whom they owe obedience; but they are not the lowest in the hierarchy since new groups have constantly been added to this structure from below to form what are known collectively as the 'untouchables'. Here, in our discussion of this grouping, we avoid using the term 'caste' because we are in fact talking about categories that differ from the real castes—called *jātis*—which are far more numerous and geographically much more diversified. The hierarchy of the jātis is nevertheless structured, for better or for worse, in accordance with the system of the four 'classes'—which are called *varṇas* (literally 'colours', since each class has its symbolic colour). The varṇas, which constitute ideally the totality of society, are each defined, simultaneously and indissolubly, by their function in society and their relation to Vedic ritual. The Śūdras are thus set completely apart since they are excluded from this ritual and in this respect they are opposed to all other varṇas. The Kṣatriyas and the Vaiśyas, on the other hand, are within orthodox society, inasmuch as they may have the Vedic rites performed on their behalf by Brahmans and may receive from them teaching of the Vedic texts which they must theoretically recite. Thus there is an opposition between the Brahmans and the two other varṇas of orthodox society, since only the Brahmans possess theoretical and practical Vedic knowledge, in other words, *Brahman*.

But it is quite clear that the most interesting opposition, the one on which brahmanic authors have endlessly speculated, is between the Brahmans and the Kṣatriyas. As early as the *Brāhmaṇas*, the Kṣatriya is the 'offerer of sacrifice' *par excellence*, the holder of a temporal power, however modest, who cannot hope to ensure the prosperity of his territory and the success of his arms without the services of the Brahman (the performer of sacrifice), who carries out the appropriate rites for him and advises him on important decisions. Conversely, the Brahman depends more or less completely on the prince for his maintenance—the priestly labourer is worthy of his hire—and his living conditions. He cannot fulfil all his duties as a Brahman unless he lives under the reign of a good prince who pays well for his services, and every good prince needs a good Brahman. Thus there is perfect reciprocity. The function of the Kṣatriya—*kṣatra*—includes in its definition the religious duties of the prince, his functions as an 'offerer of sacrifice', which do not entitle him to perform the rites himself, but oblige him to have recourse to the Brahman. So the term 'temporal power' is only a very approximate translation of this function. On the other hand, the Brahman's function, his 'power', so to speak, is *Brahman*. This is a new and final use of the term, which implies an extension of its meaning: the order which maintains the society thus structured and enables it to function is *dharma*. The Brahman is not only responsible for Vedic science, in the narrow, sacerdotal meaning of the term; through his teaching and his advice he is also responsible for the social order of dharma which he has worked out in the Tradition. That is why a king has not only a Brahman chaplain but also a Brahman minister. Only a Brahman is competent to know the religious (and other) norms of men's conduct, not least those of the prince: the texts of the Tradition are all the work of Brahmans, and the brahmanic ideal society is the idea of it that is imposed by the Brahmans.

But do they really impose it? Or is it again we who see things that way? They have neither weapons nor power of any sort, other than the power they derive from their science of values. And there is no more a 'Brahman nature' that might account for their privilege, than there is a humanity of ātman. According to the most orthodox view, one is a Brahman because one is born of Brahman parents, not by virtue of any particular intrinsic excellence. Perhaps this will serve to temper our righteous indignation: the social hierarchy is defined by an order entirely extrinsic to its members. The Brahman is not superior by nature, only by position. He may of course fall from his caste by acting contrary to his duties, but that will make him an 'outcaste', not a Kṣatriya or a Śūdra. Conversely, one cannot be born a Śūdra and aspire to wear the brahmanic 'sacred thread', although it is not unknown for a caste *as a whole* to rise in the hierarchy; but, in any case, an individual cannot but belong to his social group, otherwise his state is the most wretched there can be, reduced as he is to himself and his immediate family.

It is not very difficult to guess that the Brahmans are primarily responsible for the name of the Absolute which recalls the name of their specific domain: *Brahman*. Identity of name in such a highly structured social context raises the question of the shift from one register to the other. It is tempting to imagine that the Brahmans simply projected into the Absolute that which was seen by everyone, and *a fortiori* by themselves, as the supreme value of their society. And there is clearly an element of truth in this: the Absolute *Brahman* is 'impersonal', which, it should be noted, is a purely negative and entirely Western way of characterizing this grammatically neutral Absolute. In more positive terms, this means that the collective function of the Brahmans, their knowledge (which itself means 'Veda') of the *Veda*, was projected onto the Absolute. Whatever the case, this was a neutral principle, rather than some divine character that might have been clothed in brahmanic dignity.[1] This is a new opportunity to observe that it is not any particular Brahman who is important, but the function he inherits from his parents and which he cannot sidestep, lest he be nothing at all.

But we should distrust what seems self-evident to us: it is not so obvious what led the Brahmans to project their *Brahman* into the Absolute if we judge by what actually happened. At a moment that is difficult to situate historically and geographically, alongside the ritualistic and social religion based on the first part of the Revelation, there appeared an antithetical religious form, which all the evidence indicates was formed in the same high-caste circles in which Brahmans and Kṣatriyas competed in virtue and knowledge. Whereas the Brahman or the Kṣatriya who lives in his society—in his village or citadel—has existence and essence only through his social function, there are henceforward (and perhaps they appeared at the same time as the social structure was taking shape—Buddhism already presupposes them), men whom the social values do not satisfy and who seek more permanent and truly supreme values elsewhere. Elsewhere, in other words means, outside society as it has been constituted and the function performed within it. It means outside the bounds of village or town, in the forest which represents the terrifying and the unorganized; a permanent threat to social life; but with also unlimited possibilities of restoration. It also means solitude, as opposed to life in a group; non-action towards social duties; non-desire in relation to the multiple appetencies of social man; the resorption of man (who is only social) in pre- or post-human, infra- or supra-social undifferentiatedness. This undifferentiated Absolute would be given the name *Brahman*.

The search for the Absolute outside of the social group—which, at a distance, somewhat resembles the flight into the desert by the early Christian anchorites—is bound up with a whole philosophy which itself cannot be understood without reference to the conceptions of the society from which it breaks away. This society—of which we shall later see the very human complexity—has a sacral view of itself. Its goals are terrestrial, but its means of action, at whatever level, always have a religious or magico-religious aspect. There is always a rite—essentially a sacrifice, a vegetable or animal offering to a deity—for each goal that is aimed at, including the goal which preoccupies every man, the life hereafter. Each rite has its specific effect and—by a disquieting corollary which opens the way for reflection and questioning—the effect, like the rite, is necessarily limited. The ritualistic texts of the Vedic revelation give little information about the heaven which the rites will ensure after death, or about the length of the sojourn in heaven. They mysteriously threaten with 're-death' those who fail to perform the rites satisfactorily. The ascetics who renounce the world push such a conception to its ultimate implications: man, always driven by some desire, acts in order to realize it. Action—karman—and especially ritual action—also karman—always leads to a result, and it is the link between action and its 'fruit' which makes the stuff of an individual life. This is true of all actions, including those intended to ensure access to heaven after death (backed up by the ancestor worship subsequently offered by the living descendants) and those which seem to produce no result in this life. Thus action, and especially ritual action, condemns man (and the other living beings) to endless rebirth and redeath. The only way to escape from this perpetual flux—*saṃsāra*—is to remove oneself from the mechanism of karman, and therefore from human society, by an explicit renunciation of all that one has been up to that time. It is by this renunciation, this radical break with what constitutes him as a man, that the religious ascetic secures liberation—*mokṣa*. The non-being who is individual man in society merely divests his birth and death of all significance, to the extent of condemning them to endless repetition. At the moment when a man separates himself from his group—an individual act if ever there was—he does so not in order to recognize his individuality but in order to abolish it, to free his ātman of any individualized feature and merge it with *Brahman.*

It is immediately clear that it is far too simplistic to see renunciation of the world—*sannyāsa*—the Hindu form of the pursuit of the Absolute, as responsible for the supposed inability of Indians to adapt to modern economic imperatives. Let us leave to others the satisfaction of contrasting Hindu spiritualism with Western materialism, since it would be equally valid to reverse the elements of the problem: the specifically Hindu form of break with the world and the conceptions on which it is based are governed by the specifically Hindu way of being in the world. Logically, therefore, one would rather have to seek the source of the resistance to modernity in the ideology underlying the social organization, which is merely to pose the question in a different form without in any way simplifying it. But the links which, by virtue of their very opposition, exist between the two registers of *Brahman* do mean that each helps to cast light on the other.

But we must complicate the picture still further by introducing a second name of the Absolute, similarly fraught with social resonances. Among the accounts of the origin of the world provided by the Vedic texts, undoubtedly the one which was to have the greatest destiny was the 'Hymn to the Puruṣa' (*Rgveda*, X.90). In it we learn that the whole organized world, at the centre of which is brahmanic society, was born of the sacrifice of a cosmic Puruṣa. The term *puruṣa* was very soon to designate empirical man, but in the collection of hymns which contains the 'Hymn to the Puruṣa', man is designated in other ways and the term *puruṣa* only appears in the context of this cosmogony. It rather means 'the Male', but at the same time the description of the parts of his body, which is divided up in the sacrifice to give rise to animate beings, starting with the four human varṇas, shows that this Male has human form. So it is from someone who is a man and yet not a man that the cosmos is born, through an act of sacrifice. From him each man will soon derive his generic name, but because of his origin he will retain both a certain 'personality' and a transcendence with respect to all men, even Brahmans. When he becomes the Absolute itself, Puruṣa, or Puruṣa Nārāyaṇa, or Nārāyaṇa, he will keep these two features. In particular, we learn that he manifests himself in the cosmos through a quarter of himself, while the other three quarters are in the beyond, but the four varṇas are born of him.

Two paths to salvation

However reluctant one may be to reconstruct *a posteriori* a history, the stages of which remain largely unknown to us, the risk must nonetheless be taken. Otherwise there is a danger of concealing the initial complexity and the difficulty of understanding what happened between the oldest texts—the Revelation—and those provided by the 'finished' or, so to speak 'classical' state of Hinduism, from the first centuries AD. While almost nothing is known of the society which saw the birth of the Vedic hymns, the fact remains that the very ancient cosmogony of the 'Hymn to the Puruṣa' already contains the hierarchy of the four varṇas and their names, and that the creative act is a sacrifice, i.e. one of the rites of which the Brahmans are the priests. Thus it is much the same society which gave the Puruṣa sacrifice its central role and which also set *Brahman* in the place it occupies. So it is not surprising that '*Puruṣa*' and '*Brahman*' appear in the Upanisads as two names of the Absolute sought by the 'renouncers'. Moreover—and this seems to be a universal law—the Upaniṣadic literature is probably not the work of the 'renouncers' themselves and does not present their religious experience to us directly. Rather, it shows us, as if in its nascent state, the thinking of men who are in the process of breaking away from the world but who remain very much involved with ritualistic brahmanic society, with its numerous gods receiving sacrificial offerings. So, at first sight, there is scarcely any difference between those who give the name '*Brahman*' to the goal of their search and those who prefer the name '*Puruṣa*'. The notion of liberation is expressed in similar images: salt dissolving in water to give a single indistinct mass of salt water, rivers that lose their identity as they flow into the sea, the nectar of different flowers from which bees make a single honey, clay or iron which is the substance and the only reality of receptacles with different shapes and names. . . . It would be quite difficult to draw a distinction between these images, and therefore between concepts people have regarding liberation, in relationship to the name of the Absolute.

If, however, this apparently unstructured mass is considered from the standpoint of the subsequent developments, then it becomes possible to distinguish broadly two routes to liberation, two types of orientation towards the Absolute, which correspond fairly well to the duality of the names of the divine. These two spiritual itineraries were perhaps not clearly distinguished for people contemporary with these texts, but they probably diverged rapidly as their potentialities were explored. The path which leads to knowledge of the identity of *Brahman* and the ātman has its charter, as it were, in Chapter VI of the *Chāndogya Upaniṣad*: there one finds the teaching of monism, almost all the images just mentioned used to describe the resorption of the empirical individual into the undifferentiatedness of the All, and the famous formula *tat tvam asi*—'that thou art'—with which, after each comparison, the father teaches his son his identity with the All. The son had, however, completed his Vedic training with his master and was returning home to his father, proud of his knowledge and ready to enter the state of 'householder'. It is then that his father completes his education by imparting to him knowledge of ātman-*Brahman*. The *Upaniṣad* is clearly seen here as the 'completion of the *Veda*'—*vedānta*—and this text was to remain fundamental for what subsequently became the philosophical system of Vedānta. It defines what became known as 'the path of knowledge', in which the seeker of liberation must realize within himself his identity with the Absolute, on the basis of the teaching given to him by his master. True, he is not dispensed from personal meditation, an inward effort to perceive within himself what he is taught about himself; but none of that would be conceivable without the aid of the guru who brings him from outside the authorized testimony of the Revelation. Ultimate experience is, indeed, by definition inexpressible, since it is beyond all duality, and the authority of the Revelation embodied in the guru is needed in order to seek it without risk of error or discouragement.

In fact, this 'path of knowledge' happens to be the most orthodox, and it is no accident that the Absolute is there called *Brahman*: the role of the guru is essential for transmitting the Revelation, and it does no more than continue the teaching of the first part of the Revelation which every member of the three higher varṇas or 'twice-born' must receive, because of the initiation which makes him capable of receiving the revealed teaching. The subsequent Vedānta does not deny this interpretation. Śaṅkara only speaks to the 'twice-born' and, if he teaches that one must reject rites and adopt the life of the *sannyāsin*—'renouncer'—in order to attain liberation, his very conception of sannyāsa is only meaningful within the context of the higher varṇas, who have a share in Vedic Revelation and brahmanic practice. Sannyāsa presents itself as the fulfilment of the life of a 'twice-born'—and more particularly a Brahman, as will subsequently become clearer—just as the *Upaniṣad* is the completion of Veda. This is, moreover, explicitly systematized, to the effect that every Brahman must pass successively through four 'stages of life': that of the brahmanic student, between initiation and the end of his Vedic studies, during which time he must observe absolute chastity; that of the married householder, when he sacrifices, and begets sons, which is the social phase *par excellence*; that of the forest dweller, an intermediate and largely theoretical stage which will be examined shortly; and finally that of the thorough-going 'renouncer', sannyāsin, the stage which ensures his liberation.

The path which leads to Puruṣa, 'the supreme abode', is first and foremost that which is described in the *Kaṭha Upaniṣad*. There it is already given the name *yoga*, and the stages it distinguishes in the mystic ascent towards Puruṣa were to have an extraordinary destiny. These stages, which have to be understood as the yogin's progressive withdrawal from his empirical individuality until his resorption into Puruṣa, were reversed and used by the great mythic texts of classical Hinduism, then by the Sāṅkhya system, as phases in the emission of the cosmos from Puruṣa, which had itself become the Great Yogin. From there, they extended to practically the whole of sectarian Hinduism. In opposition to the Vedāntic path, the yoga method is characterized by a less essential relationship to the Revelation (of which it is nonetheless a part). In classical Yoga, as in every school of yoga, the guru remains necessary, but his role is not so much to repeat the revealed teaching as to guide the apprentice yogin's personal effort. Thus the methods and schools of yoga have been almost infinitely diversified as they have moved more or less far from the Vedic Revelation. It will therefore not be surprising to find all possible social origins and all degrees of ritual purity among the yogins, right up to extreme impurity.

In another vein, in Puruṣa, in accordance with the semi-anthropomorphic concept Hindus have of him, is given another name, a name which moreover points to later developments in classical Hinduism. In the *Kaṭha Upaniṣad*, he is Viṣṇu; in the *Śvetāśvatara Upaniṣad*, he is Śiva. These are two Vedic deities who were to be promoted to the rank of supreme deities, both in 'general' Hinduism and sectarian Hinduism, one or the other being superior in different cases. This simultaneous elevation of two members of the Vedic pantheon is by no means arbitrary, and their respective roles in the sacrifice introduce new distinctions into the yogic path and its relationship with brahmanic orthodoxy. But the fact that the divine is no longer a neutral principle also changes its relationship to the still empirical man who aspires to liberation. Nor is it an accident that the *Kaṭha* and the *Śvetāśvatara*[2] bring into this relationship an element of election, grace, which later acquired more or less importance in the different schools and sects. The disciple's knowledge and his assiduity in his exercises do not suffice to ensure the success of his undertaking if the Puruṣa himself does not call him. It is not hard to guess what sort of divisions such a notion encourages: the philosophical system of classical Yoga—which, like the five other *darśana* (literally, 'views, ways of seeing'), concerns only the 'twice-born'—plays down the role of the supreme God whom it nonetheless calls Īśvara, 'the Lord', and thereby reduces the importance of election. Yoga then tends to be a technique whose very perfection ensures success. By contrast, it will be seen that the more universalist current of *bhakti* emphasizes Devotion to God and the grace that the devoted may expect from it. These divergences exist even within orthodox society, but are obviously much greater when one moves from a rigorously orthodox religious movement to a sect which claims to abolish the differences between the castes.

In a kind of reaction to this, the brahmanic system *par excellence* of Mīmāṃsā—which developed its philosophical theories in order to provide a basis for the hermeneutics of the Vedic texts—paid less and less attention to the Vedic gods. Yet practically and theoretically they are essential to the ritual, as beneficiaries of the sacrificial offerings. In the revealed texts, and even in the classical myths, one has the feeling that the gods respond to men's worship with the duly codified favours that men expect. There is a reciprocity of services between gods and men which can even be said to define dharma, the socio-cosmic order for which the Brahmans are primarily responsible. The gods feed on the smoke of the sacrificial offerings poured into the fire, the mouth of the gods; in exchange, they send rain at the right time, and so on. So it seems somewhat paradoxical that the philosophers of Mīmāṃsā, rigorous guardians of brahmanic orthodoxy, eventually so diminish the role of the gods that they no longer see them as anything more than names, and put all the emphasis on sacrifice alone. Sacrifice is the technique which ensures earthly and heavenly happiness, just as yoga ensures liberation. This evolution of Mīmāṃsā would be unintelligible if one failed to locate it in the context of an increasingly pervasive religion of devotion, in which sacrifice itself has to change its meaning in order to survive.

It can already be seen that the second path towards liberation opened up by yoga is much richer in future developments, much less rigid in its framework and theoretical content than the Vedantic path. At the same time, we may observe that the intensity of speculations on liberation, and the very radicalism they brought to the fore in their break with the world, have not been without impact on this world. It is out of this very tension, a tension that obtains between these two polarities in values, that Hinduism, in its timeless form, took shape. In this way we come to the fundamental opposition that exists, without contradictions, between the religion of the *Brāhmaṇas* and that of the *Upaniṣads*.

It has already been observed that it is difficult to understand in terms of a rigorous order of succession the two aspects of the brahmanic Revelation—organization of the world and renunciation of the world—which seem rather to be given at the same time for the same society. While the ritualistic speculations of the *Brāhmaṇas* are indeed pitched at the level of this earthly world, it cannot be said that they ignore those of the *Upaniṣads*. It is always possible to imagine that the passages of the *Brāhmanas* which reveal the influence of the *Upaniṣads* are later additions intended to integrate new preoccupations. But such a historical reconstruction of the Revelation would not account for a group of intermediate revealed texts, which have already been alluded to: the *Āraṇyakas*. Traditional Vedic recitation does indeed place them between the *Brāhmanas* and the *Upaniṣads*, and some of the *Upaniṣads* would even appear to be parts of *Āraṇyakas*. In these 'Forest Books'—that is the meaning of the word—the tension between the secular pole and the renunciation pole operates at full strength, and it is impossible to see them as a phase of *historical* transition between these two extremes. On the contrary, it has to be acknowledged that the totality of the secular brahmanic Revelation is there confronted with a Revelation of liberation equally complete in its essentials, and that the structural opposition between the two gives rise to new speculations and new practices in which these two irreconcilable principles have to coexist.

The hermit Brahman

From a certain moment onwards, a moment located a few centuries before the common era, an adult Brahman's self-understanding came to take on a twofold meaning. To be a Brahman meant to be a Vedic sacrifical priest, a minister of the revealed Word, a master of the house entirely occupied in a network of obligatory ritual observances in which all was interpreted in terms of sacrifice. It would have been impossible for such an individual to follow any occupation outside of this context; in any case the Brahman knew that it was his careful accomplishment of ritual duties which ensured the prosperity of both his family and society at large. But *at the same time* he also knew of a higher sort of religion, something that lay beyond the sacrificial rites, beyond his life as head of the household, a religion which held the promise of eternal happiness. And perhaps, as a consequence, he came to realize a diminution in the value and urgency of his day-to-day activities, duties that were so tiresome and hair-splitting in their attention to detail. And with this, he would have realized the higher value of attending to his ātman, as opposed to attending to the regularity of the sun's motions or the succession of the seasons. In this situation, still within the brahmanic universe in the narrowest sense of the word, there takes shape a religious form which is made up entirely of compromises, and which may well be the starting point for all the subsequent developments: sacrifice is not abandoned, but instead of offering it to the gods, in real fire, it is offered to one's ātman, in the fire of the breath. All the outward observances are thus, partially at least, internalized and diverted from their initial application. It is obviously of enormous significance that these rites have to be performed no longer in the village, but in the forest, just far enough away for no human dwellings to be visible.

The *Āraṇyakas* are the revealed texts of brahmanism which, at present, seem to us by far the most obscure. There are many reasons for this, but perhaps the most fundamental is the fact that, as a corpus, they remain theoretical and describe, after a fashion, a no less theoretical 'stage of life' of the Brahman: that of the 'forest dweller', which would have been intermediate between the master of the house and the thorough-going renouncer. But, setting aside their impact on later Hinduism, their immediate significance is indeed as testimonies to the work of reflection that lead the household-master Brahman increasingly to resemble the renouncer. The 'mental' sacrifice—or 'oblation with the breath'—as internalized sacrifice is called, is indeed not practised by a 'forest dweller', but by a master of the house. The Brahman living in the secular world adopts practices which are only conceivable in the renouncer, and which are in fact part of the earliest observances of every renouncer.

I shall dwell here on only one of them, which was later to turn into something which the early Brahmans had certainly not foreseen: *ahiṃsā* (literally, 'absence of desire to kill'), from which we have coined 'non-violence', is strictly only conceivable from the standpoint of the renouncer. It is the direct opposite of the animal slaughter included in the major Vedic sacrifices: to kill, to cause death, or simply to come into contact with a corpse is universally felt by man to be a source of impurity. Slaughter in the Vedic sacrifice and the manipulations concerning the victim do not escape this rule, as is shown by all the precautions taken to contain the impurity of death within strict limits and to leave intact the purity of the sacrificial offerings. Despite this codification of slaughter by the *Brāhmaṇas* the tradition sought to go further and to eliminate theoretically the impurity of sacrifice by declaring that 'to sacrifice is not to kill'. At all events, it would seem that the eating of meat was closely linked to sacrificial practice. In brahmanic society, there was probably no licit animal slaughter beyond the needs of sacrifice (but any meal might be interpreted in certain conditions as a sacrifice). Now, the sacrificial rite is precisely the act—karman—which the renouncer must abandon if he is to escape from rebirth. In ceasing to sacrifice, he loses any licit occasion to kill, which means that he is obliged to adopt a vegetarian diet. Among all the defilements that he must avoid, that of death remains essential. Domestic life entails many chances of 'murder', which he will avoid as far as possible: insects burnt by the fire, crushed by the broom or mortar, drowned in water. . . . So he will cook nothing himself, prepare himself no food, filter his water. . . . Perhaps on no other point is there a more fundamental opposition between the obligations of the householder and those of the renouncer. And yet, *within* brahmanic society, the Brahman was very soon to become the main champion of the value of *ahiṃsā*, which the renouncer cannot observe rigorously without *leaving* the society based on Vedic ritual. This was apparently one of the principal reasons for the abandonment of the major Vedic sacrifices; it was certainly the decisive factor in the Brahmans' adoption of a vegetarian diet, which is still the rule today.

The Tradition was also to feel the need to give to the master of the house—who cannot abandon his ritual obligations towards the gods, the ancestors, men and all beings, without putting the world in danger—the means of expiating the defilements induced by domestic life. It is only logical that it should then precisely relate these defilements to the 'major sacrifices' which every Brahman has to perform every day for the gods, the ancestors, men, all beings and *Brahman* (i.e. the Veda). Apart from the sacrifice to *Brahman*, the first four major sacrifices centre on the household fire—which is also the sacrificial fire—and the preparation of meals, which are to be offered to all of these daily invited guests before being consumed by oneself. The very fact that insects are killed in the performance of domestic life becomes quasi licit, since this is nothing other than a set of sacrificial rites. The damage is, of course, reduced to the minimum, if not for the sake of the insects, at least for the poor master of the house, who would otherwise have to sully himself, and therefore accumulate bad karman, in the performance of his duties. We shall see that the sacrifice itself, too essential to be abandoned, emerges completely transformed from this process. We are a long way from our notion of non-violence.

Hindu man

Is there in this context a notion of man implicitly or explicitly put forward? At first sight, one is tempted to say that there cannot be a notion of man, but there are only men of this or that category, this or that varṇa. There are indeed some important distinctions to be made subsequently. However, the existence of a supra-social religion, an Absolute which has to be sought outside society, makes it impossible to accept such a simple answer. Man is not reduced to his social existence, even if the latter adheres to his very essence, and in any case social existence, based on a hierarchical and functional view, also implies *a* notion of man. It is all too clear, on the other hand, that the man who lives in society and the man who aspires to liberation are essentially one and the same and that we cannot define the one without attending to the other; in a similar vein, we have seen the Absolute appear as belonging to a particular society, even as it denied that society.

At a first level, then, it is man involved in society whom one has to try to grasp in order to discover what makes him man. This immediately reduces the scope of the investigation: from the standpoint of the Revelation, only the first three varṇas count, those which take part in the Vedic rites: the Brahmans, the Kṣatriyas and the Vaiśyas. But it is not sufficient for them to be born in order to be integrated into society. The name 'twice-born' which is given to them bears its full meaning: it is the initiation ceremony which introduces them into society, at about the age of eight. Up to that point, the rites which concern them are performed by their fathers who, in so doing, perform their own paternal duty. They themselves have no obligations; education is practically—and theoretically—absent.

Here we must leave theory behind us, with all its potential for misinterpretation, and cast a glance at contemporary Hindu society in order that we may judge what once were—and, it would appear, always have been—its practical considerations. Far from the child having a world apart, he is closely integrated into family life, especially that of the women, without having any of its responsibilities. He has no personal timetable, either for meals or for sleep, no rules of hygiene or cleanliness imposed from outside and supported by sanctions. He seems to live by pure whim, in total freedom, blissfully unaware of his surroundings. In reality, things are quite different: the child lives in perfect symbiosis with the world of the family (which moreover includes numerous children), and with the adults for whom he is often a toy passed from hand to hand. He adopts its habits, he is a *passive* participant in everything done in the household, and thus prepares to become later a master of the house fully aware of his responsibilities. Nowadays, the spread of schooling is disturbing this closed atmosphere, introducing into the child's mind the possibility of distance from family life. But for the moment, tradition still predominates and imposes its tacit rules on the school rather than the other way round. Anyone who has observed Indian primary school classes will have been struck by the collective, passive nature of the methods used to teach the basics of the 'three R's'; more weight is placed on the mechanisms of memory than on the quality of attention and understanding. How could the school introduce new norms, a different vision of the child's 'personality', and could it be *a priori* a factor of individualization? Such questions are discussed, and experts in American methods are attempting to transplant them onto the Indian soil. Will they succeed? For the moment, schooling is just one more element in Hindu society, and it duplicates the work of a traditional institution which we are now perhaps better placed to understand.

Thus the first effect of initiation is to make the child a social being. What does this mean? During the first stage, he will live with his guru (but in the case of a young Brahman, the guru may be his own father) who will teach him the revealed texts and render him capable of performing his tasks as a householder. Only then may he marry, maintain a household fire which will transform his life into a succession of rites, and perform the duties specific to his varṇa. But this is only the consequence of what initiation has made of him; to say that he has become a social being is too weak—or too strong—if by that one means entry into membership of a given social group. Surreptitiously, we would see there the recognition of his existence—at last!—as an individual within his group. In practice, this would not be completely wrong, but theoretically that would not account for the obligations incumbent on him. The young initiate is no more than a bundle of 'debts' which he will spend his life redeeming: a debt towards the gods, which he will pay off with the appropriate sacrifices; a debt towards his ancestors, which will require him to beget at least one son in order to perpetuate the cult of his ancestors; a debt towards the *ṛṣis*—the primordial 'seers' of the Revelation—which makes it his duty to learn the revealed texts (including the *Upaniṣads*) by heart and recite them for the rest of his life. So he enters into social existence only to become a link in the solid chain which binds the whole, and not solely as a member of his group. Nor is the 'whole' here limited to the totality of ritually defined human society, since it embraces the gods as well as the dead and the living in the order which structures the daily course of the world. Would the sun still rise each day if the Brahmans did not get up early in the morning and prepare its coming with the appropriate rites?

However, the full importance of ritual activity—karman—in the definition of what man is can only be measured by seeking to distinguish man from what is not man: animals and the gods. From one end to the other of Hindu religious literature, the answer is the same: it is the capacity to perform rites—and its corollary, the capacity for liberation from rites—that distinguishes man both from the animals and from the Vedic gods. Animals, not being enabled by birth to know the Revelation, also cannot perform the rites it prescribes. The *Purāṇas* tell us that animals are full of *tamas*—darkness and inertia; Mīmāṃsā observes that they are unable to set themselves a distant goal—as one must in order to perform rites whose immediate result is invisible. All philosophers agree, however, in crediting them by inference with the same capacities of perception and reasoning as man. So it is essentially the inability to perform rites or to transcend rites that makes the animal an inferior being, condemned to expiate in this way previous faults (committed in an earlier human life). Above men—since they are the inhabitants of heaven—the gods too cannot either perform rites or desire liberation. The *Purāṇas* explain this by the fact that the gods are happy and have nothing to desire that might incline them to do anything at all. Mīmāṃsā more prosaically considers that they cannot sacrifice because they have no gods other than themselves to sacrifice to.

This importance of the rite in defining humanity is taken further in the distinction which the human group makes between inhabited space and wild nature, essentially the forest. Not that the human world is opposed to nature as such: on the contrary, it is enfolded in nature like a child in its mother's arms, and the rite, as has been said, orders the physical world as well as human society. Human space, however, includes not only men but also domestic animals. The latter, which may be sacrificial victims, obviously have higher status than the wild animals pursued by the impure hunter. Among all the animals which populate human space, the cow occupies a privileged position, which is also explained by its relation to sacrifice and to the Brahman: the products of cows' milk form an important part of non-animal sacrificial offerings. Myths always symbolize the Brahman's sacerdotal function by means of a cow, and the latter eventually symbolizes the Brahman himself, since a Brahman without a cow is less than a complete Brahman. To kill a cow is almost as abominable as to kill a Brahman, although the revealed texts are categorical: certain rites included a cow as sacrificial victim. But 'to sacrifice is not to kill'.

If the rite thus serves to hierarchize beings, it is not difficult to see how it is also the basis of the hierarchical vision of man: social function is first and foremost defined, in orthodox theory, by a specific relation to the rite. The Brahman is the priest; the Kṣatriya is the 'sacrificing agent' and at the same time the possessor of the strength which protects the Brahmans and all other men; the Vaiśya, in addition to his role as a 'sacrificing agent', is the producer of the wealth required for the maintenance of the ritual activity without which there is no prosperity on earth. From this standpoint, various questions arise about the others: firstly, about women. Their case is relatively simple: they clearly do not have access to knowledge of the Revelation, and have no autonomous ritual activity; but they are necessarily associated with the rites performed by their husbands. Having no personal destiny after death (they are reunited with their husbands), they are likewise incapable of achieving liberation. To be reborn as a woman, even in a brahmanic family, is therefore another form of expiation.

As for the Śūdras, the least that can be said is that the Revelation is barely concerned with them. We shall see subsequently that they make up for this with bhakti. But it would be wrong to say that they are denied all humanity. They too have a karman inasmuch as they must serve the three higher varṇas, as the Tradition explicitly teaches. Their relationship to the rite is indirect but not entirely absent. The fact remains that rebirth as a Śūdra is one of the threats invoked against a man of high caste who fails to perform all his duties. It is no doubt a state sufficiently passive, with respect to karman, to place a man on the boundary of what is human, where there is nothing to hope for but a better rebirth. What status can be attributed to those who are even lower in the social hierarchy? There is no karman conceivable for them; they have to live away from the high castes in a space which may be either human or wild, at a level in the scale of beings which probably sets them below domestic animals. Thus one of the consequences of the ritual origin of the hierarchy of beings is that there is no clear-cut division between humanity and animality.

If the ordinary man is defined by his place in the whole as structured by rites, the logical consequence is that his own particular way of performing his obligations is the source of a certain individualization. It is possible that the this-wordly man might never have given explicit voice to this consequence if the renouncer—or, in the earliest context, the 'discussant', the Indian version of the Socratic philosopher, had not first brought it to light the better to refute it. In the world, karman is the rite which produces a determinate result, that which has to be done within the strict limits inside which it is prescribed in order to co-operate in the maintenance of dharma, the total order. The man who performs it is only aware of keeping his place in the socio-cosmic system, and he implicitly accepts limits assigned to him: life-span, membership of a certain social group, a certain lineage, etc. His social and family bonds are so strong that his troubles and joys are to a large extent those of the group to which he belongs. He cannot think of his own prosperity without thinking of that of his whole lineage (who would dare speak of nepotism in such a context?), he cannot ensure heaven after death without having done what had to be done, throughout his life, for the celestial happiness of his ancestors. Reference to himself as *ego* is scarcely made explicit outside the vicissitudes of his physical life: illness, physical suffering, or bodily enjoyment.

It was necessary to stand back in order to see things differently. And that is the paradox of brahmanic theory, a paradox *for us*, revealing in fact an anthropology different from our own: the renouncer, who refuses to keep any longer his place in the social fabric and so abandons all the rites, isolates himself from the whole and seems thus to attain a more individualized existence. His very language invites us to understand things in this way, since it condemns the accumulation of karman, sees it as the source of perpetual rebirths within a whole whose structure appears stable but whose beings pass endlessly through the processes of birth and death, synonyms of finitude and instability, of pain, in a word. The renouncer, by contrast, shaking off the whole weight of karman, seeks to recover the purity of his ātman, i.e. of the self which he essentially is. For him, the course of the world is of little account: the only thing which matters is the ātman, the only truly eternal being, which has to be detached from birth and death. The procedure is, without any doubt, that of an individual who has become aware of himself, who sees himself as something other than a flux of rites and events linked to rites, and who perceives the underlying 'personal' unity. The way in which he actualizes this awareness further accentuates its individual character: he will live as a solitary ascetic, chiefly concerned to keep himself free of any bond with any being, whether aversion or love, envy or contempt. All that counts is the final salvation of his ātman, liberation, mokṣa. One is bound to relate this option to the one which characterizes the great religions of the world, *mutatis mutandis*: entry into religious life, either solitary or monastic. It defines a level at which religion is no longer satisfied with social values and can find the deep meaning of human life only by severing the bonds with society. But in a context like brahmanism, in which social values leave so little room for individual expression, the break with the social institution can only appear even more sharply as entry into an individual religion.

Yet, in the renouncer's consciousness, at least in theory, it is the opposite that occurs. In abandoning the world, the sannyāsin abandons everything that made him an 'ego'—*ahaṃkāra*—so as to reabsorb his Self in the Absolute, where he finds no further trace of individuality. This fundamental notion, complementary to that of ātman-*Brahman* and karman, appears even in the earliest Vedantic *Upaniṣads*, in a transparent mythic form. The absolute *Brahman* 'creates' the world by becoming aware of himself as an ego: 'In the beginning, *Brahman* alone was here. It knew itself—ātman—only as 'I—*aham*—am *Brahman*'. From this, it became everything' (*Bṛhadāraṇyaka Upaniṣad*, I.4.10). A few lines further in the same text (I.4.17) we find: 'In the beginning the ātman alone was here. He was alone. He desired: "Would that I had a wife, that I might engender (a son); would that I had wealth, that I might perform the rites."

These are all the objects of desire—*kāma*'. The empirical world only comes into existence and is only maintained by virtue of its being intertwined with the 'I'—*aham*—and the 'mine'—*mama*. And the function which makes man say 'I' and 'mine' is ahaṃkāra. That is the function of desire, which not only links man to this world, but constitutes the essential part of empirical man and 'individuates' him in the eyes of the renouncer by impelling him to perform rites. Conversely, the ātman which aspires to liberation is no doubt conceived as a plenitude of being (in contrast to Buddhism, which sees it as a void), but this pure being is so divested of all determination that nothing more resembles a void. This pure consciousness, in which no subject is opposed to any object, is closer to the Hegelian in-itself than the for-itself. There is nothing individual about it, not even anything human, except the incomprehensible aspiration towards liberation that brought it where it is and even left it as it approached its end. So for some this liberated state is beatitude, whereas for others it is merely absence of pain.

So if we try to formulate the brahmanic conception of man in terms closer to our usual language, we first have to observe that humanity is detached from that which it is not, since humanity alone takes part in the rites and can renounce the rites, but that these boundaries do not run exactly where we would set them (nor do those of Aristotle, incidentally); and furthermore that the content of the notion has nothing in common with what our own notion of humanity would lead us to expect. There is nothing 'inside' man which might make him truly a thinking, willing subject. In the world, he is a desiring agent for the sannyāsin, a bundle of social responsibilities for himself. Outside the world, he is merely a transparent mirror in which nothing is reflected. For the man encumbered with desires, the renouncer is a 'free' man, who has cast off his bonds but who pays sufficiently dearly for that freedom to consider it superior and inimitable; for the ascetic, the man living in his caste thinks only of satisfying his desires and prepares only pain for himself. What the theory never explains, is the transition from one state to another: how can one conceive the act whereby one renounces acts? Moreover, the tension between the two poles never leads to a dramatic or divided picture of man. If people occasionally ask themselves why the world exists, they very quickly sidestep the question by replying that it has no beginning, and therefore no cause or *raison d'être*. The divine 'game'—*līlā*—was soon to give a definitive theological form to the idea that human life has no meaning and needs none. Those who nonetheless find it good, cling to transmigration; and they are legion. Nothing prevents the others from seeking liberation.

CHAPTER 2

The Four Goals of Man

One still remains within the brahmanic orthodoxy defined by its two poles when examining the theoretical system of values. At first sight, nothing could be more simple, since there is a single hierarchy of four terms which everyone knows by heart and must respect: liberation—mokṣa—at the very top, then dharma, the socio-cosmic order which organizes the empirical world, followed by *artha*, which includes all material interests—wealth, successful ventures and the means of ensuring them—and finally *kāma*, essentially amorous desire and pleasure. But we already know that the four of them cannot be arranged in a series, since mokṣa concerns the man who is leaving society whereas the other three are the goals pursued by man living in the world. And perhaps it is not so simple as it seems to pursue concurrently—while maintaining the hierarchy—goals as divergent as amorous pleasure, material interest, etc. But how can one designate dharma in a term which suggests to us ideas as self-evident as the first two? In fact, I would like to employ a term which could also refer to the individual, even if its semantic field also covered a higher level of individual consciousness. But one must reject all of the French or English equivalents of the term dharma that modern translations have offered in their attempts to bridge the gap between Indian realities and the western mind. It is neither morality, nor Good, nor law, nor justice. It is the socio-cosmic order, which can be said to be desirable simply inasmuch as it is necessary to the maintenance of the happy existence of the whole constituted by the 'three worlds'—*trailokya* (earth, heaven and the space between, or later, earth, heaven and the infernal regions). It is taught to men in the Revelation as mediated by the Brahmans, in principle without any reference to a transcendent Good. It is itself Good in that it ensures the continuity of the empirical world. If an individual fails to observe it, he must expect the worst disasters. If society as a whole neglects the prescriptions of dharma, then the world will perish; but the same will happen if a varṇa does not perform its proper functions or tries to take over those of other varṇas. In whatever way disorder enters the trailokya, the life of all is endangered. The absolute imperative does not pass here through a divine will or through individual consciousness; it is imposed from outside and as a totality, without any possible evasion. The constraint could not be greater.

The levels of dharma

We can immediately see that the notion of dharma resonates at different levels: to the extent that liberation is integrated into that model of human life which charts the 'four stages of life' (see p. 33), it too partakes, after a fashion, of the total cosmic order. If nothing else, it is mokṣa that maintains the universe in its proper orientation—even as it reminds man of his ultimate vocation to be reabsorbed into the undifferentiated All, at which point the cosmic order no longer has any meaning. Dharma is therefore that all-encompassing order that goes so far as to include even that which denies it, and which consists in the well-balanced hierarchy of the four goals of man, as well as in a respect for the hierarchy and proper delineation of the four varṇas. Even at this, the most comprehensive level of the notion, dharma is the business of the Brahman: it is his task to see that the totality of the cosmic order is respected. Therefore he regulates the conditions within which a man may attain sannyāsa: theoretically, this is possible only for a household master who has had a grandson, so that his descendance is ensured. This is the *sine qua non* in order for mokṣa to take its place in the overall dharma without disturbing it. Withdrawal from society requires that a man should have performed all his social duties, paid off all his congenital debts. Naturally, exceptions are provided for, not to wipe these debts off the slate, but so that they can be redeemed without passing through the householder stage, by directly attaining the state of sannyāsin. For it has to be possible for everyone's desires—kāma—to be realized, including the desire for liberation. That is why many treatises of dharma—of which *The Laws of Manu* (*Mānavadharmaśāstra*) is the best known as well as the most orthodox—include a chapter on the 'renouncer'.

It is again this comprehensive sense of the word dharma which makes the Brahman the legislator of artha and kāma. Given the close relationship between the first and second varṇas, it is not surprising to see a chapter on the dharma of the king appearing in treatises of dharma; these chapters deal mainly with the conditions which make a king a good king, one who is respectful of the objective order and of his superiors, the Brahmans. But one is less prepared for seeing the Brahmans dealing with artha and kāma for themselves. Yet the fact is that the sole treatise on artha that is known to us is attributed to a Brahman. The same is true of the famous *Kāma Sūtra* (Aphorisms on Love); and also of the many collections of rules of *nīti* (literally, 'conduct'), which complement the treatise on artha, but are addressed more generally to every man who pursues any material end and seeks success above all.

It is perhaps here that our own system of values is liable to be a real obstacle to an understanding of India. Implicitly, we set dharma—in the narrower sense of the term to which we shall shortly return—in opposition to artha and kāma, as we would the sphere of values to that of the real, semi-instinctive needs of the empirical individual. We see values as structuring all our needs, imposing transcendent norms which often hinder the satisfaction of our needs. So, while we find ourselves confronted with the painful reality which teaches us that many concrete situations flout morality and religion, we nevertheless cling obstinately to a realm where ideal values hold sway. This is not the Indian view of things. The fact that artha and kāma are inferior to dharma does not imply that they must, of necessity, yield to the dictates of dharma. Dharma does not present itself as an order of values which permeates everything, but, in its broadest sense, as a structuring of the whole of reality which leaves room for the levels of material interest and sexual desire. These are also levels of value at the same time as (and because), they are levels of reality which retain their relative autonomy. In the treatises of dharma, as in those of artha and kāma, one finds the same concern for the social hierarchy and for dharma, but also the same affirmation that none of the three ends, not even dharma, must be pursued to the detriment of the others. For us this is another reminder that dharma is not a demand of a moral type as opposed to the other two ends, but that it is itself only one of the ends pursued, limiting the others only from outside but not affecting their intrinsic nature. Without this, we would be incapable of understanding, for example, how it is that time and time again in Indian literature—and in the epic literature in particular—a woman can call upon a man to yield to her desire, her kāma, out of an imperative made *in the name of dharma*: if she is not immediately satisfied, she will die. The dharma invoked here is dharma in the most comprehensive sense of the word (which has a place for each of the goals of man) but it could also be the dharma specific to the Kṣatriyas—a third sense of the term which will shortly be discussed—since the hero to whom the woman appeals is a prince. Thus the *Arthaśāstra*, the *Nītiśastras* and the *Kāma Sūtra* are works which deal essentially with the rules of conduct which give success in business (that of the kingdom or personal business) and in love. There is no man living in the world who does not desire wealth, no king who does not seek to enlarge his power and ensure the security of his possessions, no human being who does not desire another human being. Here one has to formulate things in the most general way possible: in particular, amorous desire includes homosexual desire, which also has to find satisfaction and on which there is, in principle, no taboo.

Discussion of dharma in its most comprehensive sense has quite naturally led me to allude to dharma in a narrower sense. Dharma in this narrower definition is the end which, for each individual, must take its place between mokṣa on the one hand and artha and kāma on the other. Mokṣa is not of this world, whereas artha and kāma are concerned with visible realities, immediate and tangible satisfactions. Dharma is then the order of the invisible realities within the triple world, everything which requires of man a ritual activity or behaviour governed by something other than immediate satisfaction, a relationship to the inhabitants of the other worlds and to those of this world whom he cannot see. This is another way of saying that it is the religion of man living in the world, but a religion which is added to the rest of reality rather than that which transforms it. Here we are far removed from the lyrical or nostalgic celebrations of so-called 'primitive', 'cosmic' or 'natural' religions, as well as from their concept of an omnipresent sacred. It is likely that the sacred is present, for a Hindu, in many situations from which it is completely absent in the West. But the counterpart of this is that there exists a profane realm, that one may enjoy without afterthought, once it has been duly encompassed by the sacred as if by a rampart. We already know, moreover, that the Brahman is both the priest of this religion and the cleric who teaches all of its essential tenets. It is also the area which we have seen constituting brahman in the social sense of the word: *Brahman* is the administration of dharma, and the power which this presupposes. In this sense, the artha and kāma (in the sense of 'object of desire' and no longer 'desire') that we enjoy in the present largely depend on how we have observed dharma in the past: they are in fact the essential forms of happiness which man pursues in this world, and happiness is the fruit of the merits—again dharma (i.e., the result of the observance of dharma)— accumulated previously, in an earlier life. Conversely, unhappiness in artha and kāma stems from demerits in a past life.

The treatises on dharma in fact merge the two levels of dharma, and the reason for this soon becomes clear when one turns to a third level which is again partially confused with the first two: the hierarchical vision of human society immediately implies that dharma does not have identical content for each human group. Each has its own dharma, its *svadharma*. This follows from the distribution of functions, as outlined in Chapter I. There, svadharma appeared simply as the social function that each varṇa performed within brahmanic society: for the Brahman, there is *Brahman*, the sacerdotal function; for the Kṣatriya, kṣatra, the martial and princely function; for the Vaiśya, trade and agriculture; and for the Śūdra, the service of the higher varṇas, which implies submission to their values. The definition is absolutely constant, since it is found without any variation both in the *Laws of Manu* and in the *Arthaśāstra*.

But the same thing can now be formulated in terms of the 'goals of man'—the *puruṣārthas*—and this to our eyes is somewhat paradoxical. First of all, we should note the appearance of the term *artha* in this expression. It is translated here, in its broadest sense, as 'goal', 'goal pursued', 'object aimed at' (as such it is also used to designate what we call the meaning of a word: in fact, the things that are aimed at, pointed to, in talking). In a narrower sense, it is the goal which fits in between dharma and kāma. Initially, the four goals of man concern every individual man, and one might suppose that only the relation to dharma and mokṣa varies with the social category. In broad terms, each individual has a relationship to all four goals, even if this requires taking into account his whole series of successive lives. But the lower one descends in the social hierarchy, the more the real goals that a man can pursue are the immediate goals of artha and kāma. Thus the man who is the individual *par excellence* in terms of his daily activities and aspirations would be the Śūdra; strictly, there would be no individual except in the most empirical sense of the word, closest to the psycho-physiological level. However, the notion of svadharma significantly modifies this view, by imposing another structure on the puruṣārthas, and above all by bringing back into the theory of them the question of the social group; for at no level is the focus on the individual alone.

The correspondences drawn between svadharma and the puruṣārthas are anything but an artificial theory, some mechanical extension of the classifications and equivalences in which Hindu thought excels. Were this not the case, one would have sought, for better or worse, to generate a term-for-term relationship between the four varṇas and the four puruṣārthas. That does not exist, even if, as will become apparent, one has to assign dharma to the svadharma of the Brahman and artha to that of the Kṣatriya. But it is kāma that constitutes the most remarkable case. Though its theory is presented in only one text, the notion of kāma is omnipresent in Indian speculation and gives rise to philosophico-religious doctrines and practices in which it has a central role.

Love: women's duty

It will come as no surprise to be told that Indian civilization, like all others, is resolutely seen from the standpoint of man and that within it woman is an eternal minor. But this has probably never anywhere meant that woman did not have her indispensable and duly recognized place. The codes of laws such as that of Manu are strewn with remarks on the subject, and it is almost always a question of regulating men's attitude to women. The general opinion on women ranges from the theme of female fickleness to praise of the faithful wife—*satī*—who, in a household, is the equal of the goddess Śrī, a goddess who combines beauty, wealth and prosperity, since she is inseparable from strict observance of dharma. It is nonetheless somewhat surprising to find that woman is primarily described, for better or worse, in relation to the man on whom she depends, her husband, and second as a mother; this might be an indication that the famous all-purpose concept of the 'goddess-mother' does not have the religious importance which modern scholarship has sought to give it in India. It is true that she has to be a procreator, and especially give sons to her husband, who will need them in the life hereafter, but she can do so only if there is mutual attraction between the spouses (for example, *Manu*, III, 60–61). Thus the reproductive function is subordinated to the satisfaction of desire; there is a multitude of myths which tend to show this and which even give the initiative in desire to the woman (see p. 44). And so it is legitimate to say that the perfect woman, the satī—who appears in nineteenth century English literature as the widow who throws herself on her husband's funeral pyre—has love as her first duty, or to use a more homogeneous language, love as her svadharma. Of course, a woman's dharma is not usually expressed in this way. Her duty is summed up in a formula: to serve her husband as her principal god. However, when one knows the central place of amorous desire in the marriage bond, the deduction is self-evident and is in no way theoretical.

As is well known, prostitutes must make a more particular study of kāma, since their occupation deals with kāma. This means—and a similar modification will be seen for artha—that, despite the universally acknowledged hierarchy of the goals of man, they must attach more importance to kāma than to the other goals. It is another way of expressing their svadharma in a context in which the individual is always absorbed by his or her function. One cannot imagine the care of the kāma of all being entrusted to women without the latter having kāma as their main personal goal (although the *Treatise of Kāma* shows them also preoccupied by their earnings—artha!). But this does not only concern prostitutes: all women, including girls before their marriage, must study at least the practice of kāma. The *Kāma Sūtra* is the only traditional treatise to which they have access in fact and in theory, since, in the other areas of life, a woman is only an extension of her father before marriage and of her husband therefore. Here, women have some initiative, an existence of their own. Vātsyāyana, the Brahman of the *Kāma Sūtra*, tells us so. And we may take his word for it. According to tradition, he wrote this work when he had attained the state of 'renouncer', perhaps at Benares, in other words at an advanced age when he himself expected nothing other than liberation, mokṣa. How could a treatise so full of wisdom have been written by anyone other than a renouncer who had crossed over to the far shore of human passions?

In fact the scope of the book is much broader than the description of the sexual practices immortalized in stone by the Khajuraho temples and some others. It is explicitly stated that if a treatise on kāma is necessary, it is because all human conduct is subject both to norms—essentially those of dharma—and to technical rules, and that man and woman cannot make love to each other in the same way as the mating of beasts. Even in this area, what distinguishes humans from animals is their capacity to follow a model which is provided by the brahmanic tradition, the only way of ensuring success. Thus one of the author's first preoccupations is to state the rules of dharma which must be observed in order for the pursuit of amorous desire to be fulfilled in pleasure without entailing misfortunes. One must not solicit a married woman, according to dharma, unless she has been twice married (the second marriage is not dharmic), unless she has had five lovers, etc. The rules to be followed in order for a marriage to be dharmic are given rapidly, undoubtedly less meticulously than in the *Laws of Manu*. Legitimate wives receive their share of advice for preserving their virtue, i.e. their fidelity to their husbands, but also for maintaining their husbands' love for them, and from the initial dharmic situation, the text moves gradually into practical rules which have nothing to do with dharma, still less with what we would call morality. A wife may stop at nothing to drive away women who attract her husband or to win back the favours of a husband who has married other and younger wives. All conceivable situations are envisaged, and all the valid remedies are proposed. At the other extreme, prostitutes—whom the pursuit of kāma might lead far from all dharma—must redeem themselves by pious donations such as, building temples, water tanks and gardens, giving cows to Brahmans, holding expensive ceremonies and feasts in honour of a god, all of which are far from fictitious. Inscriptions confirm that this was part of the habitual practices of prostitutes (especially the temple prostitutes, *devadāsī*) as well as of kings.

In this way, success comes to be all that matters, once the

constraints of dharma on kāma have been reduced to a minimum. The *Treatise of Kāma* goes even beyond this, forgetting its dharmic checks and acting as if they did not exist at all. This has to be understood rather as the specialists in Vedic sacrifice endeavour to clear the Revelation of any hint of contradiction; for, despite the general obligation of ahiṃsā—'non-violence'—one finds that rites of 'black magic' intended to destroy an enemy are taught in the Revelation. How can these two teachings be reconciled? The answer is always as follows: it is forbidden to want to kill someone, but if a man is sufficiently blinded by anger or hatred, then he is shown which rite he can resort to, in order to satisfy his feeling. Without enjoining him to kill his enemy, the revealed prescription gives him the means of having his way, at his own risk, of course. If subsequently, in this life or another, a great misfortune befalls him, it will be the consequence of the rite he has performed. So even in the Revelation one finds information which belongs to the practical art of acting in such a way as to achieve a given result. This is true *a fortiori* of the *Kāma Sūtra* which is part of the Tradition.

On the other hand, the *Treatise* does not forget that the term *kāma* designates every form of desire, every object of desire, every sensory as well as sensual satisfaction. So a woman, and more especially a prostitute, must be expert in the art of satisfying all the senses—all the senses of her husband, her lover, or her client. Flowers, ointments and perfumes, music, song and dance, cuisine and needlework, are naturally part of the artifices and are put to the service of love, and what is so new about that? Or is it the arrangement in a systematic treatise that surprises us? But a woman's skills must go much further, and more especially, no doubt, those of the prostitute, although the distinction is not made: she must possess every sort of practical and theoretical knowledge (architecture, cock-fighting, languages, parlour games, etc.) that will make her company agreeable and entertaining on all occasions.

Love itself is described in the most minute detail. Not only are men and women divided into categories based on their intimate anatomy, and the chances of success of their union evaluated on the basis of this classification, but all the games of love, all the practices of seduction, all the possible (even acrobatic) forms of sexual union are meticulously enumerated. The author of the treatise never deviates from his role of guru. His aim is never to arouse, but only to instruct. He has the good sense to add, after some particularly erudite descriptions, that passion has no need of method . . . . It is difficult to say what sort of audience Vātsāyana's *Treatise* had in the classical period of Hindu civilization. But love poetry and the poetry of amorous devotion draw inspiration from it and it can scarcely be doubted that it has profoundly influenced women's behaviour. One only has to watch the actresses in modern Indian films: the sideways glances and fluttering gestures seem incongruous in otherwise seemingly virtuous heroines. Let us admit that the effect is not entirely to our own taste. But it has to be added that the modern Hindu reader of the *Kāma Sūtra* is no more innocent than the Western reader, if he ever was. In reality it is perhaps not very accurate to speak of the influence of the *Treatise of Love*: like so many other works, it has to be seen as a link in a long tradition. The text is not well established and the historical identity of the author is thoroughly obscure. It is likely that at no time did it constitute a literary event, but that it was the formalization, perhaps by stages, of a traditional art which women handed down to one another (and which was not unknown to men. That would only give more significance to this unique treatise in the cultural context in which it came into being. When we come to examine its religious extensions, we shall take care not to see it as their determinant cause: it is only part of a larger whole which is consonant and, no doubt, contemporary with it. One must also be careful not to see it as the source of a language in which certain religious conceptions were later expressed, in the way in which the *Song of Songs* was used—at a distance of many centuries—by the Christian mystics. There is a deeper relationship between this vision of human love and its religious transposition or utilization. It is probably no exaggeration to say that, in each area, a similar anthropology is being formulated. Thus, identifying the impressions which predominate, for us, in reading the *Kāma Sūtra*, may help us to understand the religious importance of kāma.

I shall concentrate on just two, which are moreover closely interrelated, although for a Western reader they may seem contradictory. First of all, if so much importance is attached to erotic techniques, this is because it is only a question of the most physical aspect of love. It would be a mistake to reverse the situation and to say that the *Treatise of Kāma* explicitly limits its scope to physical love. But it is no accident that love literature is always strongly erotic in character or that so many myths feature encounters between an ascetic exhausted by long privations and a nymph sent by the gods to tempt him: the wind only has to help by lifting the nymph's clothing and the ascetic quickly succumbs. That does not imply that deeper attachment is always absent, although polygamy must have repercussions which it is difficult for us to assess. But it is exactly as if such a feeling did not exist, or did not count. Affection clearly exists between mother and child, or between friends. As soon as a man and a woman are involved, legitimately married or not, it is physical attraction that is described, or else the text moves immediately to the level of the obligations of dharma.

In another context, this might mean the supremacy of the male viewpoint and a maximum of brutality. In India, on the contrary—and this is the second observation—conquest of a woman is nothing if it does not have as its consequence a shared pleasure. One should no doubt regard as a literary commonplace the complaints of Bhartṛhari in the *Śatakatraya* (*The Three Texts of One Hundred Verses*), in which the man seems rather the victim of female seduction, a consenting victim moreover. The author's disillusioned philosophy has something to do with this: his long 'meditation' on love (*Hundred Verses on Passionate Love*) and its undoing (*Hundred Verses on Detachment*), presupposes the doctrine of the *Kāma Sūtra* and shows, like the epic myths, that the love of women is the main obstacle to the quest for liberation (how close we are here to the temptations of Saint Anthony!). However, on the theoretical plane which is that of the *Treatise of Love*, woman is neither a dominator nor a passive instrument; she is the necessary and respected partner. Her own desire must match that of the man and find its satisfaction at the same time as his: the anatomical considerations and the classification of men and women which Vātsyāyana indulges in have no other aim than this. The experience of love is analysed as a self-dispossession, a fusion with the partner. For each partner, it is the other's pleasure which counts, and it is this sharing of pleasure which makes it possible to use expressions like 'to be but a single thought' to describe the effect of the union of bodies: 'In the world, the fruit of love is the forging of one consciousness out of two. If love leaves the consciousness (of each lover) separate, it is as if union had occurred between two corpses' (*Hundred Verses on Passionate Love*, 29). The importance of this formulation cannot be over-estimated: far from seeing it as the cause of certain religious currents, one is more inclined to see it as the analogue of Hindu mystical experiences and techniques, in which the couple reproduces the union of God and nature. Indeed, the texts make no mystery about this: 'When thought is not reabsorbed in the act of love and in yogic concentration—*samādhi*—what is the point of meditation—*dhyāna*? What is the point of the act of love?' (*Śārṅgadharapaddhati*). By the same token, this view is diametrically opposed to Greek or Roman conceptions in which woman is either the mother of children or the instrument of man's pleasure. At the same time, it has nothing in common with courtly love. India has invented her own solution to the relation between the sexes. The Indian notion of the couple reminds us both that the individual is nothing by himself and, consequently, that the specifically psychological characteristics of the individual are never valorized. The emphasis on physical love is in fact the Indian form of the humanization of sexuality.

So we return to the starting-point, in which kāma was seen as the svadharma of women: they were no more able than other members of society to achieve existence by demanding autonomy. They find their place only by fully assuming their role as sexual partners, and it is in this area that they become truly complementary to men, whereas in other areas—including motherhood—they are only extensions of men. But the social role that women thereby acquire—as wives, mistresses or prostitutes—leads to no 'sublimation', because it is essentially linked to physical love. Kāma does indeed remain a fundamental desire of the human being, which has to receive satisfaction at its own level. The 'egoistic' aspect—the individual desire to be satisfied—is maintained in its entirety, even at the theoretical level, and all possible sexual deviations are provided for to deal with every situation: for example, the women of the royal harem, too numerous for the one man to whom they are tied, must resort to other means to obtain sexual satisfaction, and here too, all means are legitimate.

The craft of kingship

Artha is the business of Kṣatriyas, kings, just as kāma is entrusted to women. But the two ends, which represent the greater part of enjoyment in this world, are not unrelated to each other. For one thing, kings have a good measure of kāma since, thanks to the artha they possess, they can have all the women they desire in the kingdom; and for another, to say that the artha of the kingdom is made their responsibility amounts to saying—and this is how it is sometimes phrased in the epics—that they enable their subjects to pursue in peace the ends common to all men. One of the mythic forms in which a king's failure to do his duty is sometimes expressed is the killing, while hunting, of a male animal about to couple with a female. He has not allowed a creature to satisfy its desire, giving priority to his own desire, a passion for hunting, which is a royal vice deriving from kāma. It is the extreme case of blameworthy violence, which it is all the more important to highlight since a king, by virtue of his function, must commit acts of violence.

The svadharma of kings is by far the one which raises the most problems, for this reason it gives rise to a vast literature that is at once didactic and mythic—the two great epics of the *Mahābhārata* and the *Rāmāyaṇa*—as well as the more technical text of the *Arthaśāstra*, the collections of aphorisms on *nīti*, the 'art of conducting oneself' or 'of conducting' (one's affairs or those of the kingdom), and the chapters in the treatises of dharma dealing with the dharma of kings.

Two aspects of artha are self-evident for every Hindu consciousness. Artha, everything which is material wealth, i.e. prosperity, is desired by every man living in the world. As well as 'goal' and 'interest', *artha* means 'that which is good, useful'. Material goods are useful to this life; they are good as objects of enjoyment and as instruments of power. But at the same time, they are difficult to acquire and preserve; concern for one's artha is for every man an occasion for using force and violence; if success is sought above all, there may be no alternative means. This observation may well be one of the self-evident facts of life which the Hindu accepts with the same realism which leads him to give its full place to sexual desire. But this is not all: it would be impossible to understand the care the

Brahmans take to free the king from every restriction in administering the artha of the kingdom if one did not at the same time refer to the figure of the ideal Brahman as indicated in the treatises of dharma: the svadharma of the king and that of the Brahman are more than ever complementary and opposed, since the former justifies the use of force and of all the apparatus which surrounds it, whereas the latter, as we shall shortly see, forbids self-defence against a direct attack. It might therefore be said that, up to a point, the Brahman denies himself the pursuit of artha, allowing the Kṣatriya to look after it for him (which is not the same thing as renouncing it), while the Kṣatriya is obliged to act in ways contrary to dharma in order to defend the artha of all.

Some have compared the *Arthaśāstra* to Machiavelli's *Prince* and claimed to see in it a teaching divergent from that of the treatises of dharma; but that is an over-simplification. First of all, it must be remembered that, because he is the guardian of artha, the king also has artha as his main end in his own right, in spite of the recognized hierarchy: once again, the individual is identified with his function, and it cannot be otherwise from the Hindu standpoint. But that does not exclude him from dharma—on the contrary. The Kṣatriya's function, in terms of dharma in which *Kṣatra* is the complement of *Brahman*, is to protect the inhabitants of his kingdom, with his life if necessary, and he cannot do this without punctiliously performing the religious duties of his status. It has already been seen that he is the 'sacrificer' *par excellence*, who must offer numerous sacrifices and generously reward the Brahmans who officiate, and that, for all his skill and efforts, he cannot ensure the prosperity of the kingdom without doing so. This prosperity is nothing other than the possibility given to each inhabitant of the kingdom of pursuing his three ends in peace. It would be unacceptable for the royal function, so central to the maintenance of the social order, not to be fully integrated into the socio-cosmic order, dharma, which unites heaven and earth, the gods and men. Having said this, the domain of artha also constitutes a plane of visible realities subject to specific techniques, in which success is the only genuine norm. In this respect, the king's attitude is little different from that of any man who pursues artha. That is why the *Nītiśāstra* (*Treatises on the practical rules of conduct*) or the *Rājanītiśāstra* (*Treatises on the practical rules of royal conduct*), which are collections of aphorisms, include maxims of folk wisdom applicable to every man as well as advice appropriate only to kings. In the aphorisms, the word *rājā*, 'king', is often replaced by *naraḥ*, 'man'. There is nonetheless a difference between the king and any other man. The latter only pursues his *sva-artha*, his personal interest, whereas the king looks after the artha of all while simultaneously pursuing his own artha (essentially the exercise of power). More than the use of techniques which seem alien to dharma from the Hindu standpoint and incompatible with morality from our standpoint, it is therefore the slippage from the advancement of the artha of all to the king's personal interest, *svārtha*, which constitutes the conceptual difficulty to Western eyes. 'Raison d'état' is not a very reputable notion for us, although it is in common use, but it becomes quite unacceptable when it really refers to the personal interest of the power-holder. The Hindu mind does not perceive this duplicity in the same way, and cannot do so, since it identifies the individual with his social function.

The *Mahābhārata* offers us one example, among others, which may save us from a misunderstanding on this point: in Book I (Chapter 140), Prince Dhṛtarāṣṭra, who, according to dharma, is unfit to reign because of his blindness,[1] wants to flout the prohibition and above all to secure for his sons the succession to the throne on the death of his brother Pāṇḍu, although Pāṇḍu's eldest son, Yudhiṣṭhira[2] is the rightful heir. Having decided in his heart to give way to the pressure of his own eldest son, the wicked Duryodhana, Dhṛtarāṣṭra asks his Brahman minister, Kaṇika, to advise him on the attitude he should take towards his nephews, particularly the eldest, whom he has himself enthroned and whom the people are acclaiming as their king. Dhṛtarāṣṭra does not ask the Brahman whether he should accept Yudhiṣṭhira as king or revolt against him; in terms of dharma, there is no point in asking the question since the answer is obvious. And so he goes straight to the level of artha: should he adopt a friendly or a hostile attitude? The unspoken implication is: in order to win the throne, for himself and his son. That is how Kaṇika understands the question, and his response leaves no doubt. The epic text says of his words that they give the answer of the *Treatises of Royalty*–the *rājaśāstras*—(v.4.). So if Dhṛtaraṣṭra wishes to triumph, he must not allow Yudhiṣṭhira to consolidate his authority, and the means at his disposal are expressed in a form that is taken, quite literally for the most part, from the *Nītiśāstra* tradition. They are presented in the aphoristic style proper to the genre: 'He should make a bow of grass and feign sleep like a hunter of antelopes. When he has brought the enemy under his power by persuasion or by any other means, he should kill him. He should not treat with compassion one who comes seeking shelter. It is in this very way that one becomes divested of all obstacles: there is nothing to fear from a dead man.' (*Mahābhārata*, 1.140, 13–14). What is most surprising to us is perhaps the fact that it takes a Brahman to give such advice. To be sure, he would never give such advice to another Brahman, but when he is preaching to a prince, his audacity knows no bounds: 'A son, a friend, a brother, a father or even a guru, if they behave like enemies, should be killed by him who desires success. He may kill an enemy with a curse, with a gift of riches (to an intermediary), or with poison or trickery. In no wise should one be negligent . . .' (1.140, 52–53). Here the pursuit of artha entails a flagrant violation of dharma: no one is sacred in the eyes of a man who seeks his interest, although, for the Hindu mind, the murder of a father or a guru is the most heinous crime imaginable. In this particular case, personal interest, svārtha, comes a long way before raison d'état, but Kaṇika does not seek to distinguish these subtleties. He replies in terms of the technical rules which must be applied by anyone who seeks to triumph over an enemy or, in terms more worthy of a prince, to win a victory.

The problem which then arises is how to situate this advice from a Brahman in relation to dharma. If the king may or must behave in a manner contrary to dharma, in a situation in which the very end he pursues is contrary to dharma (since he is blind), how can a Brahman consent to advise him? The name Kaṇika in fact probably has a pejorative value, since it means 'little speck, thing of little worth', which might suggest that the wicked prince has consulted a worthless Brahman so as to obtain from him the approval he seeks. However, the epic, whose brahmanic orthodoxy cannot be impugned, leaves no room for such an interpretation. Indeed, in Book XII one finds a speech that is partially identical in form and very similar in substance, in a radically different context.

In Chapter 140 (in the section on *āpaddharma*, 'dharma for times of distress', and not the section on *rājadharma*), it is the thoroughly dharmic Prince Bhīṣma who, shortly before his death, speaks these words of artha to the no less dharmic Yudhiṣṭhira. These *ultima verba* coming from such a totally disinterested character are explicitly intended to show a king's duty in times of distress: Yudhiṣṭhira has asked him in what circumstances a prince may violate dharma and how far he may go in such transgression. The following chapters deal with the āppaddharma of the Brahman, so there is no ambiguity about the scope of Bhīṣma's advice. Not only is Kaṇika's language in no way moderated in Bhīṣma's mouth, but he attributes the doctrine he teaches to the Brahman Bhāradvāja or Kaninka Bhāradvāja (distorted in some texts to 'Kaṇika', but it is certainly the same person). Kaṇinka Bhāradvāja is well known as an expert on artha and is quoted several times in Kauṭilya's *Arthaśāstra*, where he seems to represent the most extreme views on artha. Thus, in a situation of distress, the ordinary rules of royal dharma—for example, those which bind the king to his father, his guru or his son, if ever they were to turn against him—no longer apply. If the king is in danger of losing his throne or even his life, he moves down from dharma to artha, that is, to rules designed to ensure practical success, without other considerations. Bhīṣma does not pause for a single moment to consider what we would call the 'legitimacy' of the case in order to qualify his advice, nor does he distinguish the threat to the king's throne from the danger of death. It is clearly impossible to separate the artha of the kingdom, which the king must preserve, from the svārtha of the same king. If one applies the rule which is stated in the following chapters on the Brahman's dharma in times of distress, it can be said that the king's sole object is to return by any means to a situation in which he can perform his regal function in the closest possible conformity with dharma. But it is all too clear that there is only a difference of degree between a dharmic and an un-dharmic king, and that the very nature of artha irremediably compromises a king without entailing moral reprobation. In the epic, it is Yudhiṣṭhira's cause—the cause of dharma, therefore—which triumphs, not becaue it is intrinsically just, but because Viṣṇu and the gods, who are the ultimate upholders of the socio-cosmic order, do all that is required to make it triumph, using disreputable tactics of artha when the need arises.

Yudhiṣṭhira, the son of Dharma, shrinks in horror from the prospects opened up for him by his great-uncle Bhīṣma. The solution for him, since he refuses to violate dharma, would not be to govern more 'virtuously' than others, but to renounce the throne and become a sannyāsin. He has no illusions: a king, by virtue of being a king, has to get his hands dirty, but this judgement is based on a standard which is not of this world, the one which, beyond dharma, leads to mokṣa. The epic mythology abounds with legitimate heirs who renounce the throne to become sannyāsins. But the consequences of this action are always disastrous for the kingdom: twelve years' drought and famine, social unrest, defeat in war and so on. A Kṣatriya's dharma requires him to dirty his hands: the classical doctrine seems to have moved away from the Upaniṣadic teaching which saw Brahmans and princes vying in knowledge of ātman-*Brahman*.

Portrait of the ideal Brahman

The svadharma of the Brahman, because it relates to dharma in all senses of the word, makes dharma his main goal. One is immediately inclined to think that his specific dharma would be by far the most demanding. In theory, he must teach and not merely study the Veda, and sacrifice on behalf of others, for the king in particular, and not merely for himself. But the classical tradition goes much further: when Manu (to cite but one authority) describes each of the four 'stages of life' through which the members of the three higher varṇas should in principles pass, it very soon becomes apparent that for him the term 'twice-born' only refers to the Brahman. And the Brahman is the only one who seems to be subject to the law of the four 'stages of life'. It might even be said that he is so much the guardian of dharma that he is also the only one to practice it. It is useful to take a closer look, especially since this monopoly of dharma only better prepares the Brahman to become a sannyāsin in the last stage of his life, whereas the Kṣatriya seems condemned to the impurity of secular tasks until he dies.

We have already seen (p. 30 ff.) that the Brahman of brahmanic theory sought to appropriate for himself certain elements from the figure of the sannyāsin. Beyond this, and as a means to adapting the two ideals to each other, he probably invented an intermediate model, the *vānaprastha* or 'forest dweller', representing a third, and fictional, stage of life. It is significant that this model corresponds fairly well to the mythic *ṛṣi*—'seer'—of the epic, a Brahman living in the forest with his wife and children, devoted to ritual activities, expert in Vedic science, but more particularly versed in the *Āraṇyakas* (see chapter 2).

However, the treatises of dharma unambiguously regard the householder stage as the most important one, the one on which the others—even that of sannyāsin—are dependent. The Brahman remains a figure of this world, at least during the middle period of his life, the longest in principle. He is not even yet vegetarian in theory, but all his meals have been transformed into sacrifices to enable him not only to consume meat (particularly in the meals offered to the ancestors) but also to expiate all the minor murders of minute creatures entailed by domestic life. The practice of the five 'major sacrifices' is in this respect a masterpiece of systematization. The ritual texts apparently see them as a kind of classification of sacrificial activities. By contrast, the *Dharmaśāstra* reduce them to a symbolic grouping, one which is unimportant as regards implementation but central by virtue of its signification. If one compares them with the internalized forms of sacrifice described in the *Āraṇyakas*, halfway along the path to renunciation, one is led to see the 'major sacrifices' as another attempt at transforming the sacrifices, while still retaining their outward form and 'worldly' efficacy. Apparently the only one which remains intact is the sacrifice to *Brahman* which consists of a recitation of the Vedic texts learnt during the period of study. At the same time it has to be noted that the sacrifice to *Brahman* was perhaps rather the teaching than the recitation of the Veda. In the treatises of dharma, it is study of the text that is foregrounded, since it forms the main part of the first 'stage of life', that of the brahmanic student; the function of teacher does not reappear in the description of the householder, although it is known that it in fact continued to exist. As for the other four 'major sacrifices', they are associated with meals. The Brahman, who otherwise carefully avoids touching the remains of food because they are impure, cannot in fact partake of a meal until he has offered it to the gods, the ancestors, all creatures (especially the disquieting creatures of the invisible world) and any guests who have arrived (sannyāsins, brahmanic students, strangers etc.). He must even feed his whole household before himself. This food offered to others constitutes so many sacrifices, the remains of which he will then eat. Sacrificial activity is thus reduced to a minimum, but its efficacy is maximum: all beings are associated with it, the gods and the ancestors are satisfied, dangerous beings propitiated, the socio-cosmic order is assured, at the same time as involuntary 'murders' are expiated. One has to admire the ingenuity of the Brahmans who have thus succeeded in combining, in a very simplified rite, the essential part of their role according to dharma with the concern for ahiṃsā which they received from the sannyāsin.

However, the treatises of dharma still insist on ancestor worship. Ancestors, unlike the gods, seem not to be satisfied with the offering of their share of the daily meals. They also call for special meals on fixed dates, after having received funerals which have transformed them into ancestors. Ancestral rites still continue today among the Brahmans, and even in other castes, but the beliefs which underlie them are particularly difficult to reconcile. Originally, it was a matter of feeding the ancestor in his abode in the other world, the abode of the dead or heaven. But the Brahman, adopting the sannyāsin's belief in rebirths and liberation, is no longer sure where to place his ancestors. He nonetheless continues to offer them food while praying for their liberation (where they no longer need the fruits of the earth). Membership of the lineage is certainly one of the strongest social linkages, the one which appears last when the sannyāsin leaves the world: he himself is freed from all obligations, but his son will worship him after his death. However, the rite is transformed, and the dominant idea is that worship of the dead sannyāsin—who theoretically has no further individual existence but is reabsorbed in the Absolute—is beneficial for his descendants. At this point, liberation is close to being taken over by the world for its own ends.

In fact, the aged Brahman's abandonment of the world has probably always been the exception to the rule, and this only served to keep the ancestral rites more alive. Then it was the theory of karman, originating in sannyāsin circles, that was reversed for the benefit of the man living in the world: for the sannyāsin, past karman weighs on his shoulders and keeps him in the servitude of transmigration, and his chief concern is to cease to accumulate the residues of karman for the future, in particular by abandoning all ritual activity—karman (see p. 23 ff.). The distinction between good and bad karman would be quite irrelevant to him, since it is karman as such which is bad. The man living in the world, with the Brahman in the forefront, taking hold of this notion which seems to condemn him to a miserable servitude, develops on the contrary all the positive implications for himself: he changes the gloomy prospects into possibilities of a brilliant future and, far from seeking to suppress karman, he accumulates all the merits that it allows him, thus ensuring for himself good future rebirths. In this new perspective, the Brahman finds some satisfaction: not only can he attribute his present Brahman existence to his past merits, but he is the best placed both to obtain liberation and to secure the best rebirths as a Brahman. His concern for ritual purity, the exactness of his observances, his present 'sannyāsic' virtues—non-violence, veracity, honesty—help to orient his mind naturally, as it were, towards liberation up to the moment when he will renounce everything and seek *Brahman* alone. In practice, he alone is equipped for sannyāsa, unless he prefers to store up his merits for future lives. The *Dharmaśāstra* thus tend to 'consolidate' karman, to see the 'good' always reborn good, if they have not sought liberation, and the 'wicked' perpetuate themselves in their wickedness and their lower social status.

This ambiguity of the role of karman can be seen in all the philosophical systems. But it is particularly apparent, within the different nuances of Vedānta, in the discussions of the respective roles of rites and knowledge (of ātman-*Brahman*) in obtaining liberation. If the sannyāsin is ultimately always a Brahman, the farewell to the world is itself a rite, and it is clear that the values of the man-in-the-world were bound to force their way into those of the 'renouncer', as the Brahman living in the secular world sought to resemble the sannyāsin. In any case, the mere fact that the question of the role of rites in the journey towards liberation is raised —even if salvation is seen (as it is by Śaṅkara) only in total renunciation of rites—shows clearly that such a philosophy is closely bound up with the brahmanic universe. We started out from the idea that the Indian 'renouncer' could only be understood in terms of the man-in-the-world that he had been or might have been. The whole history of brahmanic thought—and we shall shortly reach the same conclusion for the whole of Hindu thought—confirms this premise. It is therefore logical that some great sages of Vedānta maintain a sort of balance between rites and knowledge or even, like the 'non-dualist' Maṇḍana or the 'dualist' Madhva, opt for life in the world. This having been said, modern Hindu masters subscribe totally to the universality of the Vedāntic philosophy. (But then this is no more curious a view than that of the French who might be hard put to allow that Descartes might not be widely followed outside their borders.)

That is not all. The ideal Brahman of the *Dharmaśāstra*, who is therefore a householder, is poor. He must not earn his own living, since all service is seen as degrading—a Śūdra's activity—and so forbidden. Although in theory he is the only one able to receive as well as make gifts, whereas others must give—essentially to the Brahman, but also to any 'renouncer'—Manu recommends as the most perfect path for the householder that he should collect daily only what he needs for that day's subsistence for himself and his dependants. Manu even makes a distinction between the gifts the Brahman receives for himself, which must be extremely pure, and those he receives in order to carry out his sacrificial obligations, on which he may be less punctilious, given the binding nature of his obligations. The strict ideal, however, would be to glean each day the amount of grain needed, and therefore to do without the slightest gift. On this point too, the imitation of the sannyāsin is flagrant, but so too is the contradiction, even at a theoretical level: the role of priest in the sacrifices offered by others, particularly by kings, is expressly mentioned in the definition of the Brahman's svadharma, and the epic is full of such royal sacrifices in which the Brahmans receive substantial fees—*dakṣiṇā*—if they officiate or various gifts if they merely attend. A king's excessive piety is even sometimes symbolized by over-large gifts to the Brahmans or too many sacrifices. Moreover, the texts on ritual give minute descriptions of the liturgical functions of the various categories of Brahmans. Yet the *Laws of Manu* mention only in one word the Brahman's function as officiating priest, and then make no further reference to it. Correspondingly, they do not dwell on the ritual obligations of kings, which require the services of the Brahmans. The emphasis placed on the Brahman's poverty and on the ban on serving tends, on the contrary, to leave a veil of uncertainty over the essential features of his activities and his income, in theory and in practice. But it is not certain that the contradiction here comes entirely from the proximity of the sannyāsin: a Brahman's status is bound to be somewhat degraded by the effect of rendering service and taking part in the impure aspects of sacrifice. But the model of the renouncer can only lead him to emphasize purity; the idea of poverty necessarily has the same origin in a society in which so much prestige is attached to money and to ostentatious expenditure.

The sannyāsin model also lies behind the Brahman's total inability to defend himself by force, the use of force being exclusively reserved for kings. This is only one of the applications of non-violence, which is in fact more important in the epic myths than in the theory of dharma. In practice, the Brahman has modelled himself on these contradictory demands, while taking account of harsh reality: he has consented to officiate in the various sacrifices and rites in which his presence was required, accepting the fees associated with them; he has even become priest-in-charge of a temple, which is even more degrading, but may be extremely lucrative. He has demanded proportionately greater remuneration when the function entailed greater risks for his status, for example in funeral rites. Occasionally he may have been greedy. But, as if to compensate, he has become strictly vegetarian—whereas Manu still allowed him to eat meat—and most punctilious about the minor rules of everyday purity, like the sannyāsins.

Ultimately it may wondered if this dharma, which is constantly referred to as the highest goal of man in the world, and as especially entrusted to the care of the Brahman, was ever practised in its pure form. It is rather striking that two commonly used collections of aphorisms, one in Sanskrit, the *Śatakatraya* by Bhartṛhari, the other in Tamil, the *TirukkuRal*,[3] dividing their subject into three sections, deal with nīti (which we have seen to be related to the king), erotic passion and detachment, and with a twofold dharma, that of the householder and that of the renouncer, and with artha and kāma. The *Śatakatraya* shows several times that happiness in this world is to be either a king or a renouncer, one having maximum pleasure on earth, the other having attained peace through outward and inward detachment.

Two types of men

The way in which the goals of man are distributed in brahmanic orthodoxy results in the formation of two opposed types of men, assigned to complementary tasks. The Kṣatriya, a prince and warrior, is not only committed to the use of force and to the impure works of violence; as the foremost possessor of the wealth of the kingdom, he makes it yield fruit in pious works which ensure the prosperity of all, not least that of the Brahmans. But he also spends it in the pursuit of pleasure, in increasing the number of his wives. Should his non-vegetarian diet be connected with his function of 'sacrificer'? Not necessarily, since he seems to have extended systematically the impure practices into which his functions forced him. The Kṣatriya of the epic is a meat-eater, a drinker of wine to the point of drunkenness,[4] a lover of women, a great hunter—killing for sport, therefore, and not solely out of necessity—a slayer of men in war or otherwise, and ready to die on the field of battle: rough ways and respect for the Brahmans characterize his dharma. These are features which the economically dominant castes of the various regions of India tended to adopt after his example. There is so much continuity in this portrait of the warrior-prince that even today the non-vegetarian restaurants of the east coast of the Deccan are called 'military restaurants'. The wives or concubines of princes, of very variable status, since theoretically only the first need be chosen according to the rules of caste, are assigned to his pleasure, in both the broad and narrow senses of the word: banquets, country outings, water games, music, dancing and the games of love seem to exist only for princes and their wives, if the literature is to be believed. Rich merchants, however, readily imitate them in their pleasures and their extravagances.

By contrast, the Brahman is the man whose social status is linked to purity, who keeps away from every impure person, from everything connected with death. Vegetarian and frugal, respectful of life in all its forms, he eats only with his equals so as to avoid sullying himself—which is not in contradiction with his obligation to consume only the remains of food that has become a sacrificial offering. His life is austere, because of all the observances which surround it and the theoretical absence of wealth. He is indeed the man of dharma, the man whose conduct is shaped by invisible values more than by the pursuit of pleasure or immediate gain. His wife—in theory he has only one—is likewise entirely absorbed by her husband's religious duties and must be less concerned with kāma than other women: the wretched Reṇukā, the wife of a celebrated Brahman, but the daughter of a prince, was cursed by her husband when, having gone to fetch water from the river, she lingered on the bank and longingly watched a prince playing in the water surrounded by his wives. In momentarily giving her thoughts to kāma, she fell short of the dharma of her husband, who, for once, gave way to the most violent anger and had his wife decapitated by his son: the wife's momentary frivolity prevented the husband from performing the rite at the prescribed time and provoked his deadly anger. An avalanche of sins! It takes two to be dharmic. But such a condemnation of kāma in the name of dharma in fact betrays the influence of the sannyāsin. One of the truths most often repeated, regardless of varṇa, is that none of the puruṣārthas is to be sacrificed to the others.

These two models are partly theoretical, but they well express the orthodox world view, i.e. that of the Brahmans who hold to the Revelation and the oldest Tradition. Room is made—and duly justified—within it for the 'sacred' and the 'profane' and for the whole range of human aspirations. Indeed, they are so far from pure fiction that they largely inspire the conduct of the other castes, depending on whether they live in the orbit of the princes or the Brahmans. Those who want to raise their social status imitate the Brahmans by avoiding the company of those reckoned to be impure, by restricting their range of choice in making a marriage alliance, by becoming vegetarians. In practice, however, recognition of superior status depends greatly on the Brahmans themselves. If Brahmans make themselves available to officiate in the rites of the group seeking higher status, then that group will see itself, and will eventually be seen by others, as Kṣatriya rather than Śūdra. Its members will wear the sacred thread of the twice-born. That can be done only if at the same time it gains respect by its wealth and influence—of which the Brahmans are the first beneficiaries. The Marāṭhas, for example, in west Deccan, have remained meat-eaters and drinkers of alcohol. But Śivājī, their national hero, obtained royal consecration by the appropriate Vedic rite in the seventeenth century. No one in Mahārāṣṭra would dare call these parvenus 'Śūdras'.

Renunciation and human love

Since I am endeavouring to emphasize that which differentiates the brahmanic world from our own so as to prevent ethnocentric misreadings, it is perhaps permissible here to mention what would seem to be a constant feature, in an area where one would precisely not expect to find it. Modern westerners attribute to Christianity, and especially to the great centuries of monasticism, an ethic and a spirituality which depreciate sexuality and which exert unbearable pressures on human consciousness, to the point of forcing them into hypocritical positions. We nevertheless know that medieval literature was not entirely clothed in asceticism, and this is even truer of later periods: Pascal is not the whole of the seventeenth century. Yet it would surely be wrong to attribute the sauciest fabliaux or the *Carmina Burana* to overt unbelief. The monastic ideal, on the other hand, was not defined solely by the vow of chastity, and the latter was, moreover, initially defined positively by the need to focus all attention and energy on God, more than by depreciation of women and of sexuality.

Regardless of the modern form this problem has taken, India helps us in a strange way, to look at our own cultural attitudes towards this subject in a better perspective. No one could accuse Indian culture of prudishness, puritanism or inhibition: it has given kāma its proper theoretical place and has declared, in and out of season, that amorous pleasure may not be sacrificed for the sake of supposedly higher aims. It has granted to women their place as partners in the games of love and even demanded that they learn to play their role properly in this sphere. At the same time, parallel to this and at the highest level of the hierarchy of the goals of man, it has allowed for the development of an ideal of religious life and of renunciation of the world. In this context, the exhortation to chastity is at least as strong as in the West, and has been further combined with more or less magical notions concerning the loss of physical strength through sexual activity. In fact, the perspective is very close to that of Christian monasticism, *mutatis mutandis*: Indian kāma is, as we have seen, essentially physical love, and it is the sexual act itself which provokes a weakening of the body and therefore a weakening of the mind which can no longer concentrate on the pursuit of the Absolute. The idea is at bottom the same as that of the first desert anchorites: chastity is the pre-condition which makes it possible to concentrate on a single goal. For the renouncer, there is indeed only one goal, mokṣa, which will suffer no dissipation of attention and efforts. It alone is worth sacrificing everything else. The institutionalization of chastity is even much more developed in India than in the West. Before being imposed on the sannyāsin, it is imposed on the young 'brahmanic student'—*brahmacārin*—throughout the whole period during which he has to study the Veda. *Brahmacārin*, literally perhaps, 'he who practises brahman (= Veda)', comes to mean 'committed to chastity', and it is the title borne by those who pass directly from the student stage to that of renouncer, remaining with their guru instead of going home to marry.

It is tempting to think that all the more emphasis has been placed on chastity because love was recognized as a value in the world: worldly values become alien as a whole to one who is renouncing the world, but whereas the break with dharma was difficult to make for high-caste renouncers, the renunciation of kāma has to be much more radical. As has been said in passing, in the myths, it is by provoking a sexual fallibility that the gods rid themselves of a too-powerful ascetic: once again a magical universe is manifested in which the energy accumulated by asceticism is liable to burn up the worlds, but is reduced to nothing by the loss of semen provoked by the sight of an alluring nymph. The fact remains that amorous pleasure truly does symbolize the opposite of renunciation. Moreover, it is through just such a symbolization that it also takes on a religious role in Hinduism: we will return to this point, in a context which, while quite distant from the brahmanic ideal, is one that remains within the same overarching structure. As for the Brahman, he owes it to himself to turn a deaf ear to kāma in the ideal picture he paints of himself, when it is the model of the sannyāsin that he wishes to follow.

So it seems that under all climes—for similar observations would have to be made for all religions which contain some form of renunciation of the world—human love and the pursuit of an Absolute situated somewhere beyond the world have been felt to be antagonistic. Their opposition is, in a way, that of two absolutes, each capable of polarizing all attention. However, whereas the Gospel is content to oppose God and Mammon, brahmanic orthodoxy is more radical in opposing kāma and mokṣa, one being solely of this world, the other outside the world. But Hinduism was to rework these elements in all directions, bringing mokṣa into this world by making it possible to live there without kāma and, conversely, seeking mokṣa in kāma. The Brahman would not always be able to endorse these speculations, but it would be difficult for him to deny paternity of the values involved.

CHAPTER 3

Salvation through Deeds: The Yogin Warrior

We have seen how difficult it was to maintain a univocal meaning for each of the 'goals of man'. Each of the three goals internal to this world can be seen as an all-inclusive value: there is a level at which dharma, as the total socio-cosmic order, has room for the sannyāsin and his specific end of deliverance, while in a more restricted sense it can also be the order, again social and cosmic, which is the condition of the very existence of this world, in which the ordinary man lives, and which requires one to live in harmony with the invisible beings of the 'three worlds'. Artha itself, as a 'goal' of man, may subsume mokṣa and dharma, while in another sense it is articulated with dharma and kāma to form one of the 'natural' leanings of man living in this world: concern for his material interests. Mokṣa is anyway a special case; but, whereas it ought precisely to remain apart from the 'worldly' ends, the Brahmans tended to annex it as the fulfilment of their own dharma, which would have had the effect of making liberation the all-inclusive value of this world, at least from the viewpoint of the first varṇa. This endeavour was fraught with consequences for the future of Hinduism, since the idea of a salvation outside this world was bound to have universalistic implications which tended to undermine the social hierarchy. The elucidation of these implications constitutes a large part of the religious 'history' of India; but here too, the decisive steps escape us in their actual movement and we only see their results: an imposing edifice of many dimensions—cosmogony and cosmology, theology and anthropology—forming the universe of *bhakti*, the religion of devotion. The latter, instead of taking shape alongside brahmanic orthodoxy, subsumed it and adapted its structure to take account of it, in one of those specifically Indian enveloping moves. So the Brahman can find a place for himself and his aristocratic ideas within this universe, if he will accept a broader horizon and the universalization of salvation; but he can equally well refuse it in the name of his orthodoxy.

An anthropology of desire

But all this would probably be unintelligible if we did not first pause to consider the subsuming value that kāma can become. When Bhīma, the second of the Pāṇḍavas, the younger brother of Yudhiṣṭhira Dharmarāja,[1] sings the praises of kāma in Book XII of the *Mahābhārata* (Chapter 167), it is an easy matter for him to show that kāma—desire in all its forms—is the basis of all the other ends of man: the man of artha obviously desires material goods and success; but does the man of dharma, with all his observances, have less kāma? That view would not prove tenable for long, since the Revelation is the first to link the sacrificial rites with desires: 'He who desires heaven, may he sacrifice—*svargakāmo yajeta* . . .'. For each rite, the outcome is indicated. He who desires that outcome must perform the rite. The religion of the Brahman—dharma—is therefore in fact full of kāma. Bhīma goes further: the ascetic himself would not leave the world if the desire for liberation did not impel him to do so. Sanskrit here comes to his aid, since the seeker after liberation is designated by means of a desiderative form: the *mumukṣu* is 'he-who-desires-liberation'.[2] Bhīma ('the Redoubtable'), a slayer of ogres and 'wicked' men, but a champion of women, in short a chivalrous brute, is the son of Vāyu, the Wind,[3] and shares his father's extraordinary strength and irascibility. According to the conceptions of the epic, the Wind manifests itself as the breath of life and as movement (XII.247.9). In the company of his brothers, and especially in comparison with Yudhiṣṭhira who is always tempted by deliverance, Bhīma does indeed seem to symbolize love of life on the earth on which his feet are firmly planted. He glorifies everything that his elder brother condemns, and justifies attachment to transmigration. In his own right he personifies the 'man-in-the-world'. But would he be a sufficiently acute 'moralist' to detect the omnipresence of kāma if he had not been invited to do so by the man of renunciation?

Before answering this fundamental question, let us note that the language used by the mythic Bhīma is entirely consistent with the psychology expressed by the philosophical systems. The schema set out by Nyāya—the Indian philosophical system which was constructed to serve as a basis and an exposition of logic—is more or less tacitly accepted by all the brahmanic systems: action is conceived as a kind of response by the subject to an external stimulus. Invariably the sequence is: knowledge → desire → inclination to act. There is no action that is not preceded by a desire, and the latter is never the desire to act, but desire for an object, for a precise result known to be good in itself. The knowledge which gives rise to the desire is often a perception; but this perception is of interest only inasmuch as it informs the subject of the present existence of an object within reach, which he knows in other ways to be good for him or useful to him (artha). Knowledge of the present object is inseparable from a whole halo of past experiences which gives it an index of value. Instinctive behaviour which does not seem to be preceded by either knowledge or desire (the first time a child sucks at its mother's breast, for example) is even accounted for in terms of supposed experiences from past lives. This simple structure explains sexual behaviour as well as action performed in the field of artha. But it is equally capable of accounting for actions governed by dharma which are intended to produce a desirable outcome.

The brahmanic conception of action is so well expressed in this way that it reappears, in an even more systematic form, applied by Mīmāṃsā to the analysis of dharmic conduct. Mīmāṃsā is the philosophical school which set out to draw up the rules of interpretation of the Vedic Revelation, and more specifically that part of the Revelation which deals with rites. But it really performed a work of philosophy in seeking—like Nyāya for logic—to make explicit the foundations of its hermeneutics. It starts out from the self-evident datum—it is more than a postulate—that all action is painful, since it presupposes effort and fatigue. Therefore no one would ever act if he were not convinced that by this action he would obtain a good which would significantly reward the effort expended. Let us pre-empt the misunderstanding that is likely to arise in view of the widespread prejudice that the Hindu is 'contemplative': Mīmāṃsā certainly does not draw from contemplation its conception of action as painful. The Greeks in any case taught us that contemplation is the highest form of action. But the philosophers of Mīmāṃsā did not believe in contemplation, knowledge, the pursuit of the Absolute. Up to a certain point (seventh or eight century AD?) they even refused the idea of liberation, and when they were obliged to integrate it, they still asserted that it was obtained through rites. Their conception of action as essentially painful is therefore even more remarkable. Action does not express man, it only reveals his desire, in the most egoistic sense of the term. Practically speaking, these ritualists weighted down the life of the 'twice-born' with a plethora of rites suited to every conceivable circumstance: there is the oblation for the birth of a son, the sacrifice to obtain cattle, a village, a kingdom . . . but most of these major sacrifices are aimed at securing heaven after death. The desire for this necessarily invisible result is indeed that which distinguishes man from animals. But it is neither the object nor the nature of the desire which distinguishes him, but the acceptance of an action aimed at a long-term result. However, the obligatory daily rites or those which must be performed on certain occasions (birth, marriage, death . . .) do not seem to lend themselves to such analysis of action: one does not perform them because one desires a precise result, given that they entail no result. But there is no conception of substitution: these obligatory rites are performed only because one fears misfortune in the event of abstention. Fear is the negative reverse side of desire and it can still be formulated in terms of desire: it can be said that a man acts with the desire to obtain something beneficial—*artha*—or to avoid something harmful—*anartha*. Once again, we oberve the strange overlapping of registers. We are in the midst of dharma, but it is still a question of artha. Dharma does not address a higher level of the human kind, but it is distinct from artha in that it deals with invisible objects or with actions whose efficacy is invisible, and for which the Revelation is required as a source of knowledge.

It is clearly no accident that desire is thus stripped bare, as it were, by the school of brahmanic thought that is most orthodox, but with an exclusively secular orthodoxy. Mīmāṃsā refused renunciation and would also refuse bhakti, and mention has already been made of the way in which it empties the Vedic gods of their reality in order to give full importance to the sacrificial rites. It is obviously a school of Brahmans (like all the Sanskrit philosophical schools), for whom desires and the rites intended to satisfy them highlight their priestly function. Possessing both knowledge of the rites and the monopoly of performance of them, they are the indispensable agents of the prosperity of this world. Perhaps, however, they would not have thought of systematizing their world view in this way if they had not had to contrast it with that of the renouncers and, even more, with that of the Brahmans who sought to integrate renunciation into their own philosophy. The ideal of humanity which they put forward—with entirely rational rigour and total intellectual probity, for they are talking about themselves—is ultimately somewhat impoverished, almost a caricature in its refusal of any transcendence. Man is the only being who interests them, but it is the man of their society, of high-caste brahmanic society, man as he exists in themselves and not as he ought to be or might be imagined. But by reducing the ritualistic religion of the higher castes to its essential form, they manifest it more clearly as the reverse of renunciation, as the pole of entire affirmation which is the counterpart of the pole of refusal.

The eternity of speech and the power of vision

If bhakti or the notion of a sovereign God—Īśvara—appears from time to time on the edge of their discussions, the great avowed adversary remains Buddhism, and especially the mystic Buddhism of Mahāyāna that was known to the early Mīmāṃsists. They saw it as the very culmination of renunciation, the point where renunciation really casts off its links with secular values by contesting even the validity of the Veda. Since the Buddhists claim to substitute for the Veda the word of the Buddha, it is necessary to establish the absolute truth of the brahmanic Revelation by setting it beyond all possibility of doubt, and to oppose it to the weakness of every human testimony. So we are brought back to the idea that the Veda (that is, the whole of the Revelation) is not only eternal but self-revealed: such a body of rites, placing the sorts of demands it does on people—and offering them results that are either distant or invisible (to the living human eye)—could only draw on itself for its authority. There is no man in this world who can claim a power of vision—i.e. of knowledge—superior to that of other men. Not even Manu: and for anyone who knows what this mythic law-maker represents in the eyes of an orthodox Brahman, such a declaration has to be taken seriously. This means, in particular, that even the wisest Brahman, the one whose learning carries most weight, has had no extraordinary power of knowledge. He owes his superiority solely to his deeper study of the Veda—the Veda which he received from his master like all other Brahmans. *A fortiori*, run-of-the-mill Brahmans have so special capacity for vision. They simply receive the eternal knowledge from their masters. If one asks how the Veda manifested itself in the first place, the answer is simple: the world has always existed and, since there has never been a beginning, there was never a moment when the Veda first manifested itself. It has always been passed on by word of mouth. This personal modesty and the claim of absolute authority for the Veda are aimed at all those who are credited with superhuman powers of vision thanks to which they are supposed to have 'seen' the invisible, and therefore 'composed' the Veda or some other revelation: first and foremost the Buddha, then the most powerful yogins, and finally Iśvara, the Lord, the god of Bhakti, whose respective devotees regard them as omniscient.

The refusal of omniscience even becomes a kind of touchstone of orthodoxy: the philosophers of Nyāya and Vaiseṣika, like those of classical Yoga, accept the possibility of omniscience for the original *ṛṣis* who 'saw' the Veda and transmitted it to men out of their goodness, for the yogins who acquired it through their ascetic exercises, and for Īśvara; all this has to be seen in relation to the universe of bhakti and no longer to the orthodox world view which has so far been described. On the other hand, the Vedānta of Śaṅkara takes its stand on Mīmāmsā in asserting the eternity and self-revelation of the Veda,[4] i.e. both of the Upaniṣads and of all the revealed texts which give knowledge of the Absolute. We find again here (see p. 26) the path of knowledge which was previously described as the most orthodox: the role of the guru is now grounded in doctrine. When, through the images and the formulae of the Revelation, the master teaches his disciple the identity of ātman and *Brahman*, he is not simply the extension, within the world of the renouncers, of the guru who teaches the Veda to the young *brahman*; he is the necessary intermediary, the organ of transmission of a knowledge of the Invisible *par excellence*, which man has no means of acquiring by himself. Śaṅkara's 'renouncer' has abandoned rites, but this is not sufficient to confer new powers on him. What he seeks is experimental knowledge of the Absolute, not intellectual knowledge;[5] and, by definition, that experience of an ineffable Absolute can only be beyond words. Yet it is the upaniṣadic Revelation transmitted by the guru which makes it possible to seek it in the right direction and attain it.

It is likely that Śaṅkara (seventh-eighth century?) represents a decisive moment in the renouncers' growing awareness of the demands of brahmanic orthodoxy, and that this awareness could only be achieved by following in the tracks of Mīmāṃsā. The self-revelation of the Veda is normally combined with the refusal to grant the yogins an extraordinary power of vision. However, living in a world in which bhakti is triumphant, Śaṅkara takes account of belief in a sovereign God, Īśvara, whom he makes a manifestation of Brahman at the level of *māyā*. Indeed, his non-dualism makes it relatively easy to integrate the existing religious currents, since everything that is not pure and simple *Brahman* is illusion—*māyā*—including Īśvara. This flexible orthodoxy is one of the major reasons for Śaṅkara's success up to the present day. There is not a Hindu to be found, Śaṅkarian or not, who has not learnt to distinguish the levels of reality, and who, inside a temple dedicated to a particular deity, will fail to explain to one, *ad nauseam*, that the deity worshipped in that place is but a manifestation of the supreme *Brahman*. But we shall have to return to this crucial point.

It will have been noted that the model for all knowledge is perception, particularly visual perception, of the objects present, the 'vision' of the omniscient yogin, and even the ultimate realization of the Absolute which the Śaṅkarian sannyāsin arrives at after having at great length ruminated upon the upaniṣadic teaching with the aid of his master. The knowledge which Veda gives of the invisible world of rites is itself curiously assimilated to a direct knowledge, i.e. a perception: the self-revealed Word in fact puts the hearer in immediate contact with the revealed objects. At the beginning of its exposition of logic, Nyāya recognizes that the summit of all knowledge is perception: having reached that point, thought rests, satisfied. There is never any question of intellectual understanding, inward knowledge of a thing or a being. This is one of the aspects which is logically linked to the anthropology of desire that Mīmāṃsā builds up: the desire to know—*jijñāsā*, another desiderative form—is never gratuitous, it always implies that some good is expected, not from knowledge, but from the object of knowledge. If a man does not seek to understand, that is because he does not think he needs to in order to possess: all that is useful is given, either in perception or in the the Revelation and the Tradition which completes it. And it is quite clear that the desire to know *Brahman* itself is no exception to this rule. Thus man knows essentially through his sensory organs, including his hearing, which gives him access to the revealed Word, completed by *manas*, the internal organ which also ensures the link between the external organs and the ātman. The ātman itself, which, as has already been observed, has no structure of its own since it will return to undifferentiatedness in deliverance, plays so small a part in the process of knowledge (although it preserves the record of memories and karman) that some conceive it as pure consciousness (Vedānta), while others (Nyāya) regard it as unconscious by nature—particularly so, therefore, in the liberated state—and conscious by accident. Sāṅkhya complicates this schema somewhat, as we shall see, for reasons which have nothing to do with a more refined analysis of the activity of knowledge.

However, this structure of the cognitive apparatus is linked even more deeply to the orthodox anthropology, of which the primacy of desire is only one aspect: one has to remember what individual man is in brahmanic society. Taken as a member of his group, identified with the function he inherited at birth, and integrally related to the totality of the triple world through the 'debts' he has contracted by coming into the world, he is himself a person who has no 'inside'. He learns from his group what is expected of him and the ideal for him will be to conform to it. What then is to be learnt that is not already known by someone who will teach it to you? There is never a sense of progress, other than in the explanation of what has been said in the past and which already contained all that needed to be known. Therefore philosophical and religious literature is, for the most part, a literature of commentaries in scholastic form. But the consequences of this also resonate beyond the limits of philosophy. Regardless of the manner in which the earliest scientific discoveries (in medicine, astronomy and mathematics) were formulated—discoveries that were, to be sure, no more true or false than those of ancient Greece, whatever their comparative dates may have been—the mental and, more generally, the cultural conditions never seem to have coalesced in India in such a way as to give rise to a true spirit of research and investigation. It may be granted that the history of scientific ideas in the West has been partly a matter of serendipity. But the sense this may give us of the contingency and fragility of our successes cannot mask the fact that Greece bequeathed to our Middle Ages a richer notion of individual man than that of India:[6] Plato's republic distributes its three social functions by analogy with the structure of the individual man. Even if the philosophers of that republic only contemplate ideas which exist outside themselves, the fact remains that they are capable of contemplating them, that their minds are made for that. There is an 'inside' to the individual man which Christianity only deepens, universalizes and renders more precious. We shall shortly see, by contrast, what type of man Hinduism projected, not into the human city, but into the Absolute.

One can formulate very briefly what is missing in the brahmanic vision of man, from the standpoint of the most fundamental conceptions of the West. On the one hand, the concept of reason never appears. This is a concept that allows the individual, at the very least, to appropriate for himself the ideas of his milieu. But it can also give rise to projects as ambitious as that of Descartes: to start from scratch as a means of thinking more clearly, and to base one's thinking on an unassailable initial premise. The very notion of a concept has no equivalent in Sanskrit vocabulary. Correlatively, human conduct is never considered in the light of an individual moral conscience. But it is extremely dangerous to formulate negatively in this way that which makes the originality of India. It is immediately necessary to prevent the interpretations that the ambient prejudices would encourage. If, in particular, we could abandon once and for all the absurd idea that Hindu thought does not recognize the principle of non-contradiction and that its natural mysticism even revels in the identification of contraries. . . ! This misapprehension stems from the confusion of different orders of thought, although they also exist in our thinking, where we are able to keep them distinct. Brahmanic conceptual systems are probably never what we call 'philosophy', in the sense in which this is distinguished from theology, since they are all built up within the ambient religious beliefs, themselves regarded as universal self-evidences. Their theories of knowledge all give a central place to the revealed Word without which all thought would be crippled. This is indeed still the great affirmation of contemporary Hindu thinkers in the face of the presumptions of a western civilization that is perceived overall as atheistic. Human thought can only work on foundations which are given to it and which it has to accept.[7] But this does not imply either that Hindus have not been able to think rationally or that they have never handled concepts. Not only have they used the principle of non-contradiction—it is not clear how any thought could dispense with it—but they have constructed a universe of logical coherence which is almost too perfect, both in their mythology and in their philosophy, and a system of logic that is breathtaking in its subtlety. It is my aim to give a glimpse of the former in the whole of this essay, and I shall perhaps have succeeded if the reader is left with an impression of vertigo. As for the latter, it is forever inaccessible to the non-specialist because it requires an extremely technical and rigorous language, closely linked to the resources of Sanskrit and defying translation. Each supporting the other, they have developed in a totally self-enclosed universe of thought, with very little external influence and no possibility of internal renewal. To understand this, one would have to imagine a scholasticism that never opened onto a Renaissance or a Descartes—and this in spite of the powerful originality, down to recent times, of certain thinkers.

So when Hindu or Buddhist philosophers have juxtaposed contradictory formulae such as: 'It is being and non-being, it is neither being nor non-being'; they are not ignoring the principle of non-contradiction, as some westerners, whether in mockery or in ecstatic admiration, have naïvely supposed. On the contrary, they sought, by means of a scholarly use of this principle, which they diverted from its usual applications, to express an absolute reality that eluded, by its very nature, the structures of thought. The West too has known such paradoxical formulations, and no one has ever been tempted to accuse their authors of not understanding the principle of non-contradiction. It was understood that they were seeking to express an ineffable transcendence which ordinary human language could only betray. It would only be fair to credit Nāgārjuna or other 'mystical' philosophers of India with an analogous and perfectly conscious intention. In any case, the importance of the 'mystical' philosophy of India should not be exaggerated. One sometimes has the impression that, for westerners who take an interest in the country without making it a particular object of study, Indian philosophy begins and ends with the *Upaniṣads*. In fact, at that point it has not yet begun: the *Upaniṣads* simply lay down one of its revealed foundations. But it is true that, subsequently, it was possible to write volumes of subtle dialectic on the ineffability of *Brahman*. All the brahmanic systems were built up against one adversary or another, and each of them constituted itself as a coherent whole offering a complete panoply of arguments and counter-arguments, and this is as true of the systems which speak of knowledge of *Brahman*, such as Vedānta, as it is of the others.

Instantaneity

It is generally known that Buddhism, at least in best known schools, championed the instantaneousness of all things, including human thought. This is linked to its central affirmation, that there is no permanent principle in man. But it is less well known that brahmanism as a whole, which can readily be contrasted with Buddhism as a philosophy of fullness and permanence, conserved the notion of instantaneity, applying it solely to knowledge. There are no exceptions to this: Mīmāṃsā analyses empirical knowledge as a succession of discontinuous instants, Nyāya does the same, and the others follow. This instantaneity is complemented by the absence of simultaneity between two forms of knowledge. When we have the impression of seeing and smelling a jasmine flower at the same time, in reality we have two successive, very rapid perceptions, during which *manas* moves from one organ to another to put the ātman in contact with the sight of the jasmine and with its perception through smell. Manas is as mobile as the ātman is immobile and omnipresent. It is thus the intermediary between the absolute permanence of the ātman and the fleeting knowledge of things. It is difficult to understand this universal thesis of brahmanism without referring to the values it brings into play. Since all the systems accept it, it is not brahmanic orthodoxy which directly needs this instantaneity of individual knowledge in order to oppose it, for example, to the solidity of society or of things—which does however rather well serve the interests of a secular philosophy like Mīmāṃsā. But Mīmāṃsā also needs to prove the permanence of the ātman in order to justify the desire for heaven beyond the death and cremation of the body; in addition to the testimony of the *Upaniṣads*, it then invokes the knowledge we have of ourselves when we say 'I'. The reasoning is not very convincing if knowledge itself is instantaneous: why should this knowledge of 'I' always be knowledge of the same 'I'? No doubt for Mīmāṃsā the ātman partakes of the natural stability of things, which is now extended to infinity. An instantaneous knowledge of things does not preclude their permanence; and the identity of the subject asserts itself through the evanescent perception of the 'I'.

But one observes that instantaneity is limited to empirical knowledge. Yogins who attain omniscience of Īśvara have vision simultaneously and permanently (two features absent form ordinary knowledge) of all things and all beings of the past, present and future. For it is essentially this which constitutes omniscience, a universal perception limited neither by space nor by time. This means in particular that this perception is independent of the external organs and requires only the presence of manas, in contact on the one hand with the totality of objects and on the other with the ātman. We shall shortly have to return to the question of how yogic experience is conceived. It will suffice here to regard this perception as one of the forms of so-called mental perception—*mānasapratyakṣa*—in which the totality of the objects perceived has become internal to the yogin, just as the experience of pleasure or pain commonly is. Effectively, by refining its concepts, Nyāya was to work out a theory of the mānasapratyakṣas, three of which are called 'extraordinary contacts'. One of them is intended to explain why one has the impression of smelling the scent of sandalwood when one sees it at a distance. The smell of sandalwood, which is inseparable from sandalwood, is evoked at the sight of a piece of sandalwood, and one has a mental perception—a contact— of the smell accompanying the external visual perception. The second is of much broader epistemological import, since it is one of the solutions which India offers for grounding an inference (and here we recognize our old problem of the basis of induction). This is an 'extraordinary contact' that allows for a mental perception of every possible example of a particular genus, as a means of applying a general relationship to a particular case which comes under external scrutiny. Finally, the last of these is precisely *yogipratyakṣa*, the yogic perception which transcends the limits of ordinary perception prior even to the attainment of omniscience. The yogin is, for example, reputed to know his former lives and those of others. It is difficult to prove that Nyāya conceived the other forms of mānasapratyakṣa along the lines of yogic perception, but the latter was known before the others and also extends far beyond the school of logic. This is, regardless of the school it belongs to, the sole form of knowledge in which time stands still and space becomes boundless. It is also the one which represents the state of consciousness closest to the delivered state, although it is still part of empirical life. Mīmāṃsā, moreover, refuses both of them: it no more understands what is meant by a consciousness unadulterated by any object or an ātman that is no longer conscious (Nyāya) than it accepts yogic perception.

It is then very tempting to think that the idea of the instantaneity of empirical knowledge takes on its full meaning in the opposition that is thus established between the temporality, and therefore the essential limitation, of any consciousness engaged in the life of this world and the eternity of the pure consciousness which is ātman, or of the unconscious ātman. Would it even have been so strange for the ultra-orthodox thinkers of Mīmāṃsā to have purely and simply borrowed this idea in order to adapt it to suit both the needs of polemics and the demands of their own system? The history of the philosophical ideas of India is largely the history of the borrowings which the systems have made from each other in order the better to defend their own positions. But there is more than that involved: we initially posited that the values of liberation in India were only intelligible within their relationship of opposition to secular brahmanism, but it very quickly had to be added that the world of the sannyāsin had served as an example, or even as a fertilizing element, at the deepest level of the life of the secular Brahman. We have seen Mīmāṃsā being preoccupied with ahiṃsā, which orthodox thought nonetheless strove to keep outside the sphere of the sacrificial rites. This in fact leads us to suspect that there perhaps never has been a pure Mīmāṃsist, whose religion would have been entirely dominated by his system of ideas—a limit case system which, apart form the hermeneutics of the Vedic texts which it provides, was consciously constructed as the 'anti-renunciation' by borrowing weapons from its adversaries. It is not necessary to posit a system of Vedāntic or yogic type, entirely constituted at the conceptual level, and to imagine that Mīmāṃsā there found ready-made the idea of instantaneity. The latter is more likely, both in Mīmāṃsā and in the systems centred on renunciation, to have been one of the conceptual transpositions of a value-judgement by the renouncers on the empirical world. Who was the first to make this transposition? The history of the polemics between religious currents or currents of ideas might be able to decide the question for us, if only we knew enough about it.

Linked to the instantaneity of knowledge is another characteristic which gives rise to the same kind of reflexion on our part: the brahmanic texts, Mīmāṃsā, Vedānta or others, repeat that knowledge is itself without form, and that it is the known object which lends it its form. This thesis is directly opposed to the 'idealist' Buddhist school of Vijñānavāda, for which knowledge constructs its objects, whose form is thus inseparable from knowledge and has no external reality. However, the importance taken by this idea of the formlessness of knowledge cannot be justified solely by the needs of polemics with Buddhism. It certainly has a more direct value in the constellation of brahmanic theses. In fact, in Mīmāṃsā, it serves to support the affirmation of the objective reality of things independently of all knowledge. But in Vedānta and in any system which seeks to safeguard the existence of an ātman independent of empirical life, it is on the contrary the formlessness of knowledge which is directly valorized: it is indeed in complete agreement with the notion of an ātman that is pure, totally unlimited consciousness, which is that of Vedānta. It is equally congruent with the idea of a *samādhi*—'concentration of the mind'—in which there remains no 'mental construction', the ultimate stage which the yogin attains. We thus find ourselves in the same situation as with the thesis of instantaneity: both the most orthodox Brahmans and the systems which were constituted around renunciation used the same idea to meet the respective—and sometimes contrary—needs of their systems. This idea certainly has a role to play in the polemics with Buddhism, but this is not its whole justification.

In particular one cannot avoid evoking the fifth material element, *ākāśa*, which the brahmanic philosophies, and more especially the Vaiśeṣika and Sāṅkhya systems, add to the four well-known elements—earth, water, fire and air—making it the material medium of sound.[8] But ākāśā, before entering this conceptual systematization, is empty space and, as such, in the *Upaniṣads*, it is the analogue of ātman inasmuch as it is omnipresent, unlimited and without internal structure. Once it became the material substrate of sound (where and when?), ākāśā kept its unstructured and, one might say, 'formless' character, whereas Vaiśeṣika develops a theory of the atomic structure of the other constitutent elements of matter. Owing to this peculiarity, which introduces a surprising asymmetry into the system, the ether remains the analogue of ātman and makes it possible to specify some of its properties. So it seems here too that the formlessness of knowledge was one of the conceptual transpositions of the opposition which the renouncers saw between ātman and the diversity of empirical knowledge. From the beginning it must have been linked to the negative value assigned to the multiplicity of names and forms: 'Just as, my son, by one clod of clay all that is made of clay becomes known, the modification being only a name arising from speech, whereas only that which is called 'clay' is real; just as, my son, by one lump of metal all that is made of metal becomes known, the modification being only a name arising from speech, whereas only that which is called "metal" is real; just as, my son, by one pair of nail scissors all that is made of iron becomes known, the modification being only a name arising from speech, whereas only that which is called "iron" is real; so it is with the teaching on that (=Brahman)' (*Chāndogya Upaniṣad*, VI.1.4–6). If one remained within brahmanism, corresponding to the objective unreality of names and forms was their accidental character within thought and the possibility for the latter of freeing itself from them. It will be noted that Uddālaka's teaching to his son, in the *Chāndogya*, states that the multiple forms have speech as their medium, and not thought, as Buddhism would assert.

So there is every likelihood that Mīmāṃsā again took up and used for its own purposes a notion which it derived from the thinking of the brahmanic renouncer. Furthermore it is clear on what, in its ritualistic speculations, it could have constructed a metaphysics and devised a language capable of entering into a relationship, albeit one of hostility, with the brahmanic or Buddhist renouncers. It is exactly as if it had accepted up to a point the gaze which the renouncers brought to bear on the secular world and the value-judgement they applied to it. To be sure, its religious universe was somewhat changed by this. However, we can also say that it did the same for the sannyāsin since, in the strict sense of the term, it is the Brahman alone who can become a sannyāsin. This he effects through a rite in which he renounces his householder status; and by this means he retains, in his life as a sannyāsin, the memory of his social origins. This give and take, which was sometimes effected at cross-purposes, and which we have seen occurring at the conceptual level between the two poles of brahmanic thought, was in fact fully played out on a religious level, where it provoked vast upheavals. Neither the world of the renouncers nor secular life remained unscathed, and what is called 'Hinduism' rather than 'brahmanism' emerged from the process. Once again renunciation played a decisive role through the new prospects it offered to men living in the world.

From renunciation to bhakti

Up to now, in fact, the debates we have followed took place almost entirely among and for the benefit of Brahmans, all the more so since the great Buddhist philosophers of the first centuries AD were Brahmans by birth. By contrast, the concepts of the puruṣārthas laid greater stress on the princes and indirectly, no doubt, on the lower castes, at least as regards kāma and artha. It had long been understood that the Brahman was above all the man of dharma, but now he was also claiming for himself a kind of monopoly over liberation and modifying his dharma in this direction.

However, renunciation, because it sought liberation outside society, could scarcely exhaust all its possibilities and its power of attraction in this special relationship with the Brahmans. It could not fail to be the carrier of a more universal expectation: the major *Upaniṣads* present Kṣatriyas who, though 'offerers of sacrifice', nonetheless have the same preoccupations as their officiating Brahmans, and seek to know more about liberation from karman. Their very piety, however, forbids them to renounce their kingly duties which seem to condemn them to accumulate the worst sort of karman there can be. We shall indeed see that the first foundations of bhakti—since it is this which was to burst the framework of orthodoxy—are laid down in the epics which depict a turbulent society of princes and Brahmans who argue about war and salvation. But it would be simplistic to see the emergence of bhakti as essentially a reorganization of the prospects of salvation in favour first of the Kṣatriyas, and then the lower castes. The upheaval is much more radical.

To persuade oneself that renunciation was really felt to be universal in scope, one only has to turn to various passages in the great Vedāntic *Upaniṣads*—texts, in other words, which were to become the charter of the path of knowledge, the most orthodox of the forms of renunciation, that of the old-style sannyāsin. Assertions such as the following, applied to someone who has experienced ātman, have incalculable resonances for brahmanic ears: 'There, a father becomes a non-father, a mother becomes a non-mother; the worlds (to be conquered through sacrifice) are no longer worlds, the gods (beneficiaries of the sacrifice) become non-gods. . . . There, the thief becomes a non-thief, the murderer a non-murderer, the *Caṇḍāla* a non-*Caṇḍāla*, the *Paulkasa* a non-*Paulkasa*,[9] the ascetic a non-ascetic, the *tapasvin* a non-*tapasvin*.[10] He is followed neither by blessing nor by sin, for he has then passed beyond all the sorrows of the heart.' Śaṅkara, commenting on this passage from the *Bṛhadāraṇyaka Upaniṣad* (IV.3.22), more faithful to the spirit of renunciation than to the orthodoxy which he has to integrate, allows no ambiguity to persist. Each term denied is explained by its relationship to karman: the knower of ātman, being freed from all karman, is no longer that which he was before: the father-son relation no longer exists, nor does the mother-son relation. One notes in passing that woman seems here to have access to liberation, i.e. to an individual destiny which secular conceptions of life hereafter did not grant her. Women are indeed not absent from the Upaniṣadic literature, and it is the same *Bṛhadāraṇyaka Upaniṣad* which gives us the very beautiful dialogue between Yājñavalkya and his wife Maitreyī (II.4). The next terms which are denied designate objective aspects of the universe of sacrifice: the spheres—*lokas*—that are won through rites, the gods to whom offerings are made. Thus the thief, the Caṇḍāla, etc., might be taken for examples of impure beings who are no longer impure for the renouncer. But Śaṅkara's reading is different, and his view, as the guru of the 'twice-born', has to be taken seriously: a Caṇḍāla who knows ātman is no longer a Caṇḍāla. Thus impurity no longer exists in renunciation, and this ought immediately to imply that *anyone* can become a sannyāsin. But the contradiction is flagrant, since the path of knowledge, as it was institutionalized, would require that one have access to the Upaniṣadic Revelation, from which a Caṇḍāla is forever excluded. This teaching might therefore have remained purely theoretical if another path had not been offered to those whom the orthodoxy would leave in outer darkness. From this standpoint, it is particularly interesting to note that Śaṅkara, following the *Upaniṣad*, regards the various ascetic exercises as reduced to insignificance by access to knowledge: he does not condemn them, but the way in which he places the śramaṇas and the tapasvins in the same series as the thief and the Caṇḍāla suggests that the suffering they undertake is not what brings them to knowledge (the Buddha said nothing different). On the other hand, the word *yoga* is never used.

This is not all, and we return, after a detour, to the question from which we started: from whence does Bhīma, in the *Mahābhārata*, get the insight that leads him to see desire at the basis of all human activity, of every stage of life? In fact—since it is probably more convincing to remain with what subsequently constituted the most orthodox reference of renunciation—the same *Upaniṣad*, which is very clearly earlier than the classical systematization of the goals of man, readily uses the language of kāma to refer to the love of ātman. In particular this is what Yājñavalkya does when instructing the worried Maitreyī (II.4.5), and it is surely no accident that the term *kāma* is endlessly used in a speech addressed to a woman: 'It is not for the love—*kāma*—of the husband that the husband is dear, but it is for the love of the ātman that the husband is dear. It is not for the love of the wife that the wife is dear, but it is for the love of the ātman that the wife is dear. It is not for the love of sons that sons are dear, but it is for the love of the ātman that sons are dear. It is not for the love of wealth that wealth is dear, but it is for the love of the ātman that wealth is dear. It is not for the love of the *Brahman* that the *Brahman* is dear, but it is for the love of the ātman that the *Brahman* is dear. It is not for the love of the *Kṣatra* that the *Kṣatra* is dear, but it is for the love of the ātman that the *Kṣatra* is dear. It is not for the love of the worlds—the *lokas*—that the worlds are dear, but it is for the love of the ātman that the worlds are dear. It is not for the love of the gods that the gods are dear, but it is for the love of the ātman that the gods are dear. It is not for the love of beings—*bhūtas*—that beings are dear, but it is for the love of the ātman that beings are dear. It is not for the love of the universe—*sarvam*—that the universe is dear, but it is for the love of the ātman that the universe is dear. Indeed, it is the ātman that must be seen, that must be heard, that must be thought upon, that must be concentrated upon, O Maitreyī, since it is by the vision of, the hearing of, the contemplation of and the knowledge of the ātman that all this is known.'[11] Yājñavalkya, on the point of abandoning his two wives in order to go and live in the forest as a hermit, is trying to explain to one of them that shining through the desire or love for the things and beings of this transient world—one notes in passing the key terms of 'worldly' language—is a more essential love for which it is worth leaving everything. Later on, however, when polemics have refined the conceptual tools (more than the conceptions themselves), philosophers hesitate to use the term *kāma* to designate the desire for liberation or the love of ātman. They emphasize, in any case, the uniqueness of this desire, its radical difference from earthly desires, inasmuch as it entails no karman. So they cannot agree with Bhīma in his generalization; yet Bhīma was drawing on the best sources in his apologia for kāma, and the reflexion on desire could only come from those who had distanced themselves from it, even if they no longer recognized their work in the words of Vāyu's son.

On this point, much more than on philosophical theses such the instantaneity or the lack of form of knowledge, it is quite clear that the common problematic of the sannyāsin and the man in the world had to develop into a total opposition. Bhīma glorifies kāma, whereas his brother Yudhiṣṭhira (in the same chapter of the *Mahābhārata*) opposes to it mokṣa, which sweeps away all the other puruṣārthas. The hierarchy of the four goals of man could only satisfy the man in the world, determined to keep mokṣa on the horizon, but also to pursue worldly ends as fully as possible. The fact that, metaphysically, these have only a relative value does not prevent them from being good and desirable. The renouncer, by contrast, when he turns back to look at the world, sees it entirely governed by desire, from which he has to liberate himself. We have seen (see p. 38) how, again in the same *Bṛhadāraṇyaka Upaniṣad*,[12] kāma is linked to the ego—*ahamkāra*—and how it is through kāma that the world of the relative, of metaphysical ignorance, appears. In the sannyāsin's perspective, kāma is the all-encompassing value in this world, whereas for the orthodox

Brahman, it is dharma alone that can fulfil this role. We thus arrive at the paradox whereby the cow, the symbol of the Brahman's sacrificial power, is most often called Kāmadhenu, 'she from whom one milks all that one desires'. Thus there emerges another level of kāma—where it is no longer solely erotic desire but desire in all its forms—which re-establishes the essential discontinuity between mokṣa and the other ends of man. Kāma is what has to be renounced in order to break free from the bonds of karman and of transmigration.

Whereas the starting-point of the sannyāsin's speculations was karman, the analysis he conducted, parallel to that of the Brahman, on human actions and goals, has shifted the focus of interest. It is this notion of kāma—in the all-encompassing sense which the renouncer attributes to it—together with the whole constellation of associated ideas, which comes to constitute a golden thread that runs through all speculations about true universal salvation. Bhakti would seek a solution in the abolition of kāma in the very heart of man's ordinary activity. In other words, it would seek to imbue secular life with the sannyāsin's ideal. By contrast, what has been referred to under the excessively vague term of tantrism was to be the attempt to place kāma (in all senses of the word) and the associated values at the service of liberation.

The universe of bhakti

In the epics, in the *Purāṇas* (accounts of the origins)[13], in an abundant devotional and hagiographic literature in Sanskrit and in all the great modern languages of India, there was expressed and developed, over the centuries, in its different aspects, what is generally known as Hinduism. In fact, bhakti, the religion of devotion which has covered India with its most beautiful temples, is only one of the major currents of Hinduism, but one can no more understand the structures of sectarian Vedānta (Rāmānuja, Madhva . . .), or the tantric sects, than those of classical Sāṅkhya, without starting from the doctrinal edifice which it has built up in an essentially mythical language.

Because this religion of devotion is completely absent from what are regarded as the most ancient texts of the Vedic Revelation, and presupposes, in particular, a conception of deity of which the Vedic rites offer no example, there is a tendency to seek its origin outside Vedic circles, or more precisely to hypothesize about the existence of a religion contemporary with the Vedic literature, of which no trace remains. Its popular character might explain the total silence of the Veda on the subject. This theory appears entirely plausible, until we realize that it implies, of itself, a complete reconstruction of bhakti as we know it. Such a reconstruction would either be wholly unconvincing or would even be ruled out by textual data as well as by our present knowledge of brahmanic socio-religious concepts. It would in fact attempt to view bhakti as a religion of more or less unbridled emotions, a religion whose true colours do not appear until such texts as the *Bhāgavata-purāṇa* or, more exactly, until the vernacular literature. This would further oblige us to characterize the epics and the more 'intellectual' *Purāṇa*s as the first imperfect articulations of a bhakti of lower-caste origins, which slowly pushed its way into upper-caste circles.

As has already been said, there is no question of denying that India saw religious forms other than brahmanism, both before and after the coming of the 'Aryans'. Were these popular learned forms which the conqueror condemned to inferiority? Local or even tribal cults, rather than a unified set of beliefs? We are here in the area of pure conjecture, and it is pointless to linger in it. Two things seem clear: firstly, it would be very difficult to understand how such a hierarchical society, in which the norms always come from above, could have yielded to pressure from below to the extent of allowing itself to be won over to a reputedly inferior religious form. On the contrary, the only intelligible process would be one in which the conquerors accept the religious forms which they find on their arrival, integrating them into their own structures, but in a subordinate place. We have already seen such a process of hierarchization and envelopment at work in the reciprocal integration of renunciation and secular religion, and it also applied in other areas. Historically, the conquests of the great sovereigns did not, in general, lead to the substitution of one power for another, but to a subordination of the vanquished to the victor—which prepared the ground for a possible reversal of the situation, always theoretically conceivable since this took place in the limited domain of artha. But reversal is no longer possible when it is a question of imposing socio-religious norms which structure the whole of society. The superior has to remain the superior, but his hierarchical vision precisely enables him to integrate almost anything with a minimal change in structure. This can be proposed as a principle of functioning and no doubt as a model of all historical change within Indian society. On the other hand, there are no grounds for supposing a vanquished-victor relationship comparable to what happened between Greece and Rome. Brahmanism has never admired anything that was alien to it. In particular one cannot invoke against this what happened in the fifteenth and sixteenth centuries, under the domination of the Muslim emperors, since by then bhakti was already solidly implanted in India and it was bhakti which made possible the osmosis between Muslim and Hindu mysticism.[14]

Furthermore—and this is the second point we can take as given—when we honestly attempt to accept and understand the phenomenon of bhakti as a whole, together with the epics and *Purāṇas* that serve as its basic doctrinal texts, we realize that its structures are unintelligible so long as they are cut off from Vedic Revelation. This is not to say that these structures developed out of it in a direct linear fashion; and in this sense it is still possible for us to say that the Vedas knew nothing of bhakti. But bhakti was constituted by a re-reading of the Revelation which gave birth to a mythic and ritual universe of very great complexity, even if for the moment one only takes account of the pan-Indian and not the sectarian structures. It is even possible to be more specific: the data of the Revelation have not all been reworked with the same care and consistency. There is no doubt that the *Yajurveda*[15] was particularly at the centre of the speculations of bhakti, both in its ritualistic part and in its *Upaniṣads*, and this cannot be a pure accident: the *Yajurveda* is the Veda of the *adhvaryu*, the priest who, in the sacrifice, is charged with all the ritual manipulations, the actor *par excellence*, whose every gesture must receive a symbolic interpretation. This will be one of the threads to guide us through the labyrinth of bhakti.

If it is true that the structures of bhakti were thus the work of Brahmans—this being the direct implication of its essential relationship to Vedic Revelation—and that they were, as such, normative for all of Hinduism, then we should expect to find them throughout Hindu India and at every level, from the high-caste temples to the humblest of shrines, the unhewn stones one finds at the base of trees. And this is exactly the case. It is clear that in this impressive flowering of temples and holy places—which can be systematically recorded only on the scale of a local land registry—there must be shrines of all origins. But bhakti has so well integrated all these elements that it would be thoroughly unsound to seek to distinguish what is Aryan or indigenous or Dravidian, or what is pan-Indian or local or 'popular'. For my part, I know of no so-called 'local' cult which does not contain the general beliefs of bhakti. At the same time, it naturally has to be recognized that the generality of the beliefs allows a multiplicity of different levels which betray greater or lesser remoteness from the apex of the social pyramid. But we thereby simply rediscover the hierarchical structure of Hindu society. This multi-tiered structuring of levels translates particularly into the most widely varying transformations of the classic myths,[16] myths which have yet to find their Lévi-Strauss: the language and the story are often barely recognizable if the intermediate links in the transformation are missing; but on the other hand, under the names of different characters one finds some remarkably stable mythic structures. As for the values at stake, they become degraded without ever entirely disappearing, for one remains within the same cultural unity and the same religion. In the rites, the major division runs between vegetable offerings and animal sacrifices but precisely that which might be expected to bring out an insuperable duality within Hinduism between high-caste and low-caste deities only serves to manifest its unity, which is fundamental as that of society. Vegetarian gods and carnivorous gods associated—and duly set in a hierarchy—in the temples and cults. In the process, it is clear that local elements, and even historical events or characters, have been integrated, but that they become just as quickly unrecognizable. The 'learned' Brahman reacts to this situation by following one of two strategies. He either balks at recognizing his heritage when it is patently his own; or he finds a subtle brahmanic reinterpretation of what are apparently the most far-fetched of popular beliefs.

God as yogin and creator

The appearance of Viṣṇu and Śiva as major gods of bhakti cannot be entirely fortuitous, since the two *Upaniṣad*s which constitute the revealed foundation of the yogic path to salvation call the ultimate goal of the yogic ascension in one case Viṣṇu and in the other Śiva (see p. 28). These deities of the yogin reappear in bhakti, each being conceived not only as the culmination of the yogic experience and of the movement towards liberation—or, in mythic language, as the site of liberation—but also as supreme Yogins. This does not occur, however, without a radical shift in perspectives, and it is their broad outlines that we must analyse if we are to understand what has taken place.[17] It is the *Kaṭha Upaniṣad* (3.10–11 and, with a variant reading, 6.7–8) that supplies the initial categories. The yogin progressively withdraws from the senses and their objects, and the manas—and then from other levels of being (or consciousness?) whose correspondences in the realm of yogic experience are difficult to determine. However, beyond a certain level, the one called *mahān ātmā*—'the great ātman'—it is certain that 'perception' is no longer limited to the body but extends to the whole of being. The omniscience attributed to the yogin no doubt corresponds to this level of experience, but this is not the ultimate level, the one towards which yogic endeavour strives. Beyond it is a level called 'the Undifferentiated' or 'the Non-distinct'—*avyakta*—and finally, beyond this, the supreme Puruṣa, Viṣṇu, in which the yogin is absorbed. This is indeed a yogic process culminating in samādhi, total concentration, and not in bodily death, since the *Kaṭha* adds that one has to attain total immobility of thought, that this is the supreme path. It then offers a definition of yoga which was to go far (6.11): 'Yoga is considered to be this maintenance of the immobility of the senses. Then one becomes undistracted, because yoga is appearance and disappearance.' Coming after the enumeration of the stages of the ascent to Puruṣa—who, we are told elsewhere, is inside the heart—this verse can only mean one thing: yoga takes the subject through phases in which external and internal objects disappear in order that the Puruṣa may appear, and opposite phases in which the subject returns to an ordinary level of experience. A yogin who has gone into a definitive samādhi is dead: indeed this is the way his death is usually expressed. So yoga is normally conceived as an oscillation of the levels of consciousness which range from ordinary experience to the ultimate experience of fusion with the Absolute. Compared with the definition of the *Yogasūtra* (the basic text of the classical system of Yoga)—'Yoga is the stopping of all the movements of thought'—the formula of the *Katha* is more dynamic and more complete. It takes account of the processes as well as of the result that is aimed at.

First cosmogony Moving now to the cosmogony presented by the main *Purāṇas*, we have the surprise of finding these stages of yogic experience transformed into successive planes of manifestation of the cosmos, to form together the initial phase of the cosmogony, which we shall call the 'first cosmogony'. Thus the stages of an individual ascent have become the stages of a progressive descent of the supreme Puruṣa into the cosmos: the Puruṣa has become the yogin, and the process of creation is assimilated to the yogin's return from samādhi to ordinary experience. There are, however, two important differences to be noted in this transposition: the Puruṣa is no longer, as in the *Upaniṣad*, set in a series with the other planes. It is no longer simply the final stage in the ascension, or the starting point, of the cosmic manifestation. Rather, it is the immutable principle, spiritual and transcendent, which remains so in a certain sense even as it gives a primary impulse to the *avyakta*, the 'Unmanifest', through its yoga. The *avyakta* is also called *pradhāna*, 'primary ground', and *prakṛti*, 'primordial form'; henceforth, we shall refer to this either as 'original Nature' or as 'Nature', according to the stage of manifestation in question. This designation will serve both to highlight the distinction between the evolutionary principle and the immutable Puruṣa, and to point out the fact that the former would be unconsciousness were it not for the light that it borrows from the pure Consciousness of the Puruṣa, which is Light. The Puruṣa thus involves itself in each of its phases without ceasing to be the great Yogin. The *Kaṭha Upaniṣad* seemed resolutely monistic (but not 'illusionistic', like Śaṅkarian Vedānta); the *Purāṇas* are not, but nor are they completely dualistic: God is and is not his creation, God manifests himself but remains the 'beyond' of all manifestation; or again, in more psychological terms, God takes an interest in his creation while remaining indifferent. But this is precisely what the *Bhagavad Gītā* teaches through the words of Kṛṣṇa (IX.4): 'All of this world is pervaded by my unmanifest form. All beings dwell in me, but I do not dwell in them'; 'I am dear above all else to him who has knowledge, and he is dear to me' (VII. 17b); but also (IX.29): 'I am alike towards all beings. There is none who is hateful or dear to me. But those who worship (*bhaj*—literally, take part in) me with devotion (*bhakti*), they are in me and I am in them.'

If anyone is surprised by the contradiction, they may reflect that our Western theologians expended great efforts in explaining that God had no need of humankind, although he took the trouble to create it and save it. The gratuitous character of the creation in India nonetheless introduces maximum tension between the two aspects of deity, inasmuch as the yogin, the image of its supreme form, can have no attachment of any sort for the world he has left, and it becomes difficult to conceive of a creation out of love. However, to this too Hinduism has sought an answer within the terms of its system of problems: the human yogin, having reached a certain degree of mystic experience, precisely the one at which he has moved beyond the bounds of his empirical individuality, seems to feel a strong sense of pity or compassion—*kāruṇya*—for all the beings which are still held in the bonds of Ignorance (which, it is scarcely necessary to point out, is reminiscent of the compassion which Buddhists ascribe to the *bodhisattva*). It is also this sentiment which Hindus attribute to God, sometimes to account for the creation, sometimes to explain an end of the world—since the latter is obviously implied in the cosmic and divine transposition of the two phases of yoga. It is in order to save his creatures—or to enable them to attain liberation—that God emits the worlds, and it is also in order to save them that he reabsorbs them into himself. Arjuna's 'awful' vision of Kṛṣṇa in Chapter XI of the *Bhagavad Gītā* has no other meaning: as the yogin makes the external world disappear from his consciousness so to plunge ever deeper into himself until he reaches the essential core, so the Puruṣa (here Kṛṣṇa, which is the form Viṣṇu takes in the *Mahābhārata*) reabsorbs his creatures into himself so as to commune with himself, but this movement is liberation for the creatures since they are thus united with the Puruṣa.[18]

However, a second difference appears in the transposition of individual yoga into divine yoga, which only accentuates the quite deliberate intentions behind this work. While the *Purāṇas* identify two of the higher stages of the *Upaniṣad*, they add a new one which does not figure in the *Kaṭha* but whose significance has already become apparent to us—*ahamkāra*, the function of the ego. And they add it exactly where one might expect, just below *mahān ātmā* (which becomes *mahān* or *mahat* in the *Purāṇas*),[19] in the progressive manifestation of the cosmos, in other words at the moment when the Puruṣa constitutes itself as the cosmic ego. Whereas the term *ahaṃkāra* seems to occur for the first time in the *Chāndogya Upanisad* (VII.25.1), one of the great Vedāntic *Upaniṣads*, and then later in the *Śvetāśvatara* (V.8), it is essentially in the *Brhadāraṇyaka Upaniṣad* (I.4.10 and 17; see p. 38) that its mythic explanation appears in a recognizable form: 'In the beginning, the *Brahman* alone was here. It knew itself—*ātman*—only as: "I—*aham*—am *Brahman*". From this, it became everything. . . . In the beginning, the ātman alone was here. He was alone, he desired—*akāmayata*: "Would that I had a wife, would that I might engender (a son); would that I had wealth, that I might perform the rites." These are all the objects of desire—*kāma*.' To say 'I' and to desire that something be 'mine' are inseparable notions. The world of ego is also that of desire, and therefore of the metaphysical Ignorance which turns its back on liberation.

This introduction of a Vedāntic mythic theme—presented from the first as a cosmogony—into the yogic schema has numerous implications. Perhaps this is the moment to point out that the *Kaṭha Upanisad* and the *Śvetāśvatara* belong to the *Black Yajurveda*, whereas the *Bṛhadāraṇyaka* belongs to the *White Yajurveda*. What we have distinguished as two paths to salvation (pp. 25ff.) is thus first formulated within the same mythico-ritual whole. And the two routes to salvation might be expected to be integrated into a single structure. The cosmic transposition of the individual yogic process may have been helped by the cosmogonic value attributed to the ego of *Brahman*. Moreover, the very importance which this ego and its desire take on in the creation explains why the insertion of ahaṃkāra into the *Kaṭha* schema introduces a critical point into the process of manifestation. It is the ego, in fact, that is the starting-point for cosmic manifestation, which follows two parallel lines of development (these are absent from the *Kaṭha*, in which the progression is linear). One line consists of the sense organs and the organs of activity (hand, foot, etc.), together with manas; the other is made up of the five sensorial properties and the corresponding material elements (see note 8). Ahaṃkāra, precisely inasmuch as it is the starting point of the components of the empirical world, no longer has a single, simple texture. It has three different aspects or *guṇas*:[20] the purest and most luminous, the most transparent to the light of Puruṣa is *sattva* (literally, the abstract cognate of *sat*, 'being'; it is therefore 'the fact of being' or 'the sum of all beings'); by contrast, the heaviest and darkest, the most unconscious, is *tamas* ('darkness'). Both of these would forever remain inert, one through excess of knowledge, the other for lack of it, if there were not, interposed between them, *rajas* (literally, 'dust', probably that which obscures the light refracted in sattva), the active element *par excellence*, which predominates in particular in mankind. The sattva and the rajas of ahaṃkāra combine to produce the organs of sense and action, while tamas and rajas give rise to the sensorial qualities and the elements (starting with sound and ākāśa). The reversal of the yogic process in the cosmogonic schema now takes on its full significance: the authors of the Purāṇic cosmogony (for there is only one, despite the multiplicity of texts) seek to explain the world in terms of the renouncer's vision of it. But, not being renouncers themselves, they obviously tend to valorize ahaṃkāra in the work of creation—even if this means seeing it as the source of metaphysical ignorance and condemning it in practical life. In one way or another, one has to return to the world one knows, where one lives and is at the centre. There is seemingly a wilful misunderstanding in turning the divine yoga towards the world; but in reality there is neither misunderstanding nor bad faith, since, as we shall see, the same tension between yoga and the world is introduced at the same time into human action.

Viṣṇu and Śiva While it is thus fairly clear how the notion of a sovereign God came to be constituted, we still have to account for the proper name given to this God—sometimes Viṣṇu, sometimes Śiva. The *Purāṇas* are sometimes divided into Śaivite *Purāṇas* and Vaiṣṇavite *Purāṇas*, according to the name they give to the supreme deity. They may differ in content and composition as much as one wants, but the same could be said of the Vaiṣṇavite or Śaivite *Purāṇas* among themselves; the structure of the total cosmogony (including, therefore, the second phase, which we still have to examine), that of the cosmology, the different levels of manifestation of deity, and the organization of the cosmic periods, remain identical. One must therefore hesitate to speak of the main *Purāṇas* as sectarian, for the sects in the strict sense would not leave this schema intact. Each one modified, or rather multiplied, the levels of being and of its manifestation, not to mention the specific myths and philosophical elaborations which conceptually specify their mythologies. The main *Purāṇas* build up a conceptual universe which is fundamentally one and the same, whereas each sect was to construct its own closed world which aspires to be defined against those of the other. Moreover—but this is also true of the sects—the choice of either Viṣṇu or Śiva as supreme God does not mean that the other is not present at a lower level.

Viṣṇu and Śiva, needless to say, are present in the Vedic Revelation, even before the yogic *Upaniṣads* in which they have already become supreme deities. Apparently they do not have a prime role in the ritual and mythology of the *Brāhmaṇas*, and it is certain that at this level one could not foresee their subsequent promotion. But when we look more closely, aided by what we know of subsequent events, we observe that there they occupy key positions with respect to Vedic sacrifice. While Viṣṇu is frequently identified with the sacrifice, and represents (perhaps even etymologically) the scope of the beneficent effects of the sacrifice, Śiva by contrast—under the name he then bears, Rudra ('the Terrible', whereas Śiva means 'benevolent') or Paśupati ('master of the cattle', but more probably 'of the sacrificial victims', since *paśu* means both)—personifies the impure and dangerous aspects of the sacrifice: it is he who receives the part of the victim damaged by the slaughter, which is handled in such a way as to avoid contaminating the other pieces of the victim. This opposition between the two gods is clearly so fundamental only because sacrifice is the essential ritual act, and therefore one of the poles (renunciation being the other) of brahmanic speculations, to which one always has to return in order to understand the subsequent transformations. Because Viṣṇu is the sacrifice and is thus intrinsically linked to the prosperity and splendour (*śrī* or *lakṣmī*) of a reign, he is at the heart of all organized social life. There he is the deity which represents the union of the two higher varṇas. So even when the yogin calls the supreme Puruṣa 'Viṣṇu' and when bhakti may thus make him a yogin, Viṣṇu retains his link with brahmanic orthodoxy and in his temples he has a royal air emphasized by the tiara he wears. By contrast, the Rudra of the *Brāhmaṇas* can only remain outside human space. He is the 'forest-dweller' or the 'mountain-dweller' like the renouncer, which predestines him to become a yogin and a renouncer in a much more radical sense than Viṣṇu. It is the ascetic's topknot that naturally befits him when he is depicted in his human form. Bhakti registers these oppositions and would draw from them endless implications and myths. So on this point, that of the choice between the two deities, bhakti merely reworked the data provided by the Revelation, preserving their original meaning within a larger whole.

Second cosmogony The first cosmogony which so far has been discussed, and which only implements categories derived from the renouncers, leads to the constitution of a cosmic egg, and not yet the 'triple world' with which we are familiar. The cosmogonic theme of the egg is not specifically Hindu. In India itself, it is already found in the revealed texts, the *Brāhmaṇas* and *Upaniṣads*, where it generally constitutes a starting point rather than an end point. Here, however, the egg which appears is not just any cosmogonic egg, since it is called 'the egg of Brahmā'. A familiar figure reappears. More precisely, *Brahman* (neutral) has become a divine personage, a level of divine manifestation. It will be recalled (see pp. 17–25) that *Brahman* became the name of the Absolute only because it also designated Vedic knowledge and its efficacy, i.e. the totality of the Brahman's function, centred on sacrifice. Here, it is both these levels at once, but the Absolute which it represents is in any case relativized with respect to the great Yogin. Its appearance within the cosmic egg clearly indicates the resurgence of the brahmanic world within the universe of bhakti.

In effect, it is this which the second phase of the cosmogonic narrative, or 'second cosmogony', portrays. There is never any narrative linkage between this and the first cosmogony; and the second cosmogony seems to be self-sufficient. The egg no longer plays any role here; we again find Brahmā 'wishing to create' (*sisṛkṣu*, yet another desiderative form). So it is the very same kāma which, yet again, appears at the origin of the creative process, just as it did in the *Bṛhadāraṇyaka Upaniṣad* (see p. 38). Here, Brahmā turns himself into a boar in order to bring back the Earth to the surface of the ocean which had covered it in a previous flood.[21]

While we cannot give a step-by-step summary of the narrative here, we will highlight those points which give the most meaning to the whole. First of all, the boar (a cosmogonic motif borrowed from the *Saṃhitās* and *Brāhmaṇas* of the *Black* and *White Yajurveda*) is identified, in every *Purāṇa* in which this account occurs, with the Sacrifice. Sacrifice is thus the creative principle which presides over the re-establishment and ordering of the 'triple world', the fate of the earth always being bound up with the fate of heaven and the infernal regions. When Brahmā has thus retrieved the earth from the sea-bed, he starts by creating Ignorance. One might have rather expected the sequence Ignorance-Sacrifice, since we have been taught that knowledge implies the abandonment of sacrifices; only metaphysical Ignorance could explain the practice of sacrificial rites—*karman*. This reversal seems to indicate a new upgrading of sacrifice which will enable it to continue when the veil of Ignorance has been lifted. But, at the same time, the reappearance of Ignorance shows clearly that the prospect of liberation has not been lost sight of. This is confirmed by Brahmā's creation of man, the only one of his creatures who satisfies him because, spurred by pain, he seeks liberation. This results from the high proportion of rajas in man, which impels him to action. Here too one notices a curious reversal of ideas, whereby men are made fit for liberation by their capacity to act, whereas previously the renouncer was he who abandoned all 'action'. All this will become clearer when we come to examine the anthropological implications of this new theology.

Furthermore, the second cosmogony is linked to a specific level of deity. At the highest level, it was a yogin, and the two phases of its yoga accounted for the emission and reabsorption of the world. Now it has to preside over the world of sacrifice. It is the deity which takes the form of Brahmā in order to create; normally it is then predominantly 'rājasic', as always when action is involved. But when the world is created, it is again the deity which keeps it in existence by assuming the form of Viṣṇu. This is the phase in which the regular performance of sacrifices enables the world to continue in existence; it is therefore natural that Viṣṇu—who is sacrifice—should be its protecting deity. Perhaps it is less obvious that, in this function, he should be 'sāttvic', since sattva predisposes towards inaction. But sattva was inactive only insofar as knowledge led to inaction, and its first characteristic is that it is transparent to the Light shed by Puruṣa. From now on, the Light seems to accept the sacrifice.[22] Finally, since the process of evolution and involution is perpetually repeated, the supreme deity has a third form at this same level of manifestation, which presides this time over the destruction of the world. It is of course Rudra the 'tāmasic' who incarnates this third aspect which brings on the cosmic night. These three forms taken by the Absolute—not concomitant in their operation but of the same level of being and indissociable—have been recognized as what is called the Trimūrti ('triple form') or, to put it in more Christian terms, the Trinity. The fact is that, despite the few unfortunate attempts made to connect them, there is little in common between this three-fold divine manifestation and the Christian Trinity. The Trimūrti too appears with the same constancy in all the *Purāṇas*, whatever the name given to the supreme form of deity. In other words, either Viṣṇu or Śiva may be found at both levels, but not Brahmā, who only intervenes at the level of the Trimūrti. Brahmā effectively never presents himself as the great Yogin and, correspondingly, is not the God of bhakti. Rather than wonder at the extreme rarity of his temples in India, one should wonder how there can be any at all.

Cyclic time

In ancient Western thinking, the idea of cyclic time seems to have been associated with the idea of a cosmology governed by the movement of the stars. Astronomy is clearly not absent from Indian speculations, which need fairly precise data for the performance of the rites: it is even part of the ancillary sciences of the Veda, along with grammar, metrics and the detailed description of ritual acts. The annual cycle of the seasons and the feasts which punctuate them also favours a conception of time which always returns identical to itself. However, the model on which Hinduism constructs its cosmic periods owes very little to astronomy, apart from the distinction between days and nights and the choice of the year as one of the units of time. Furthermore, the temporal divisions are first presented in their totality in the context of the Purāṇic cosmogony, a fact which would lead one to associate them with the conceptual framework of bhakti. Indeed, it would be unintelligible if it were not linked to the idea that the creation and reabsorption of the world are endlessly repeated as the phases of the yoga of the eternal Puruṣa. But it can also be seen at the same time that further complications have to be brought into the structure of cosmic periods in order to account for the two quite distinct stages of the genesis of the world and of the levels of manifestation of divinity.

Thus, the period between the start of a first cosmogony and a total reabsorption into the Puruṣa—the cosmic and divine transposition of the twofold phase of yoga—is but an instant of the supreme Puruṣa, but this instant measures a life of Brahmā. Since the length of an ideal individual human life is a hundred human years, the life of Brahmā is a hundred of Brahmā's years. But one of Brahmā's years is itself made up of three hundred and sixty-five of Brahmā's days or *kalpas*. A kalpa measures the period between a second cosmogony and the symmetrical reabsorption (see p. 100). i.e. the period dominated by the manifestation of the divinity at the level of the Trimūrti. Kalpa—from the root *kḷp*, to be adjusted—is also the noun which designates a set of texts describing domestic ritual and the rules of dharma. If Brahmā, waking at the end of a night, creates the world of sacrifice, the day which is thus initiated is fairly logically called kalpa, whereas the night, corresponding to a cosmic reabsorption of equal length but during which nothing happens, is never called kalpa. The life of Brahmā, which thus contains one hundred times three hundred and sixty-five kalpas, constitutes a *mahākalpa* or 'great kalpa', as opposed to the great reabsorption of equal length. The life of Brahmā is the cosmic period dominated by ritual activity but provoked by the act of yoga of the supreme Puruṣa.

The perpetual return of the cosmos is thus in fact the perpetual transmigration of the deity, which has manifested itself to the extent of constituting itself as a cosmic ego, endowed with the desire to act, to say 'I' and 'mine'. Thus, in the interlocking of the great periods of time of the universe, we find a mythic aspect correlative with the double cosmogony. Brahmā does indeed play the active—rājasic—role transposed from the myth of the *Bṛhadāraṇyaka Upaniṣad*. There is creation only because the deity constitutes itself as (to use an oxymoron) a cosmic individual. The supreme Puruṣa is the Yogin whom no act can sully or bind. He is *par excellence* the Liberated One, who should therefore, for all eternity, be subject to no further rebirths. Yet the theology of bhakti has him involved as if voluntarily in a perpetual transmigration, in which he does not cease to be himself liberated but which transforms him into a Saviour: the beings of our triple world are reborn, or attain liberation, within his transmigration. Thus the ineluctable flow of discontinuous instants is grasped within a perspective of eternity, thanks to an eternal return. The instant exists only for eternity, just as life in this world acquires its meaning only through the liberation which denies it.

But the structuring of cosmic time does not stop there. A kalpa is in turn made up of a thousand times four *yugas* or a thousand 'great yugas' which, this time, are measured in years of the gods—the gods of Vedic sacrifice; the 'great yuga', amounting to twelve thousand years of the gods, is divided into four yugas of unequal length and unequal value, separated by 'twilights'. Finally, it is said that one human year is a day and a night of the gods, which means that one year of the gods is equivalent to three hundred and sixty-five human years. The fantastic figures one arrives at by counting each great period in human years manage to present a reassuring image of the universe. Present-day man is always at the centre of a cosmic period sufficiently long for no universal cataclysm to be in sight.

The level of the yuga itself corresponds to another level of manifestation of deity which again highlights the tension characteristic of the world of bhakti. Expressed here is the very widespread idea of successive ages of humanity which is created in a state of perfection and progressively deteriorates. The four yugas are named after the four throws of a die, and Hindus concur with all the peoples of the world in saying that we live in the worst age, the one in which social disorder is at its peak—an idea which bears witness to the sense of the gap between the norm and the reality. Dharma is so weakened, the Vedas are so forgotten and the Brahmans so little respected that the supreme Puruṣa has to incarnate itself specially in the 'triple world' so as to come and restore order: this 'descent' of the deity is the *avatāra*. The real unit of time must here be the 'great yuga', since there are a thousand of them in one kalpa: an avatāra myth—such as that of Kṛṣṇa which forms the core of the *Mahābhārata*—seems to belong at the point of transition between the fourth yuga (*Kaliyuga*) of one 'great yuga' and the first of the next 'great yuga', which is naturally a sort of golden age (*kṛtayuga*, literally 'perfect age'). The avatāra is often a prince—or a Brahman with warlike qualities—who provokes the destruction of humanity through war, so as to enable the world to start anew. This war of catastrophic dimensions presents itself as a pale image of the reabsorption of the world at the end of a kalpa, and the order of 'salvation' which it promises remains sharply defined: the loss suffered by the wicked ought to ensure the triumph of the good. Thus even Buddha can become an avatāra of Viṣṇu: he came to earth to complete the misleading of the wicked by his false doctrine and so provoke momentary chaos which only the good will survive.

However, the myths situate the different known avatāras at the transition between the yugas themselves. In the *Mahābhārata*, Kṛṣṇa appears at the point where the third yuga gives way to the fourth—the latter being the worst, which is not very consistent with the idea, actually echoed by the myth, that he brings a new golden age. In fact, the four-yuga structure which describes the progressive decline of dharma has to follow not only the model of the throws of the die but also a more general quadripartite model (there are four varṇas, four stages of life, four goals of man, four Vedas, etc.) Besides, the avatāra theory did not spring from a Brahman's brain in its fully-fledged form. Even the classical list of the ten avatāras of Viṣṇu (which has regional variants) leaves one to guess the use made of the different motifs. The Fish, the Tortoise, the Boar and the Dwarf, for example, are well-known cosmogonic themes from the Revelation, re-used as avatāras by means of the addition of a demonic figure—the *asura*—which symbolizes social Evil and which they must overcome, whereas Narasiṃha ('Lion-man', or rather, no doubt: 'lion among men', i.e. 'king'), Kṛṣṇa and Rāma are probably major gods of a given territory within the geographical area occupied by Hindu society. In the contemporary religion there is in fact an unlimited number of avatāras, and one finds avatāras of Śiva as well as of Viṣṇu. But the classical theory could only acknowledge the avatāras of Viṣṇu, in view of the avatāra's role as restorer of the dharmic order and Viṣṇu's essential link with the society based on sacrifice, and therefore on brahmanic dharma.

One already sees the essential function of the yugas in the structure of time, thanks to the direct intervention in our world of the supreme deity which it makes possible, thanks also to the unlimited possibilities it offers for integrating local deities into mainstream Hinduism: a local divinity of the high castes is immediately declared an avatāra.[23] Śiva and Viṣṇu appear in the temples under very varied names which sometimes recall their initial functions in the Revelation, and sometimes link them to a particular place. As a result, the forms in which they are worshipped are also very varied: for example, the Veṅkateśvara of Tirupati (near Madras) cannot be confused with the Viṭhobā of Pandharpur (in Mahārāṣṭra); but they are both Viṣṇu.

Salvation

This open structure, so rich in possibilities, is also one of the weak points in the theology of bhakti: the effort to integrate 'worldly' concerns into a religion of salvation leaves some of the joins clearly visible. The texts do not agree on the values predominating in each yuga; but it is no surprise to see Knowledge or tapas in the first yuga, and sacrifice in one of the later yuga, whereas our epoch, Kali, is characterized rather by an all-purpose substitute for sacrifices, the gift—to the Brahmans, of course. The gift is conceived as the minimum performance of dharma, short of which there is no dharma left at all. However, this systematization still remains set within the orthodox perspective, which indeed presides over the whole theory of the four yugas, and gives no clue as to how it integrates with the conception of bhakti. In fact it cannot be separated from it, once it is recalled that it is the god of bhakti who is incarnated on earth to save dharma.

The *Viṣṇu-purāṇa* (Book VI), one of the great Purāṇas in which Vaiṣṇavite bhakti is unfolded, offers one of the most striking presentations in this respect. Since it has to end, as theoretically every good Purāṇa should, with an account of the end of the world, the last part of it opens with a description of the Kali age, which duly includes all the evils which afflict a declining society:[24] neither the Brahmans nor the Kṣatriyas are doing their duty; the Śūdras no longer obey the higher castes and couple with Brahman women (so peopling the soil of India with Caṇḍālas!); the Vedas are no longer recited, and so on. It is a familiar story and as usual the Kaliyuga is the worst of all yugas. And yet, the next chapter introduces, without any transition, the great Brahman 'seer' Vyāsa, whom tradition credits with the 'unfolding' of the Vedas in their present form, as well as the compilation of the epics and the Purāṇas. Such a figure cannot be suspected of non-conformity with dharma. Yet, while performing his ablutions in the Ganges, he utters such strange exclamations that his disciples ask him to explain, which he does: the Kaliyuga is the most blessed age, because it is now that salvation is most easily obtained. One only has to invoke the name of God—one of the names of Viṣṇu, of course, in this context—in order to obtain supreme grace. But this Hindu version of the Beatitudes goes still further: 'Blessed are the Śūdras'! Vyāsa proclaims, 'Blessed too are women.' We prick up our ears: no doubt he is going to explain that in the Kaliyuga Śūdras and women can, like anybody else, invoke the name of God and so achieve salvation. But no, that is not what he says: Śūdras and women are blessed (i.e. now, in the Kaliyuga) because they only have to do their duty—*svadharma*—in order to be saved. Whereas in a strictly orthodox view the castes outside the three higher varṇas, and even ultimately those outside the first varṇa, were excluded from liberation, bhakti grants even Śūdras and women access to liberation by the simple performance of their traditional function. They have indeed come up in the world; and not in the way one might have expected within the logic of bhakti. It is clearly not self-evident that devotion to God purely and simply replaces the traditional secular religion. Rather, it is the latter which seeks new vigour within the framework of bhakti.

The remarkable thing about these words of Vyāsa's is that they highlight, within a single speech, both the explosive potential which bhakti contains if its logic is followed through to its conclusions, and also its role of conserving the order of dharma. They give the key to the tension, which can be felt in the major currents of bhakti, between the concern for a thoroughly orthodox purity and the opening-up to the Śūdras.[25] So it is that South Indian Śaivism, as well as the Vaiṣṇavism of the Śrīvaiṣṇavas, combine vegetarianism with an underlying liberal outlook. In the first case, the Śūdras are, moreover, integrated not so much in the name of a negation of impurity as in the name of the conception of the divine Yogin as transcending the pure and the impure. The mythology readily presents Śiva in impure guises which shock the Brahmans, in order to teach that the salvation of bhakti is beyond secular distinctions of caste and of purity: for example, he is a hunter, and his four hounds are the Vedas. There could be no clearer image of the reversal of 'worldly' values, according to which hunting is a vice, grudgingly allowed to kings, and the dog, an impure creature the mere sight of which puts a modern-day Brahman to flight. The legend of Kaṇṇapa, the Śaivite saint of Kāḷahasti, has the same implication: Kaṇṇapa is a professional huntsman, a great devotee of Śiva to whom he offers the flesh of animals killed in the hunt, after having tasted it; the faults of impurity are compounded. The *liṅga*, a symbol of Śiva, receives no animal sacrifice. The animal victim offered up in the Vedic sacrifices was in any case normally a domestic animal, not game. Furthermore, the god is always the first to be served, and his worshippers may only have the remains (which, in temple worship, become the sign of his grace—*prasāda*). But Śiva accepts his bhakta's offering and one day, to test his sincerity, produces tears in one of the eyes of the liṅga. Kaṇṇapa at once plucks out one of his own eyes and offers it to God. The tears instantly stop. Shortly afterwards, the other eye of the liṅga also seems to weep. Kaṇṇapa wants to offer his second eye, but to be sure of finding the weeping eye when he is blind, he puts his left foot on it. Yet another abominable impurity: his foot on the liṅga and, worse still, his left foot! But Śiva then appears to his bhakta and restores his sight, showing that he has received his gesture with favour.

At the same time, present-day popular imagery portrays the head and torso of Śiva (and his wife) as they stand over the cow Kāmadhenu, a symbol of 'this-worldly' values. Depicted within the cow are all the great deities of the Vedic pantheon, as well as the Trimūrti, including Śiva: it is clear that the supreme form of Śiva transcends the Trimūrti and the whole complex of values and deities which accompanies it, but does not abolish them. Therefore, although the Śūdras are admitted to the Śaivite 'sacraments' which are linked to salvation, they do not have access to all the degrees of these sacraments. The social hierarchy still counts.

The case of the Śrīvaiṣṇavas reveals an even more contemporary tension. These Brahman inheritors of Tamil-language Vaiṣṇavite bhakti, which flourished in the south for several centuries before it spread northwards, had at the end of the eleventh century a great theologian and reformer in the person of Rāmānuja. If the legend is to be believed, Rāmānuja was concerned to put into practice the teachings of bhakti (which he developed into a Vedāntic system) and to break the taboos which prevented him from mingling with people of lower caste. The community of bhaktas could not admit the prevailing social hierarchy. Today, the Śrivaiṣṇavas are divided into two violently opposed groups, those of the north and those of the south. The former, who write in Sanskrit, have a justified reputation for orthodoxy. Their temples remain largely closed to non-Hindus. When one inquires—of other Brahmans—the reasons for their extreme rigidity, the answer is always the same: they want it to be forgotten that at one time in the past they opened their ranks to Śūdras, and that one cannot be entirely sure of the purity of their birth. So we have here a case of a sectarian caste which preferred its social status to the community between brothers which bhakti seemed to call for.

This is only an extreme example of what happened in virtually all sectors of bhakti: the universality of salvation had to accommodate itself to the secular hierarchy. This is all the more striking in that the Hinduism of South India was for centuries cheek by jowl with a powerful Buddhism and with a Jainism which has not entirely disappeared, in other words religions of salvation for which Vedic orthodoxy lacked any basis. In spite of the fact that Śaivites and Vaiṣṇavites have had their own authoritative texts, a total rejection of their Vedic origins would have spelled the loss of their identity as Hindus. In fact they incorporated the Vedas without denying them, and with them a whole conception of society. In practice, the temples are not only distinguished as Vaiṣṇavite or Śaivite. They are also differentiated as high-caste temples, both Vaiṣṇavite and Śaivite, where the offerings are vegetable, and low-caste temples, where animal victims are sacrificed even today, despite the multitude of official bans. We recognize here the opposition between the vegetarianism of the Brahmans and the meat diet of the lower castes, but also theoretically of the warrior princes. Between deities of the high and the low castes relations are established that are reminiscent of the social hierarchy of their respective devotees. It is also natural, in view of what we know of the relationship of Viṣṇu and Śiva to Vedic sacrifice, and therefore to the dharmic order, that low-caste deities should be more related to Śiva or to deities connected with Śiva. Symmetrically, Śiva welcomes Viṣṇu into his temple, whereas the opposite rarely occurs (especially in South India, where sectarian oppositions have been violent): Viṣṇu tolerates Śiva in his vicinity rather than in his temple, but he does tolerate him. Likewise, if the low-caste deities are excluded from the pure temple, they are not far from it. On these close interconnections, which reflect those of the social fabric, bhakti has built up mythic themes which explain the very real universality of salvation: the low-caste god becomes a minister and therefore a servant of the high-caste god. Or again, the low-caste god is a demon who is converted to the pure god; the latter gives him salvation and makes him his guardian. Through these motifs one recognizes the idea expressed by Vyāsa, that the Śūdra secures salvation by serving the higher castes.

Faced with these demands of orthodoxy, bhakti aroused religious movements of opposition to the Brahmans, tending to deny all hierarchy. Rāmānuja's attempt was taken up again tirelessly and more radically by reformers from all points of the compass, seeking to establish a community of devotees. In the twelfth century, for example, the Śaivite Brahman Basava founded in the Deccan the Liṅgāyat sect which, even today, is distinguished by it opposition to the Brahmans—particularly in the political field. The fact that this movement of bhakti, in spite of its negations, still draws inspiration from brahmanic renunciation can be seen in its attachment to vegetarianism, and in the practice of burying the dead in the seated posture (i.e. like yogins). Moreover it has its own renouncers, married or living in monasteries, who serve as priests. The coming of Islam provoked in North India, from the fifteenth century, a series of reforming movements, either syncretic or revivalist. Kṛṣṇaite bhakti soon dominated from east to west. But whatever the intentions of the founders, the caste is always reborn from its ashes within the sect, unless the sect finally coincides with the caste.

The end of the world and individual salvation

But what really is this salvation which bhakti grants to all? Brahmanic liberation is the fusion of the individual ātman into Ātman or the supreme Puruṣa. Bhakti transposes this idea into mythical terms and promises the faithful 'the world of Viṣṇu' or 'the world of Śiva'. This is the last paradise from which one is no longer reborn. In principle it is granted instantaneously by divine grace, and the hagiographic legends leave no hint of any delay between death and access to the supreme abode. But if we turn back to the Purāṇas, on which we saw the cosmogonic and cosmological framework of bhakti being built up, the situation is different. Since the supreme Puruṣa is the yogin who manifests himself in the rhythm of the great temporal periods by manifesting the universe, individual salvation has to be integrated into this rhythm and must also translate in its own way the hierarchy of the values which the successive levels of the cosmogony brought to light. It is the accounts of cosmic reabsorption which inform us about this, and, at the same time, they reveal a whole structure of the cosmos which has not so far become apparent.

It will be recalled that the Vedic revelation had a 'heaven'—*svarga*—where the ancestors dwelt with the gods, and that the *Upaniṣads* opposed to this heaven gained through rites a liberation from rebirths through knowledge or yoga which caused empirical man to lose his individuality and united him for ever with *Brahman* or the supreme Puruṣa. None of this is suppressed, everything is left in its place, and svarga itself becomes a stage in liberation, just as the empirical world only has meaning in relation to that liberation. This necessarily entails the mingling of some seemingly opposed values: at the end of the kalpa, dwelling in svarga are the Vedic gods, all the well-born people who have observed dharma and who receive regular ancestor worship from their descendants, their 'clientele', which no doubt means the inferiors who have served them well, and also the renouncers—if this is the correct interpretation of the less technical and more mythical terms used in the Purāṇas. It is the end of the world, at the beginning of a night of Brahmā, which enables all this host to rise to higher spheres from which they will not be reborn. The highest sphere to which they then rise is the 'world of Brahmā' or 'of the *Brahman*', where they are all equal with Brahmā or the *Brahman*, without a sovereign, filled with joy and purity. The mythical transposition is clear: from the idea of liberation through renunciation of all individual identity and all social hierarchy, we have moved to the notion of a world in which all the members are equal and indistinguishable. This does not yet represent final liberation, but only the second stage, the one which seems to correspond to the orthodox idea of individual liberation. But it must not be forgotten that a cosmic period is also involved: the end of a kalpa leads to access to a world in which one has to dwell while waiting for a mahākalpa in order to go 'higher' in liberation.

The rhythm of the days and nights of Brahmā is linked, as we have seen, to the manifestation of deity in the form of the Trimūrti. It is natural that the 'world of Brahmā' should appear at this level, where Brahmā is both the higher *Brahman* of liberation (when he turns towards the cosmic night) and the lower Brahman who creates by individualizing himself. But the 'world of Śiva' or the 'world of Viṣṇu' can only be attained at the end of a life of Brahmā or mahākalpa. So at the level of the Trimūrti, when the cosmic night comes, the deity gathers into itself, in different 'worlds', the totality of ātmans, both liberated and non-liberated. Only the liberated rise within it to the 'world of Brahmā'; the others will be reborn at the next dawn of Brahmā. After Rudra-Śiva has destroyed the world by fire, thus allowing the exodus of the liberated, and the flood has covered all that remains, the form of the deity that presides over the cosmic night and bears all creatures within it is called Nārāyaṇa. This Nārāyaṇa, which is already abundantly attested in the revealed texts as identical with the supreme Puruṣa, is thus, as it were, the fourth form of the Trimūrti. In fact, it is very quickly identified with Viṣṇu, and in the *Purāṇas* we find the conservative function of the Viṣṇu of the Trimūrti interpreted as presiding over the cosmic night. Nārāyaṇa is a yogic form of Viṣṇu. He is depicted reclining on the ocean of the flood, and his sleep is a yogic concentration, shallow enough to retain the memory of the creatures who are to be reborn. The traditional iconography adds a further symbol to this picture: between Nārāyaṇa and the ocean is the snake Śeṣa, which serves as a couch for the sleeping god. The snake universally symbolizes the formless, the chaos which precedes the cosmos. Its name Śeṣa, 'remainder', points explicitly back to India: the cosmic fire presided over by Rudra-Śiva is assimilated to a monstrous sacrifice, a sacrifice which is no longer Viṣṇu because it destroys the cosmos instead of keeping it in a state of prosperity: the charred residue is conceived as the remnants of what has been offered to the deity, which in a normal sacrifice is consumed by the officiating priests and the 'offerer' of sacrifice, so as to ensure them the beneficial effects of the sacrifice. Thus the snake Śeṣa is here the promise of a coming renewal of the cosmos, the assurance that the destruction is not final. It is the correlative of Nārāyaṇa, who bears within him the ātmans destined to be reborn.

From this very complicated schema, a few essential features may be extracted. First, the practice of dharma prepares directly for liberation, which is as one might expect if the religion of bhakti is truly the attempt to introduce renunciation into secular life. We shall in fact see how it succeeds in combining the demands of dharma, essentially the performance of rites, with renunciation: for was this world not created under the sign of the Vedic sacrifice, and does not the deity 'descend'—*avatṝ*—into this world in order to rescue an imperilled dharma? This does not mean that bhakti cannot be defined by an attitude of love towards God, but this love, in accordance with Purāṇic conceptions, may be manifested in rites—*karman*. On the other hand, and this is again a logical consequence, liberation cannot be a purely individual matter. It is collective, although obtaining it on earth depends at least as much on individual attitude as on social category. The definitive abolition of the empirical ego, on the death of the liberated, makes any individual transformation meaningless, and it is the totality of the inhabitants of heaven, including the gods, who rise through the spheres. None of those living on earth at the moment of the cosmic cataclysm are saved, because their presence on earth implies that they are not without karman. So there is also a sort of equality of the non-liberated who are condemned to be reborn, which will last as long as the cosmic night.

But it is perhaps more important to note that, ultimately, access to liberation is withdrawn to a fabulous distance, to which the authors of the *Purāṇas* seem readily to resign themselves. One is almost inclined to see here a subtle devaluation of liberation. This is probably true of our Brahmans, who were content with their place in society and readily accepted the idea of being reborn in it. The prospect of liberation becomes as remote in time as the prospect of an end of the world. One might even say that its content is degraded in the mythic transposition and that it loses much of its interest. Was this not inevitable in this compromise with the world . . .? But this would be too hasty a judgement. The theoretical framework of the *Purāṇas* is inspired by bhakti, that is, by a renewed notion of God and of his relation to his creatures. Liberation can no doubt not remain exactly what it was in the *Upaniṣads*. Even if it is difficult to bring together all the variants of bhakti under a single heading, it can be seen in a general way that it displaces the devotee's aspirations. Whether the latter's love dictates to him a clear and definite line of conduct in the world—as is the case in the doctrine of the *Bhagavad Gītā* which we shall shortly examine—or whether it is so violent as to lead him to seek inward union with the hidden God in mystical experience, bhakti has the effect of bringing attention back to the present instant and therefore to this life. What the bhakta cannot endure is the absence of his God *hic et nunc*; he wants to feel that He is present. Kṛṣṇa has to show himself to Arjuna in all his glory and power in order to satisfy him (this is the vision of Chapter XI of the *Bhagavad Gītā*), and the most mystical of bhaktas asks nothing more than the inward experience of divine presence. This presence so fulfils him that he wishes for nothing more, and endless rebirths as a bhakta constitute for him the most blessed prospect imaginable. While being a man-in-the-world different from others, the bhakta too thus ultimately accepts this life. *His* renunciation is of another sort. The hagiography of bhakti shows us saints totally unsuited for normal life: bad husbands and bad fathers, they are only fit to sing the praises of God or contemplate him in ecstasy. But Hindu society, living on the same beliefs as them, integrates these 'deviants'—who are not figures of pure legend—with astonishing ease.

There is a corollary not to be forgotten: if salvation has become universal, the Brahman has nothing to lose, since the rites and the love of God give him a twofold guarantee for the future. It is therefore not surprising that the devotees of bhakti include very orthodox Brahmans like the Śrīvaiṣṇavas, who are perhaps not among the 'madmen of God', but who have nonetheless accepted the idea of a god who sanctifies their karman and this world. The Vedānta of Śaṅkara could dispense with bhakti and integrated it only at a lower level. That of Rāmānuja, by contrast, modifies the conception of the Absolute in such a way as to identify the supreme *Brahman* with the Viṣṇu of bhakti. That of Madhva (twelfth century) takes the opposite course and goes so far as to introduce the hierarchy into paradise, abandoning all monism.

Desireless activity

Although it draws the attention of its devotees back towards this world, bhakti does not jettison the Upaniṣadic renouncer's analysis of desire as the motivating force behind human acts; however, its conclusions run in the opposite direction. If, in the act, it is desire which is bad and alienating, then it is desire which must be suppressed rather than the act. The problem is clearly that of knowing whether there is any further reason to act once there is no more desire. The anthropology from which we started provides only a negative answer, since all human activity has been placed under the sign of kāma.

It is theology which would give rise, not to a new anthropology—India has only ever had one—but to a divine model for a human activity apparently devoid of foundation. This is the teaching of the *Bhagavad Gītā* in which, in the battle between the enemy cousins, the avatāra Kṛṣṇa plays the part of the charioteer who drives the chariot of Arjuna, the third Pāṇḍava, the ideal prince and a close friend of Kṛṣṇa. The image of the charioteer in fact expresses the function of spiritual guide performed by the human form of the supreme God, in this battle for dharma: it is simply a transparent symbol of the very function of the avatāra. Of the three levels of divine manifestation which the *Purāṇas* or the epic offer us, supreme Yogin, Trimūrti and avatāra, it is clearly the last one, the closest to man since it is incarnated on this earth, that presents itself as a model to imitate. But the avatāra is essentially identical to the supreme God, it is the manifestation of his 'interest' in the world. It is therefore the God of bhakti who reveals himself in this way, and he offers himself so well as a model only because there is a relationship of love between him and his worshipper. This relationship is itself the transposition of the desire for liberation. God, in making himself accessible to his worshipper and granting him his grace, becomes the object of the supreme desire, the one which suppresses all other desires. So it is impossible to explain the teaching of the *Gītā* on activity without desire without this precondition of a transfer of man's whole capacity for desire onto God—a desire for God which is expressed always in very Indian terms by the desire to see God, but which is made explicit, in conformity with the renouncer's move towards liberation, as an identification with Him. 'I desire—*icchāmi*—to see thee with thy tiara, and with mace and disc in hand. Assume that same four-armed form', Arjuna implores in the *Gītā* (XI. 46). But Kṛṣṇa's language is less naive: 'Many are they who—freed from attachment, fear and anger—are made of me, are grounded in me and, purified by the austerities of knowledge, have attained my being. In whatever way they come before me, in that same way do I communicate—*bhajāmi*—myself to them. Men on all sides follow my path' (IV. 10–11). The vocabulary is that of the most traditional renunciation, but it is God who speaks directly and makes himself a guru. To identify oneself with God now means first of all behaving like Him as far as possible, and when one is a prince, who has to protect dharma at the point of the sword, like Arjuna, much is possible: 'There is nothing that I have to do in the three worlds, nothing that I have not obtained, nothing that I have to gain; yet I am involved in activity. If indeed I should ever not be tirelessly engaged in activity, men on all sides would follow my path. These worlds would be plunged into oblivion if I were to do no work. I would be the author of (universal) confusion. I would cause the ruin of these creatures' (III. 22–4). Such is the ideal of action that is put forward: to act without having any personal goal, any desire for any 'fruit' for oneself. 'The four-fold varṇa was created by me, through the differentiation of their qualities and acts. Although I am the author of this, know me to be one who does nothing and who does not change. Acts do not stain me; nor do I desire the fruits of acts. Thus he who knows me is not fettered by acts. Knowing that the ancients, desirous of liberation—*mumukṣu*—performed acts, you should therefore perform acts—*kuru karma*—as the ancients did in former times' (IV. 13–15). The phrase *kuru karma* can be translated both as 'to act, to perform works' and as 'to perform rites'. And the double meaning is even more apparent when Kṛṣṇa says clearly: 'He who performs an obligatory act without leaning toward the fruit of his act—he is more a sannyāsin and a yogin than one who is without (the sacrificial) fire, or one who is without rites (*kriyā*)' (VI. 1). The new ideal is indeed formulated in relation to traditional renunciation: you have been told that the sannyāsin or the yogin was he who abandoned his fire or his rites, but I, Kṛṣṇa the avatāra, I say to you that you should keep your fires and your observances, do your ritual and other duty, without any desire for reward. You should act, like me, for the good of the worlds.

The context is well known: this dialogue, by turns anguished and passionate on Arjuna's side, but supremely impassive on Kṛṣṇa's side, takes place as the great battle for dharma is about to begin between the camp of the Pāṇḍavas and that of their cousins, the Kauravas, in the *Mahābhārata*.[26] All the negotiations have failed, the troops are in position, and only the signal is awaited to begin the fight. It is then that Arjuna hesitates at the task before him. To ensure the triumph of his elder brother, the son of the god Dharma, he must, with his army, kill members of his family, his first cousins, his revered great-uncle Bhīṣma, his guru Droṇa.[27] Unlike Yudhiṣṭhira, he is not tempted to escape by renouncing the world, but his duty is not clear to him. It is then that his friend Kṛṣṇa encourages him and proves to him that he must do what he has to do: are not those whom he must kill immortal in any case, through their ātmans? Is it not his svadharma to fight, to kill and, if need be, to be killed on the field of battle? We again encounter the ethical problems which cropped up previously, and this time presented in dramatic form. Kṛṣṇa does not simply declare that one cannot escape one's svadharma; he proves that in performing it, one also performs the holiest action from the standpoint of salvation, so long as one acts without anger or hatred, without any desire for reward beyond the divine friendship. But Kṛṣṇa never forgets that he is talking to a prince, whose svadharma has two inseparable aspects: the task of the warrior, with all the violence and horror this entails—there is never any question of a morality brought into war to soften its brutality; only the warrior's inward attitude has to be modified with a view to his salvation—and the ritual function of the 'sacrificer', who must be exact in his observances in order to ensure the prosperity of the country.

In other words, the universalizing of salvation by bhakti, the consecration of violence in its impurest forms, comes through the avatāra who offers himself as a model to the king and thereby provides the reason for this final level of divine manifestation. The specifically royal values had to be justified, brought into the orbit of salvation, in order for the two types of men distinguished at the beginning (see p. 64) to have equal access, each in his own role, to divine grace.

The vision which Kṛṣṇa gives of himself in Chapter XI helps to unify the two aspects of the warrior's ethic within the general framework of bhakti: he then appears in the terrifying form of Time 'swallowing up' the worlds at the end of a cosmic period. Arjuna sees all the combatants in this war, good and bad alike, rushing into its gaping mouth. It is an awesome apparition, reserved in the *Purāṇas* for Rudra-Śiva, of deity reabsorbing the creatures into itself.[28] The war, in which Kṛṣṇa will play a major role right up to the end without directly taking part in the fighting, prefigures the end of the world which we have already seen assimilated to a cosmic sacrifice. In associating himself with Kṛṣṇa in the battle of dharma, Arjuna also becomes the 'sacrificer' of this war, he who will ensure the victory of dharma and so enable the three worlds to be maintained. Every action becomes a ritual, just as every effort to kill desire becomes a war. It is therefore not surprising to see in the *Bhagavad Gītā* a generalization of the use of the term *yoga* which makes it more than ever impossible to translate. Arjuna's action must be an act of yoga, like the act of the supreme deity. Because it is action, his yoga is a *karmayoga*, a yoga of the act. But because this action is performed in full awareness of what it has to be, this yoga is also a *jñānayoga*, a yoga of knowledge. Finally, because this disinterested action which even runs counter to the warrior's natural feelings is only possible through an unconditional surrender of self to God, it is also a *bhaktiyoga*, a yoga of devotion. Subsequently these three terms became the names of three separate paths to liberation, and this is the case even today. But here they only designate three aspects of the action of the prince: it is surely no accident that the yoga in which the three elements are held in equilibrium is still today called *rājayoga*, 'royal yoga'.

This yoga within-the-world does not exclude the other yoga: the *Gītā* recognizes and recommends the usual practices of yoga—postures, breath control and mental concentration. Perhaps they have to be regarded as exercises which make perfectly disinterested action possible? The result, in any case, must be an activity without residue, a karman which gives rise to no future rebirths, which does not bind its author but, on the contrary, leads him to liberation: 'He who is devoid of attachment, who is liberated, whose mind is grounded in wisdom, who acts for the sake of sacrifice—all of his karman dissolves away. The act of offering is the *Brahman*, the oblation, which is the *Brahman*, is offered by the *Brahman* into the fire of the *Brahman*. It is to the *Brahman* alone that he should go, he who concentrates himself—*samādhi*—upon the act of the *Brahman*' (IV.23–4). Have we really left Upaniṣadic speculations behind us? Or have they rather been applied to justify in absolute terms human activity defined according to the secular brahmanical perspective?

Even today the *Bhagavad Gītā* is the pious Hindu's bedside book. Even if his practices are no longer those of narrowly defined orthodoxy, he will always find something in this text to reassure him. It is clear that this gospel of bhakti in fact preserves the orthodox values, by promising salvation to him who observes his dharma. Dharma triumphs all the more since there is nothing else to offer as a goal to the man who lives in the world: to observe dharma is to help to maintain the world, to do the work of Viṣṇu. But it must also lead to liberation. Here too one feels that liberation is liable to remain somewhat theoretical, and that action for the world is bound to bring the world back to the centre of the stage. The prince remains first and foremost a prince. The tension inherent in bhakti is only resolved on a theoretical level. All it can offer this world is a mere supplementary guarantee, since it fails to provide it with a *raison d'être*.[29] These words of Kṛṣṇa's, again from the *Gītā*, highlight this situation: 'This world is fettered by acts—*karman*—other than those performed for the sake of sacrifice. Therefore, perform acts towards that end, freed from all attachment. In the beginning, having emitted the creatures together with the sacrifice, the Lord of creatures said, "May you increase through this. May this be the milch cow of your desires" ' (III, 9–10). This image of the cow Kāmadhenu is inevitably associated with sacrifice. But can one then sacrifice, being freed from all attachment?

We have seen how the world of bhakti was bound up with renunciation, and more specifically with yoga. There is however another term which appears in the epic and the *Purāṇas*, and which the *Bhagavad Gītā* returns to several times, opposing it to *yoga*: Sāṅkhya is in fact, in the list of classical philosophical systems, always associated with Yoga while at the same time distinct from it.[30] In the *Gītā*, it can be seen fairly clearly that yoga deals mainly with practice, with action as I have sought to analyse it, whereas Sāṅkhya is concerned with knowledge. This would be clearer if the two terms did not serve to distinguish two groups of people rather than two aspects of a single mode of action. At all events, it is in relatively late systematic treatises that one sees the two orthodox systems of Yoga and Sāṅkhya being constituted. They continue to be linked in theory as they were in the epic, but this does not mean that they hold similar positions on all points. Moreover, although they seem to have their roots in an ancient tradition, it would not be easy to relate them to sectors of Hindu society which profess them. They provide few texts, although their categories and the questions they deal with, pervade the other systems, classical or sectarian, and inspire many polemics. One finds no continuous tradition which explicitly claims descent from them, but rather a diffuse utilization of them. Thus, starting with Rāmānuja, Vaiṣṇavite Vedānta integrated Sāṅkhya categories; yoga was very soon admitted alongside the path of pure knowledge preached by Śaṅkara, and this 'orthodox' yoga referred back principally to the classical yoga of Patañjali. The sectarian systems which constituted their own Revelation, the Śaivite *Āgamas* or the Vaiṣṇavite *Saṃhitās*, only complicate the Sāṅkhya categories, in particular by adding new categories from above.

Sāṅkhya proper is nothing other than a reworking, half-conceptual and half-mythical, of the Purāṇic categories of primary cosmogony; and, as we have seen, this was itself an appropriation of the *Kaṭha Upaniṣad* stages of yogic ascension, with the added element of *ahaṃkāra*. It also makes them the successive planes of manifestation of the cosmos, but with one important modification: the structure is decapitated, losing the supreme Puruṣa from which formerly everything issued and in which everything had to be reabsorbed. The system becomes overtly dualistic: opposed to a primordial Nature which evolves in the rhythm of the Purāṇic cosmic periods are *puruṣas*, individual 'souls', which have to liberate themselves from the processes of Nature to which they are fettered. If we hold to the teachings of the *Sāṅkhyakārikās*,—a short basic text of this system, but one which is somewhat obscure on certain points—we find that while yoga perhaps constitutes the required method for liberation, bhakti seems to be wholly excluded, since the supreme Puruṣa is no longer present. Nor does anything suggest a collective exodus of the liberated towards the supreme abode. There is, however, a curious link between a verse of the *Sāṅkhyakārikā*—in which Nature withdraws from the puruṣa which has achieved knowledge of its true identity, as a modest woman hides because a man has seen her—and a mythic theme of Kṛṣṇaite bhakti (*Bhāgavata-purāṇa*' (X) which shows the mischievous child Kṛṣṇa stealing the cowherdesses' clothes as they splash in the river, so that they have to climb out of the water in embarrassed nakedness and look for their garments. Moreover, Sāṅkhya develops a theory of causality emphasizing the pre-existence of the effect in its cause, which greatly attenuates the consequences of Nature-puruṣa dualism, while consecrating it. Nature, evolved and 'involved', is always the same; it evolves only with a view to the liberation of the puruṣas, but nothing happens apart from this liberation. The cosmic periods have lost their link with the yoga of the supreme Puruṣa, but they have not thereby gained any new meaning; on the contrary, they have lost that which made their structure intelligible. Although the monistic Vedānta philosopher, Śaṅkara, argued extensively against the Sāṅkhya theory of causality, this theory was no doubt the 'realist' equivalent of his own theory of *māyā*, 'cosmic illusion'. The set of problems is still the same, to such an extent that one of the most ancient commentators on the *Sāṅkhyakārikā* already glosses the term *pradhāna*, 'original Nature', as *māyā* and *Brahman*!

Overall, therefore, this system looks like an artificial construct, an attempt by the Brahmans to take over the framework of bhakti while precisely emptying it of its bhakti. We have seen how the notion of a supreme God, omniscient and omnipotent, was rejected by the most orthodox-minded Brahmans. Sāṅkhya may be an orthodox endeavour of the same order, an empty systematization intended to 'co-opt' a godless form of bhakti. Yoga seems to be an endeavour of the same sort. It does in itself constitute a complete yogic system, it does not even use any longer the categories of Sāṅkhya, but it minimizes the importance of the supreme God, Īśvara, the 'Lord'. He is little more than an object of meditation. When he is also made the 'controller' of the mechanics of the creatures' karman, no one is taken in: karman is precisely that which operates automatically, and the very idea of control is in contradiction with its nature. We see therefore, once again, the efforts of orthodox thought to remove all content from the notion of God. In practical terms, this makes yoga a system in which the values of the traditional renouncer are revived—the virtues initially demanded, purity, asceticism—and which can thus serve as a frame of reference for Brahmans' yogas, whose concrete disciplines are developed partly outside of it.

Although one essential dimension of the Hindu universe is still missing, we already see the proliferation of divine forms which leads the western reader to raise the eternal question of monotheism and polytheism. Everything has been said in this area. Sometimes commentators frankly assert the polytheism of a religion which has covered India with shrines dedicated to innumerable deities, whose mythology creates gods out of any notion or value. One is indeed struck by the seriousness with which pilgrimages are conducted, each shrine in a given set being duly visited. Each sacred site is a reduced image of the complexity of the Hindu's concrete beliefs and the diversity of the deities to whom he gives worship. At other times one hears the rather well-known refrain that all these gods are nothing other than the *Brahman.* But we should distrust this abstract—and orthodox—rationalization of living beliefs. Moreover, the bhakta is almost always more particularly attached to a given form of the deity. He worships Viṣṇu, but the Viṣṇu of Śrīraṅgam rather than another, the linga of Śiva, but that of Cidambaram or Kāḷahasti. Or he is a devotee of Veṅkaṭeśvara at Tirupati, of Viṭhoba at Paṇḍharpur. . . . His devotion even multiplies the forms at will: the infant god who arouses paternal or maternal feelings, the young-man god, the yogin god, the hunter god, the terrible god . . . all the themes evoked around bhakti give rise to a divine form and a particular feeling on the part of the worshipper.[31] But he speaks of his God as of God: the Lord, the Blessed, the supreme Puruṣa. The names with which he invokes Him make Him the one and only God. This is what has sometimes led to the idea that the polytheism is only apparent and that, even if the Hindu accepts a multiplicity of gods, every time he addresses one of them, he considers him as unique.

However, this debate perhaps still leaves us too much in a western perspective. We have so far taken care to see Hinduism in essential relationship with a particular anthropology. We must maintain this relationship more than ever and understand in the light of it what happens in the Hindu's religious consciousness. We started out from the observation that at the level of secular society, both theoretical and concrete, there was no place for the human individual as such; the individual is only a unit within his group, caste or lineage, which determines his place in the hierarchy.[32] His place, in other words his relationship to all others, whether higher, lower or equal, is more important than what he is in himself. However, from his group he receives a certain idea of his duty, and of all the invisible realities on which it is based. The day he feels too strongly the relativity, or indeed the vanity, of what is expected of him, he breaks away from the group and attends to what is most essential and permanent within himself—the ātman, or the puruṣa. But this ātman, which still receives from the social group the revelation of its existence, does not thereby acquire determinations which, from our standpoint, would be characteristically human. On the contrary, it attains liberation, through knowledge or yoga, only by shedding all differentiation, by being absorbed into the Absolute where it finally loses all that remains of empirical individuality. The god of bhakti, the projection of the yogin into the absolute, partakes of the same inner void, the same lack of intrinsic unity. Even the devotee's relationship with this god cannot give him a 'personal' density which the devotee does not have and cannot even conceive of. Thus the most anthropomorphic forms are acceptable inasmuch as they are never more than 'names and forms', no more human than man himself is.

On the other hand, if the bhakta remains a man in the world, his relationship to deity cannot be defined simply as a mystical relationship to the one God.[33] God, like society, is bound up in a network of relationships in which his place defines the essential part of his nature. In particular we have seen that Vedic sacrifice remains the central reference point in relation to which Viṣṇu and Śiva are differentiated (although within the sects, the hierarchy that is established may be the opposite of what one might expect). The deity is also situated by vegetarian or carnivorous diet: the pure god is higher than the impure god, but neither can be isolated from the other. In such a context, one cannot really pose the question of monotheism or polytheism: the choice between alternatives is not pertinent. Each Hindu deity is part of a complex. If the Absolute is located anywhere, it is this complex and not one or another of its members. It is in this sense that 'all the gods are merely forms of *Brahman*'. Let us say that together they all constitute *Brahman*.

CHAPTER 4

Divine Loves

To anyone at all familiar with Indian realities, it must seem strange that I have so far refrained from mentioning an omnipresent figure in the Hindu pantheon, the goddess, and also the religious movements which tend to give her pre-eminence over the male aspect—*Puruṣa*—of deity. This might be taken to imply acceptance of the theory which sees the female deity as an element external to brahmanism and its Vedic sources. According to this view, brahmanism is 'Aryan' and the goddess 'Dravidian'[1]. Likewise, tantrism[2] would be seen as an extra-Vedic, and probably older, religious form. Something analogous has, after all, already been said about bhakti. It must therefore be firmly restated that we are not entitled to isolate what presents itself to us as an integral part of the total structure of Hinduism. When one seeks to show the lines of force of such a complex religion, one necessarily adopts a particular order of exposition. But what comes last is no less essential; on the contrary, everything that precedes is needed in order to understand it. This is not to say that there were no goddesses before brahmanism—perhaps personifying mountains, for example—any more than one would deny the likelihood of there having been older gods. In any case, the historical data on this point provide hints rather than facts, and it is certainly more fruitful to see how the goddess's place is established within Hinduism, and how the tantric currents are linked to this whole set of ideas. That is certainly within our scope and forces us to acknowledge that to assert the alien origin of these elements casts no light whatsoever on what they may have been outside of the structure which now gives meaning to them.

On the other hand, it is perhaps useful to emphasize—in the light of the present state of 'dilettante' literature that appears on India, its goddesses and its tantrism—the fact that it is impossible to cause the Hindu goddess to spring, fully armed, out of the Vedas. What she presupposes, at all levels of her conception and her worship is, first of all, the clearly asserted complementarity between the inactive

Male and the female Nature which emanates from it and transforms itself until it ultimately gives rise to our tangible world; but also the paradoxical conjunction of the most bloodthirsty war-making and of total detachment in the ideal king, who is himself a replica of the avatāra of the supreme god. To insist on this twofold foundation is to contradict every attempt to explain exaltation of the goddess as the esoteric face of a Vedic Revelation opening up in outward practices. The goddess, like the major gods of bhakti, only takes on her full scale in a confrontation between renunciation and the world of sacrifice. It remains to be understood how she is truly complementary to Viṣṇu and Śiva, and not simply a redundancy or an accretion, when the avatāric form of Viṣṇu has already presented itself as the model to be imitated in action in the person of Kṛṣṇa in the *Bhagavad Gītā*.

Privileged experiences

As we have seen, the Hindu religious consciousness has centred its thinking and its endeavour on ahaṃkāra, the function of the ego, and on the desire which is the everyday expression of it. The renouncer suppresses ahaṃkāra by breaking away from everything which gives him a place in society—his duties, but also his rights. The bhakta seeks to achieve the same result by replacing desire as the motor of his activity with the love and imitation of God. His love may take a mystical turn, but it is above all the quality of his acts — *karman*—which characterizes him, even if these amount to no more than worshipping God in a particular temple—for temple worship is performed for the good of the worlds, both for material prosperity and for the deliverance of all. The sannyāsin and the bhakta seek salvation in an exit from self, in an extension of the ātman beyond the bounds of the empirical 'ego', *aham*. But nothing forbids the search for other paths which may lead to this result, or rather, certain areas of experience which point to other possibilities.

It has already been observed (see p. 51) that desire, in the particular form of amorous desire, was not necessarily an assertion of the ego. Whereas, in 'moralizing' literature, human love is often contrasted with renunciation as its main enemy, erotic experience, essentially shared physical pleasure, is analysed as an experience of self-dispossession. And this dispossession is immediately associated with that achieved through yogic concentration; it is the analogue of the religious experience pursued by the renouncer: 'When thought is not reabsorbed in the act of love and in yogic concentration, what is the point of meditation? What is the point of the act of love?' The linkage between the two orders of experience goes much further than the search for an expression of mystic union in terms of human love. It is already clear that if the figure of the yogin can be projected into the deity, the act of love can also be transposed into the divine to express the union of the Puruṣa with the world, or more precisely with original Nature. The Puruṣa and Prakṛti[3] merge into one another, but, parallel to this, there must then be a spiritual path for man (and woman) which passes through the act of love. This is one of the mainstays of tantric practices in the Hindu consciousness.

Another area that has been explored at great length is that of aesthetic emotion. In point of fact, I hesitate to translate the Sanskrit term *rasa* by such an approximation. Is this, for the Hindu, a question of what we call the Beautiful, in other words an area of experience distinct from those of the True and the Good? Rather than seek to answer such an outrageously Western question, perhaps it is more useful to try to pin down the notion as it appears in Hindu literature. Etymologically, the term evokes flavour, the sensation given by the organ of taste, as well as the plant juice which has this flavour. But for the Hindu it immediately has an Upaniṣadic resonance: *Brahman* is *rasaghana*, 'a mass of flavour', and the term *rasa* is thus from the beginning very close to the term *ānanda*, the beatitude consubstantial with *Brahman* (cf. in particular *Taittirīya Upaniṣad*, II. 7.1). One cannot say definitely that this is why the term is consecrated to express aesthetic emotion as early as the oldest treatise we have on the subject, the *Nāṭyaśāstra* attributed to the mythical sage Bharata (first centuries AD?) and remains the only term used to designate this notion throughout all the schools of aesthetics—or rather, poetics.

Indeed, it seems essential to start with this observation: dramatic literature is at the heart of all Hindu aesthetic reflexion. Bharata's treatise includes dance in drama (*nāṭya* designates both), but dance is only the visual accompaniment of dramatic expression, and the latter is not separable from poetry proper. Song and its instrumental support are also part of the complex which constitutes dramatic art (and, nowadays, Indian cinema). The specifically visual arts are associated with architecture and are only discussed in normative accounts which pay little attention to the aesthetic effect on the beholder and user. This pre-eminence of the spoken word, and of a spoken word which tells a story at the same time as moving the listener, is not entirely accidental. The subjects of stage plays are largely taken from the epics—edifying and glorious subjects which strengthen the emotional bond between the sources of the Hindu tradition and the audience. The text of the *Mahābhārata* itself, as a totality, is regarded by the best theoreticians as capable of inducing *śāntarasa*, the rasa of peacefulness, in the listener, through the light it casts on the events of this world. What we call an 'epic' because it deals with princes and battles, is something quite different for the Hindu mind. But it is no doubt banal to conclude that Hindu literature is not a gratuitous art; art for art's sake is a product of the modern Western mind.

We are brought back more specifically to Hindu, and even brahmanic, reality when we look for the roots of this preponderance of the spoken word. If there is one female aspect of the divine which is clearly present in Vedic literature, it is precisely the word. It is the personification of the Revelation itself, the source of all knowledge of the invisible, as indispensable for living as is the sensory perception that brings us into contact with the sensible (and essentially visual) world. As the Vedic Word, the Upaniṣadic Word, it is the guide for 'worldly' life as for life outside the world, for the enjoyment of earthly goods through sacrifice as for renunciation of this enjoyment. Under the name of Sarasvatī, she is the wife of Brahmā. Bhakti also identifies her more or less explicitly with original nature, the Goddess. She is the expression of the Puruṣa which turns towards cosmic manifestation.

It may be thought that to connect this revealed Word with poetic or dramatic speech is to force more coherence on the Hindu mind than it has ever really had. To be sure, the connection is not a direct and conscious one, but it is nevertheless present, as may be witnessed in the history of doctrines: towards the end of the fifth century of the common era, a philosopher and grammarian named Bhartṛhari attempted to reverse perspectives in the concept of the Word. It is moreover probable that he drew his inspiration from earlier speculations, no longer extant, of which the greater part were perhaps not expressed in written works, but may rather have been integrated into yogic practices. Until Bhartṛhari, the revealed word was essentially conceived as being transmitted by word of mouth. The Nyāya school attributes to God the function of revealing it, and to the mythic 'seers' (*ṛṣis*) the power of perceiving it. In the orthodox systematisation that was presented in many late Upaniṣads, the revealed Word constitutes the lower *Brahman* (of which the syllable *Oṃ* is thus the epitome), in opposition to the higher *Brahman*, to which it lends access. It is a revolutionary perspective that Bhartṛhari introduces; yet he perceives himself as following the same brahmanic Revelation as the most orthodox of Brahmans. For him, the revealed Word is internal to *every* man (and here we may glimpse the workings of the universalist tendency of renunciation), and even to every living being. It is this which accounts for all instinctive knowledge found among animals and babies, and all spontaneous behaviour. It is supreme Reality itself—or at least there appears not to be any *Brahman* other than it. It is the stuff of all consciousness, eternal, indivisible, and undifferentiated. It only fragments itself into concrete words, into carriers of distinct meanings, in order to communicate itself outside of a given consciousness. It then manifests itself with the help of audible sounds, called *dhvanis*, which are themselves evanescent.

This innovative and audacious philosophy was not followed in orthodox brahmanic circles, and it was not taken up by Sanskrit grammarians until it had first been appropriated by the Śaivite philosophers of Kashmir. And it is precisely in this context that it came to enrich speculation on poetics. This was due, in essence, to the work of the rasa theoreticians, Ānandavardhana (ninth century) and Abhinavagupta (eleventh century), of which the latter was also known as a tantric philosopher. Abhinavagupta does nothing more than to give a commentary on the work of Ānandavardhana (as well as that of Bharata), and it is Ānandavardhana who borrows Bhartṛhari's vocabulary in order to apply it to poetics. For him, rasa, the emotion experienced by the hearer, has no connection whatsoever with expressed meaning; it occurs in the order of suggestion[4] and, as such, is identical with the *dhvani*, that internal resonance of words from which all temporal sequence has disappeared. Rasa thus takes on an objective consistency, becoming the surplus of meaning proper to sounds, rather than what the hearer experiences. Words may express a human emotion, but this is not what rasa produces directly for the hearer. Previously, rhetoricians had concentrated their efforts in establishing inventories of figures of style and of the processes by which poetic language could be generated. With the dhvani theory, rasa arises out of a property of the word not subject to analysis, a property that eludes all process, but one that is related to a certain internal intent on the part of the poet.

However—and here is the second point we wish to make—this is never a case of generating a text's poetic value out of a particular mood, and even less out of an unconscious that is secret and more personal than the conscious and social ego. Every analysis of rasa—analyses which are never connected, moreover, with that which takes place within the hearer — emphasize that which differentiates rasa from ordinary emotion. We feel pleasure when we hear a play or a poem, even when these are describing a hero's sorrows. Characters' happy emotions themselves, most especially feelings of love, that most frequent of themes, are also experienced in a way wholly different from that in which we would directly experience them. We are only able to experience them because they awaken in us the dormant memories of similar personal emotions or feelings—if necessary those of a previous life. Yet, at the same time, all reference to one's self is quashed: each and every one of the spectators may feel the same thing at the same time and, for each of them, the emotion that has thus been depersonalized becomes divested of every spatial or temporal dimension. The compelling drama suspends the passage of time, suppressing concrete circumstances as well as waking memories. This is what the theoreticians of rasa describe as the universalization of emotion: the aesthetic enjoyment obtained through the poetic word is but another case of the dispossession of the self, in which the ego forgets itself in the emotions and feelings represented on stage or in a poem. This is one of the experiences that help an individual to transcend his ahaṃkāra: an analysis of this sort, like that of the act of love, clearly presupposes that the transcendence of the ego is not primarily a question of an ethical order. This has been demonstrated from the outset. We hereby come to understand how the enjoyment of rasa—*rasāsvāda*—can be so easily paralleled with the enjoyment of the *Brahman—Brahmāsvāda*. The sudden wonder—*camatkāra*—

created by dramatic action or verse is felt as an expansion of thought beyond its normal limits, in much the same way as the yogin or mystic (especially in Kashmir Śaivism) instantaneously accedes to an experience, a *camatkāra*, in which he transcends his ego.

The religious implications of this are immediate. In the classification of the different kinds of rasa, it is the rasa of love that is most highly prized, even if Abhinavagupta places greater emphasis on the śāntarasa which, for him, has a direct religious value. As for bhakti, it would also come to use the notion of rasa to typify the (essentially unselfish) feelings held by the bhakta towards the divinity, with the śāntarasa being common to both aesthetics and bhakti. At the same time, the convergence of bhakti on the one hand, and the analysis of love and of aesthetic enjoyment as the dispossession of self on the other, would bring the creation of a very abundant erotico-poetic mysticism of which the celebrated *Gītagovinda* of Jayadeva (twelfth century) remains the model. In order that he might better love Kṛṣṇa, it is necessary for the devotee to imagine his love play with Rādhā. The poet offers him a poetic and highly erotic description of their play, which the devotee cannot savour in the same way as he would the love play of any lesser character. This serves to draw him out of himself and to love God for himself. Here, the bhakta takes the place of the spectator.

The Goddess

For methodological reasons, we will begin by turning our backs on the dichotomy—which is taken to be self-evident—that exists between Śrī or Lakṣmī, the consort of Viṣṇu; and Parvatī or Durgā, who is considered to be Śaivite even if she is not always Śiva's wife. We will return to this dichotomy, properly delineated, in due course. We must first, however, establish the place of the deity who is worshipped in her innumerable independent temples, under a wide variety of names, as the Goddess. A second methodological imperative requires that we clearly separate our treatment of this Goddess from the problems posed by that extreme form of tantrism known as śāktism, until such time as we can reiterate the real connections that exist between the great Hindu temples (and not only those of the goddess) and tantric practices.

On the mythological level, we will begin by briefly evoking the

Goddess's birth legends, without attempting to go back to the origins of such accounts, or to produce an exhaustive list of her appearances. The first known myth of her birth is in fact that of the *Harivaṃśa*, that appendix to the *Mahābhārata* whose explicit aim is to recount the acts of Krṣṇa in such a way as to flesh out their epic allusions. At the moment in which Viṣṇu is to incarnate himself in the womb of Devakī in order to become the avatāra Kṛṣṇa, Kaṃsa—who is, of course, an asura incarnate, as well as the son of Devaki's brother—vows that he must die, for it has been fortold to him that Kṛṣṇa would kill him. Viṣṇu asks his sister Kālī (also called Kauśikī, Kātyāyanī, Ekānaṃśa, Nidrā, Vindhyavāsinī, etc.), his divine sister, to incarnate herself at the same time, in the womb of Yaśodā, in order that the two might be exchanged on the night of their birth. This substitution having been effected, Kaṃsa seizes the infant he believes to be Devakī's child, but who is in fact an incarnation of Kālī, and smashes it by striking it against a boulder—a *śilā*. She escapes from him, laughing, and rises up into the sky as she announces to Kaṃsa that his slayer has been born. The role of the goddess is limited to this role (in this part of Kṛṣṇa's biography, at any rate), and it is this episode that is invoked whenever the argument is made that the goddess is Viṣṇu's sister. She is sacrificed in order that her brother might fulfil his role of avatāra against Kaṃsa, and it would be a mistake to see hers as a purely passive role here: at the very least, she is a consenting party in this episode. Here she is a virgin goddess, and the worship that is promised to her in exchange is a bloody worship. More than this, she is attributed the discus and the conch, the weapons of Viṣṇu. It may nevertheless be supposed that she bears a relationship to Śiva's wife Pārvatī, the daughter of Parvata 'the mountain': a synonym for *parvata* is *śaila*, 'boulder, outcropping' and Pārvatī is consequently known as Śailajā, daughter of the Mountain. Here we find an echo of the boulder—*śilā*—upon which Kaṃsa sacrificed the infant and thereby caused her rebirth into her celestial existence.

Without a doubt, the *Devīmāhātmya* (a portion of the *Mārkaṇḍeya Purāṇa*) is a later source, even if a *Mahābhārata* hymn to the Goddess already portrays her as enjoying the blood of the buffalo, and in spite of the fact that the iconography of the goddess as slayer of the buffalo goes back to the second century AD. This contains two juxtaposed birth myths, of which one reiterates her familial ties to Viṣṇu, albeit in a different form from that of the *Harivaṃśa*. This time, the setting is purely Purāṇic: Viṣṇu is sleeping on the serpent Śeṣa, who is himself resting upon the waters of the flood. From Viṣṇu's navel there arises a lotus which, when it opens, reveals Brahmā. This god watches, horrified, as two asuras, born from the impurities of Viṣṇu's ears,[5] prepare to attack him. He then begins to invoke Yoganidrā who, inside Viṣṇu, suspends him in his state of 'yogic sleep'—this is the meaning of her name—during the cosmic night. But it is also Yoganidrā who, emerging out of Viṣṇu, awakens him and 'deceives' the creatures: she is the cosmic Great Illusion—Mahāmāyā—who allows beings to exist in a world which believes itself to be distinct from the god. In this case, Yoganidrā awakens Viṣṇu when she emerges from his eyes, and he easily slays the asuras. To this point, the goddess, the still unwed sister of Viṣṇu, limits herself to helping the god in the service of creation. At first blush, the second *Devīmāhātmya* myth is more problematic, since the goddess here seems purely and simply to replace the avatāra in his role as saviour of the social and cosmic order. Her kinship with Viṣṇu dissolves into an all-encompassing bond with the world of the gods in which are counted Viṣṇu and Śiva, but also the Vedic pantheon. Yet, we should not be taken in by these appearances, for the emergence of the goddess is directly subordinated to the war between the gods and the demons, and the king of the demons who must be defeated is Mahiṣāsura, that buffalo demon whose iconography and worship both demand our attention. In this new account, Devī, who is Caṇḍikā ('the Terrible'), Bhadrakālī ('the Black Goddess,' but with a beneficent—*bhadra*—connotation), Mahāmāyā, etc., is formed from a portion of *tejas*, from that fiery and luminous energy that is the intimate stuff of the gods.[6] Their combined *tejas* is fused into a single shining mass which takes the form of the goddess. This is done upon the initiative of Brahmā, who goes to ask for help from Viṣṇu and Śiva against the demons 'in order to perform the work of the gods.' Here again, Devī is in her virgin form, and her privileged relationship with Viṣṇu remains explicit in her name Nārāyaṇī. But here she appears in her full-fledged form as a warrior goddess and an avatāra.

A primary conclusion which must be drawn, on the strength of these myths alone, is that the goddess is not Śaivite in those mythic forms in which she is Śiva's wife and that she is primarily a relative of Viṣṇu—though we dare not say of his lineage—in her function as defender of the socio-cosmic order. On the one hand, she helps him and even supplies him with the sort of sacrificial victim he needs in his role as avatāra; on the other, she awakens him as she emerges from his body in order that he might take up the fight against the asuras who threaten Brahmā, the personification of Vedic knowledge and ritual practice. Finally, she also seems purely and simply to take the place of the avatāra in his battle against the asuras. Here, Mahisāsura appears to be the demon who is reserved especially for her,[7] with her function in this case being all that remains of her kinship with Viṣṇu. Across these various scenarios, she remains possessed of a single and unchanging 'nature', one which closely corresponds to the Purāṇic cosmic cycles and to concepts proper to bhakti. Inside the sleeping Viṣṇu, she is his yogic sleep; outside of him she is cosmic Illusion, primordial Nature. In a word, she is the feminine principle as opposed to the Male or to the man—Purūṣa—who is Viṣṇu. We know that the avatāra's mission is to initiate a nearly total destruction of the world, as a means to re-establishing an overturned order; and this is the significance of the role that Kālī must play as victim in the hands of Kaṃsa, the demon incarnate.

The problem that remains here is one of finding a unifying principle for these apparently differentiated functions; also problematic is her role as avatāra, as saviour of the socio-cosmic order in the recurring battle against the asuras. A rapid typologization of goddess temples will enrich the mythic data and allow us to move forward in our search for answers to these questions.

Without completely neglecting the multitude of family goddesses, local goddesses, or goddesses who fulfil special functions (regarding female sterility, various diseases, crossroads, mountain-tops, etc.), here we will deal solely with those goddesses whose functions are all-embracing for a given territorial unit, since it is these alone who can help us to delineate the socio-cosmic role of the Goddess. At the humblest level, it is to the tutelary Goddess of a village that we must turn. Athough she does not bear the name of 'village deity'—a name attributed to her on the eastern marches of the Deccan—in all her locations, she nevertheless seems to be found everywhere. She appears in single or multiple forms; and all across India, in the north and south as well, we find the recurring theme of seven sisters, who are grouped together in a single place or who distribute their roles across several different villages. At times they may appear in pairs or in groups of three, together in their temples, or divided among separate shrines. What is absolutely characteristic of this form of the Goddess is that her place of worship is always located on the limits of a populated area. As the protectress of a site, she should in fact be found on the border, prepared to challenge the enemy. Of course, in the details of her worship, she is also connected with the centre of the village, that place in which the crucial moments in the life of the group are played out. But she herself is first and foremost the goddess of the boundary—and this is the meaning of one of her names, Ellamma, a name found across the whole of the Deccan. Presently, her festival is in an advanced state of decay, well on the way to disappearing, a phenomenon that may be best understood in the light of the fact that its essential ritual observance, the buffalo sacrifice, is a rite that has been prohibited. In this function, she is always a virgin goddess, in accordance with her mythological description.[8] The enemies against whom she fights, and who are personified by the buffalo demon of myth, are essentially epidemics that afflict man and beast alike, and the droughts or excessive rains that threaten harvests; in short, all that concerns the life of a locale. She is close to her devotees, who know very well that they can turn to her for all that concerns the local prosperity, but nothing more. It would be wrong for us to see in this a 'popular' specialization of the goddess, or a reproduction of her on a village scale. What the villagers ask of her is in fact the shape that dharma—the socio-cosmic order, that well-tempered functioning of the universe in which each village must play its role and take part—will take for them on a local level. The buffalo sacrifice bears witness to the fact that, here too, the goddess is the victorious and consequently the royal warrior of mythic fame.[9]

By virtue of this, it is she whom we find on the scale of the kingdom itself, in the form of the protector goddess of the royal family. Here, she is less of a territorial goddess than she is a divinity of a family lineage; but this is a case of a particular lineage, one which identifies itself with its kingdom and its prosperity. The royal goddess's shrine is generally located in the interior of the royal palace, at the centre of the capital, and only receives worship from the princely family. If her worship is executed properly, the goddess bestows her benedictions upon the king, and thereby upon his kingdom, which is itself especially symbolized by the kings's primary wife. But she can also be found on the boundary of the royal territories, where her role is homologous with that of the village protector goddess. Her worship also betrays this homology, since the king presides over Durgā Pūjā celebrations in the same way as does a village chief in his role as the mandatory 'sacrificer' at the local goddess's festival. In both cases, it is likely that the buffalo sacrifice was rigorously observed nearly everywhere in India, even if we cannot prove this irrefutably today. Another possibility is that the royal goddess produces a double of herself. As the protectress of the royal line, she has her temple at the centre of the capital; however, she also bears a relationship to a boundary goddess—often her younger sister—over whose cultus the king also presides. In this light, the capital, inasmuch as it is a centre, becomes the symbol of the entire kingdom. At the time of the autumnal Durgā Pūjā, the festival of the royal goddess includes a ceremony in which the king's weapons are worshipped; and this constitutes the occasion for vassals to renew their allegiance to their lord by their presence. This festival, which culminates in the buffalo sacrifice, marks, at the end of the harvests, the beginning of military expeditions. This period is itself distinguished, in certain places, by the rite of 'crossing the border'. Military operations are thus perceived as passing under the direct protection of the goddess who of course is, here as in the village, a solitary virgin dwelling in her shrine.

Yet, in the great bhakti temples, those belonging to Viṣṇu and Śiva as well as to regional gods who are territorial guardians—gods whose protection, in any case, extends to the entire universe—the goddess is transformed into the wife of the god, and appears to be associated with him, of necessity, in subtle ways which we will undertake to describe. It is at this level, of the great pan-Indian or regional pilgrimage centres, that we find an opposition made between Lakṣmī or Śrī, and Umā or Pārvatī, as the respective wives of Viṣṇu and Śiva.[10] The god himself has, within a single site, an entire complex of shrines in which he appears under different forms. If the grouping is organized on a hillside, an upper temple is almost invariably placed in opposition to a lower one. The upper temple, much less visited than the lower one, contains a 'terrible' or ascetic representation of the god who is without any consort. At the foot of the hill, on the contrary, that place to which the god has descended in order to make himself more accessible, he is accompanied by a goddess—a wife, sister or mother—and the devotees come in droves, their hands filled with offerings and their minds filled with hopes and desires. Many are the possibilities for organizing such shrines, and these have varied with place and time. As a general rule, however, we can say that the god and the goddess maintain separate shrines, even when they are found within the same enclosure, as if to remind the devotee that the higher form of the god is an ascetic one. At the same time, it is from the goddess that one expects the most tangible blessings, blessings which bear a relationship to the world in which we live: even when he makes his request to a god, the devotee knows that it is through the channel of the goddess that he has access to him. In the local myths connected with every great temple, one regularly finds the goddess being substituted for the god—or helping him to wield his weapon—in order to kill the demons whom the latter has defeated at the site. It is as if, in order to maintain his ascetic purity and his salvific power, he must be discharged of his 'mundane' and especially his military duties. The divine couple is never truly brought together, apart from the time of their annual processions in which the god and goddess solemnly move through four streets which, forming a quadrilateral, symbolize the Earth. It is at this time that one may hope to gain from them their fullest blessings, for this world as well as for the world beyond.

There exists, however, another spatial configuration of shrines, one encountered too frequently to be passed over without comment, and one which recurs too often to be without significance. This is the case in which, for one reason or another—and many are the myths that account for this situation— the goddess and the god do not inhabit the interior of the same temple enclosure. Sometimes it is the god who has driven off his sinful wife, and sometimes it is the goddess who has refused to follow her lord and master as far as he has wanted to lead her. It is here that the goddess is invariably exiled to the outer confines of the 'Earth', that is, of the locality. It is tempting to see in this, yet again, the goddess in her primary function as guardian of a site; and this in opposition to the god, whose eminent protection extends over the entire universe. There is certainly an intentional complementarity here, one that is described in spatial terms. This complementarity undoubtedly translates itself into feelings held by devotees who find themselves unable to address to the god the same prayers as they do to the goddess, even though both are necessary. This bisexuality of the divine is all the more striking when one recalls that the great god of bhakti, in his temple, is most often represented in the form of one of his avatāras; that is, of a warrior who intercedes in order to destroy the demon of a given place. The goddess too is a warrior before all else, a warrior who battles against the buffalo demon and ensures the king his victory: it is possible to see in this the doubling of a single theme, down to its specific variants.

There is a real problem here, one of the tangled webs that Hinduism weaves for us, a conundrum that defies analysis. We therefore do not presume to be providing the last word here; we even have the distinct feeling that we must go much further in our investigations if we are to account for the god-goddess duality in all its dimensions. It is nevertheless possible to clarify the data of this problem, even as we point out the different levels of this complementarity.

At the deepest level, it is obvious that we are once again in the presence of the supreme Puruṣa, the Yogin who is turned toward liberation; and of the primal Nature who emanates out of him and who periodically returns into him to the cadence of the great cosmic pulsations which rhythmically control the divine Yogin. The god of the great pilgrimage temple is—regardless of his name and his myth—the pure divinity, withdrawn into himself, the god of ultimate salvation. Furthermore, his most 'terrible' forms border on being considered improper for worship, so dangerous are they even for the devotees themselves. These are relegated to the most inaccessible of locations, where they are surrounded by all kinds of taboos, and only appeased by the appropriate offerings. As for the god's great temple, it contains Śiva's phallic emblem, which is inserted into the female sexual organ—the *yoni*—for the perpetual procreation of the world. Alternatively, it contains a Viṣṇu who, although he is still lying on his serpent Śeṣa, is waking up, with a little Brahmā seated on the lotus that has grown up out of his navel. Rāma or Subrăhmaṇya is divested of his weapons in his images: often the name of the divinity or his cultic attributes evoke his ascetic form. In short, even though the god is the master of the universe of which his temple is the centre, he does not have a direct function as its protector *hic et nunc*. This role is delegated to an inferior god, with Bhairava being the classic territorial guardian or *kṣetrapāla*. The main sanctuary does not presume to represent the god in his supreme form—for such would be a contradiction in terms—but at most suggests his renunciant nature as the final cause of the world. Whence his purity, his exclusively vegetarian diet and his apparent inability, on a local level, to fulfil his function as an avatāra. It is for this reason that the goddess is required to take on various unclean tasks, notably the slaying of mythic demons. Compared to him, the goddess, regardless of her kinship relationship with him, is the whole of this universe, as well as the divinity who ensures its harmonious functioning and its essential order. By nature, she is active, bending to fulfil human needs, and on her guard against the evildoers who threaten her devotees. Vegetarian in theory if such is the case with the god with whom she is associated, she is amenable to certain compromises if the situation can be amended without damaging the purity of the god. At Puri, we find the surprising example of Vimalā, that goddess whose shrine is adjacent to that of Jagannāth, who, on the Eighth Night of Durgā Pūjā, secretly receives a sacrificial male goat through a hidden door. Elsewhere, we find the shrine of the non-vegetarian wife of the god located outside of the enclosure of the pure temple. This carnivorous diet obviously goes hand in hand with her warrior function. In simple terms—which we will develop in greater detail later—she remains foreign to yoga and to any form of asceticism. She is the cosmic manifestation of, and thereby personifies, that phase of the god's yoga in which he returns to a level of empirical consciousness. Here we can understand how she constitutes the devotee's only hope, and why he addresses her with innumerable hymns in which the names which describe all of her aspects form the leitmotiv: she is the Mother of the world—even though she has no children—Mahāmāya, the Great Illusion; Mohinī, 'she who leads astray' (while allowing the world to exist in a form that is distinct from the god himself); Ādiśakti, the Primordial Energy; Mahālasā, the Great Active One, etc.

In another sense, we have seen this complementarity of the god and the goddess described in spatial terms: if the god is the master of the universe, the goddess is more often associated with a determined territory, village or kingdom (this latter being in fact represented by the royal lineage or by its capital). Here, appearances can be deceiving: the innumerable temples with liṅga (the phallic emblem of Śiva) most often attribute to that god the name of 'lord—*īśvara* or *nātha*—of such and such a place', and a local myth has him battle with a demon who he has dethroned. This we have already said, in so many words: it is in his form as an avatāra that the supreme god may have a localized shrine attributed to him; but this becomes, *ipso facto*, the centre of the world, by which the god's sovereignty is perceived as limitless. Conversely, the goddess's power of intercession is strictly limited to the territory of whoever presides over her cult. That is, her realm is in fact circumscribed by the power of the goddesses who protect neighbouring localities. This is why the consort of a great god like Viṣṇu or Śiva, cannot, in the strict sense of the word, take on this concrete function. She is obliged to associate herself with the goddess of the place. The relationship between goddess and territory is easy to understand if we remember that the world is not a territory *plus* its inhabitants, but the earth-together-with-its-inhabitants. The whole of a kingdom is called *janapada*, the ground-together-with-its-inhabitants. It is the same symbol that at once refers to the kingdom as both territory and as people; and not even dharma can dissociate the fate of the two facets of this entity. The goddess, she who slays the buffalo demon and who gives victory to the king, is therefore that very Nature in which men have their place and from which they await the satisfaction of their needs. The multifold manifestations of the goddess are at least in part connected to the fragmentation of political power. Elsewhere, the god-avatāra reminds the king that, following the consecration of his power by Brahmans, he is symbolically the universal sovereign.

Finally, we find an ultimate aspect of this bisexuality of the divinity in the complementarity, internal to the Puruṣa, of Viṣṇu and Śiva. We should recall that Viṣṇu, who is identical to the Vedic Sacrifice, has not only retained, through this function, a connection to the brahmanic orthodoxy,[11] but that he also bears a properly royal aspect, by which it befits him to wear a kind of tiara. When only one goddess is associated with him, she is always Lakṣmī—Prosperity, the Brilliant and Effulgent One who brings Sacrifice into the world. This alone suffices to place her on the cosmic manifestation side of the equation, and to associate her closely with dharma.[12] Often however, and especially in the context of processional imagery, she doubles herself into Śrī (Lakṣmī) and Bhū. In this latter manifestation, she is Earth; and here she is placed to the left of the god, the position traditionally accorded to the wife of the divinity. This serves as a means of integrating Śrī with Viṣṇu—from whom she is in fact inseparable—and to depicting at the same time the relationship between the sacrifice and the prosperity of this world. In theory, Śrī is never alone in her temples; in other words, she is never a virgin goddess. Correlatively, her myths never depict her as a warrior goddess.

We must nevertheless qualify this general statement with two corrective remarks: there do exist in India temples dedicated to Lakṣmī in her twofold role of virgin and warrior, but in these cases she bears the name of Mahālakṣmī. We have already noted, moreover, that she can at times figure among the seven sister guardians of village India. In these two cases, she is always Lakṣmī, and never Śrī; that is, she is undoubtedly that goddess who at once encompasses in herself, both the Earth and its prosperity. But the epic also speaks of a human incarnation of Śrī. This is the princess Kṛṣṇā Draupadī, the common wife of the five Pāṇḍava brothers and the sister of the god Agni, the sacrificial Fire; and here we see that she is not a simple mirror image of Viṣṇu's wife, in spite of her kinship with the sacrificial fire. Black—like the avatāra Kṛṣṇa—she is born 'for the destruction of the Kṣatriyas'; her favourite husband is Arjuna, the incarnation of Nara and the son of Indra, the Pāṇḍava who is closest to Kṛṣṇa-Viṣṇu and the epitome of the ideal king. Without a doubt, she is not a warrior in the immediate sense of the word, but her quickness to anger and the impatience with which she tolerates her own and her husbands' sorrows stand in marked contrast to Yudhiṣṭhira's boundless ability to forgive and Arjuna's manifest repugnance to the thought of doing battle with his family relations. On the contrary, she gets along famously with hot-headed Bhīma, who is always ready to cross swords, especially when it is to please and avenge her. She is thus an active character in the war. She is unaware of the god's great plan (as is proper for a woman), capable of placing Bhīma in impossible situations, and is the mistress of faulty reasoning—in a word, she behaves as Māyā ought to behave. But when all is said and done, she is categorically opposed to seeing herself reduced to slavery by her husbands' enemies, and chooses, once and for all times, the side of dharma. It is thanks to her that the dreaded dice game of Book II is annulled and then begun anew, so as to end with a glimmer of hope for salvation: for is she not ironically hailed as her husbands' saviour, as the raft that is to keep them afloat? It is therefore not surprising also to find, in a part of the Tamil region, temples to Draupadī where, surrounded by her five husbands and Kṛṣṇa, she is nonetheless the temple's principal deity. Her ambiguity is total here: having been carried off by a low caste individual with royal pretensions (she herself is a Kṣatriya), she is nevertheless at no time the recipient of a buffalo sacrifice, or of any animal sacrifice in the strict sense of the word. Her festival ends, however, with a fire walk, which is but one of a great number of substitutes for human sacrifice found in temple worship. We must thus be very careful in speaking about the passivity of Śrī, as opposed to the more active Goddess.

As for Śiva's consort, by whatever name she is known—Pārvatī, Umā, or Rudrāṇī (in the *Mahābhārata* when Śiva is still simply Rudra), or again by some local designation—she is always the goddess, the sister of Viṣṇu who has become the wife of the ascetic god. In this way, the latter becomes Viṣṇu's brother-in-law, a theme which is consciously intimated, in south India at least. This alliance between the god of the Sacrifice and that of Renunciation is not without its consequences for the Hindu concept of the nature of the goddess who seals it. The ferocious warrior—in the *Harivaṃśa*, Viṣṇu names her Kālī, 'the Black One'—who has refused the amorous advances of demons in order that she might place herself in the service of the gods, falls so much in love with Śiva that she even takes up the life of an ascetic to draw his attention, in the hope of making him her husband. With the goddess then, we run the gamut of the entire typology of masculine divinities. Starting with Kālī, wearer of a garland of skulls, naked and black, drunk with blood and alcohol—for she is so portrayed in her famous Kālīghāt temple in Calcutta, with her long red tongue[13]—we eventually come, at the other end of the spectrum, to the pure, vegetarian goddess. Yet, for all this, she remains a single goddess, for she is now Yogeśvarī, the Mistress of Yoga, who rivals with Śiva in her austerities and purity. When she has at last become the wife of the ascetic god, living together or apart from him, she returns to her vegetarian diet, but finds herself obliged to subordinate an inferior goddess to herself—in some cases, Kālī—in order to accomplish the bloody tasks that she has renounced.

Interpreting this multitude of the Goddess's forms, as virgin or wife, impure or pure, violent or pacified, now becomes relatively easy. Sociologically, it is generally not the same castes who worship her in all of her forms, and we find among her worshippers the same sort of cleavage as that found in her various depictions. We nevertheless encounter variants that cannot be explained on the simple basis of the general atmosphere of tantrism that obtains in India. So it is that a pure temple, such as that of Cāmuṇḍesvarī, on the hill that dominates the royal city of Mysore (in which we recognize the goddess of boundaries, of whom Cāmuṇḍā is a 'terrible' name) in South India, portrays the Goddess in her shrine in her 'terrible' form as the slayer of the buffalo demon. We can now say that she performs this function in the service of the gods and of dharma. Her cultus, in the hands of the Śaiva Brahmans,[14] is strictly vegetarian inside the temple precincts. But, like the goddess of the *Devī Māhātmya*, Cāmuṇḍeśvarī is attributed a younger sister, whose shrine is a few kilometres away. It is she who, according to the myth, licked up the drops of the demon's blood (therefore her long tongue), and it is also she who receives the buffalo sacrifice each year. This sacrifice is now limited to a very low-caste village; but in an earlier time, it took place *outside* the temple itself, during which time the Śaiva Brahman priests of Cāmuṇḍeśvarī came to stay, *inside* the temple, for two days. Preceding the buffalo sacrifice, which is always a communal affair, the local non-vegetarian castes make individual votive offerings of male goats and cocks. Some of these take place in front of Cāmuṇḍeśvarī's temple itself, on the outside of course, and out of view of the goddess and her priests. Here we can see the infinity of permutations that are possible within her cult, permutations that allow for the establishment of a connection between the pure vegetarian and the impure bloody forms of worship, as well as between high and low castes. This leads us to a more theological level of interpretation, one which doctrinally founds the unity of Hindu society, both in its complexity and in its impeccable ordering. The relationship between high and low castes should first of all be understood in terms of the relationship that obtains between Brahmans, a group that has long imitated the renouncer in its concerns for purity, its vegetarian diet and Kṣatriyas. Within caste society, the Brahmans bear living witness to the classic ideal of renunciation, whereas the Kṣatriyas are, in principle and by virtue of their warrior tradition, non-vegetarians, hunters, etc., and are thereby tainted with impurity. Strictly speaking, it would be untrue to present Viṣṇu as the god of Brahmans and Rudra-Śiva as that of Kṣatriyas; yet, there are a good number of cases in which the mythological division is of this order. It would undoubtedly be more exact to say, in spite of all this, that Viṣṇu—who probably first became a yogin in his Nārāyana form[15]—incarnates the proper relationship between the Brahman and the Kṣatriya, a relationship in which each of the two higher varṇas has its privileged function in the sacrifice and in its own appropriate form of renunciation. From the perspective of status, the Brahman's being the higher one, Viṣṇu may appear to be the god of Brahmans, even as his avatāric form sacralises the royal model. In this light, Rudra-Śiva necessarily remains, in spite of his yogic purity, associated with the dangerous aspects of the sacrifice which he symbolizes, and with the forest areas haunted by hunters and outlaws. He is nonetheless the Yogin god *par excellence*, in comparison to the royal Viṣṇu who reigns over dharmic society; and it is he who because of his position, incarnates renunciation in the classical Hindu perspective. The complementarity of the two gods is expressed through their family alliance, which is hypostasized in the Goddess. She is the 'marriage' of secular values dominated by the Sacrifice, and those of renunciation of which Rudra is the incarnation: that is, she is the principle of integration between asceticism and the world, a principle we have seen operating from the outset. The Goddess who transforms herself into an ascetic out of her love for Rudra-Śiva is the perfect symbol of this absorption of renunciation by society. This is the very way in which it is expressed: it is the Goddess who chooses and who wins the good fight, like the great warrior that she is, for her husband. This she does however with the weapons of yoga, while he, withdrawn into himself, long resists her assaults in a state of total impassivity. But it is in his role as Yogin that the Puruṣa emits the worlds in order that he might insert them into the process of liberation—and this is the symbolism of Śiva's phallus (behind which we may glimpse that of the sacrificial post), inserted into the female sex organ. With the myth and cultus deciphered in this way, we find a society that continues to be dominated by Brahmans and by the Sacrifice, a society that recognizes the preeminence of the renouncer and which sees itself as being enriched by this ideal. And this society cannot help but recognize itself in and through the goddess.

To this point, we have been able to confine our analysis of the major structures of Hinduism to a unified framework. If this is a matter of locating values and beliefs on a theoretical level, the overarching picture so generated corresponds to yet another practice that is common among the Hindu masses. Here, at pan-Indian and local pilgrimage temples, devotees visit local shrines, where they do not fail to worship the Śiva who is the neighbour of some celebrated Viṣṇu, or vice versa; and who also show their devotion to the guardian goddess of the place, regardless of their caste or sectarian affiliation. Elsewhere, the introduction of bisexuality into godhead does not give immediate rise to a notion of divine sexuality; for the goddess, tied to the world and this-worldly interests, has come to occupy a niche that has been hers alone in the functioning of the pantheon, most especially with regard to the yogin Puruṣa. We should nevertheless note that an important step was taken when the virgin goddess was transformed into the wife of Śiva. In this case, sexuality was introduced within the context of the divine life, as is clearly attested by the presence of the millions of liṅgas that spangle the Indian landscape (even though the great majority of devotees deny the sexual interpretation of this symbol). This notion bears important consequences for the Hindu concept of the divine. To be sure, it is particularly necessary that a connection be drawn between this and the eroticism that displays itself unabashedly in religious art, in temples as well as in popular iconography. The moment has arrived in which we must discuss that which is designated under the generic heading of tantrism. Since the relationship between Viṣṇu and Śrī or Lakṣmī has all in all shown itself to be but minimally sexualized, we might expect a Śaivite dominance in those religious currents which emphasize the masculine-feminine relationship within godhead. And yet . . .

The divine game

What the classical doctrine and its cultic extensions teach us regarding relationships with the god and the goddess in fact only concerns their relationship with those beings whom they have allowed to fall into empirical existence. When we return to the supreme Puruṣa who is withdrawn into his yogic trance (and it is always to him that we must return if we are to comprehend the apparently disparate facets of Hinduism) we find that the initial impulse which he gives to primal Nature in order to bring the cosmos into a manifest state—as well as his more direct interventions in this world for the restoration of a weakened dharma—do not find sufficient justification. Let us recall the words of Kṛṣṇa in the *Bhagavad Gītā* (3.22): 'There is nothing that I have to do in the three worlds, nothing that I have not obtained, nothing that I have to gain; yet I am involved in activity'; and (9.29) 'I am alike towards all beings. There is none who is hateful or dear to me. But those who worship me with devotion (*bhakti*), they are in me and I am in them.' As a yogin, the Puruṣa can have no attachments, and consequently he can have no reason for which to act. Yet it is asserted that he engages himself in cosmic manifestation for the salvation of beings, most especially for the salvation of his devotees. But the manner in which Kṛṣṇa formulates his relationship to the devotee strangely appears to give the initiative to the latter. In fact, the idea that is most impressed upon the Hindu mind is that God creates freely and for no reason, as a form of play. The notion of a divine game—which is still rendered in the Sanskrit by the feminine term, *līlā*—as the origin of this world is not the least bit shocking in a context in which man's sole duty consists in maintaining that which exists through acts that are ritual in origin and essence, with the proviso that he never creates anything new from that which already is. The idea is solidly grounded in the most orthodox of traditions, as indicated by the use which the *Brahma Sūtra* (2.1.33) makes of it, as well as by Śaṅkara's commentary on this *sūtra* in which the creation of the world is specifically explained.[16] It is, correlatively, the source of numerous mythic themes which transpose, with equal efficacy, the terrible (but salutary) acts as well as the blessings of the God, into dances or other forms of play. Each of the great gods has his dance: that of Śiva Naṭarājan, 'king of the dance', is renowned. This is a violent and terrible dance in which the god treads upon a demon: here Śiva dances on the worlds that he has just finished destroying. The infant Kṛṣṇa dances on the serpent he has just defeated, a serpent who also represents a demon, perhaps the symbol of the Kali Yuga. He also dances with joy when he has stolen a lump of butter from his mother. Gaṇeśa dances with his enormous paunch and his short legs; and it is perhaps a dancing pose which the monkey god Hanumān strikes when he treads upon another demonic figure, at a much more popular iconographic level. This theme becomes so widespread that a Tamil *Purāṇa*, for example, comes to describe Śiva's manifold incursions into this world as so many games.

Yet, it is rare that the god plays alone. The terrible dance of Śiva itself takes place in the presence of the Goddess. The divine līlā in fact bears immediate relationships to māyā, to primal Nature; and this is inevitable because it also describes the relationship between the god and cosmic manifestation, his 'activity'. When we move from myth to philosophy, the connection between līlā and māyā is also present: the two are often purely and simply identified with one another. God's play is also play with the goddess: to wit, the dice game played by Śiva and Pārvatī, a game in which they indulge themselves in their Himalayan paradise, and from which they will rarely brook disturbance. It is the destiny of the world that is being played out here (the game of dice evoking the succession of the yugas), but it is also a moment of loving intimacy between the god and the goddess: the game is the attention which Śiva lends towards cosmic manifestation, of which the goddess is the very hypostasis.

Nevertheless, it is Kṛṣṇa's bhakti tradition which most abundantly illustrates the theme of play. Kṛṣṇa, in the form of a young flute-playing cowherd, charms his childhood friends, most especially his girlfriends. The *Bhāgavata Purāṇa* (book 10) mentions the cowherding boys (including Kṛṣṇa's older brother, Balarāma), but the cowherdesses are clearly of much greater importance: at first maternal in their love for baby Kṛṣṇa, their love quickly becomes erotic. The *gopīs*—'cowherdesses'—clearly represent his devotees, whose souls experience feelings for Kṛṣṇa that are duly categorized by the bhakti tradition. The legends of his infancy develop—throughout all of the literature recorded in modern languages and especially in north India—in such a way as to allow for a free expression of the devotee's 'maternal' feelings. But it is the very erotic love of the gopīs for the young Kṛṣṇa that quickly comes to the fore: already in the *Bhāgavata Purāṇa* we find a description of the *rāsa līlā*, 'the game (made) of rasa'. We find this literary theme adapted into modern languages, translated into a ritual dance, and commentated by such theoreticians of Kṛṣṇa bhakti as the gosvāmins who were heirs to Caitanya (sixteenth century) in Bengal and in the Mathurā region. In the language of the *Bhāgavata Purāṇa* as well as in the writings of the gosvāmins,[17] we find the subliminal notion of the poetic rasa. This is that 'ultra-mundane'—*alaukika*—aesthetic emotion which causes the individual to leave himself even as it causes him to feel that which all of the other listeners or spectators are feeling along with him. In the play of rasa, Kṛṣṇa dances with all of the gopīs at the same time, so that each of them rejoices in his presence as if she were the only one who was so rejoicing, without jealousy for the other gopīs. In spite of the erotic overtones of the poetry that describes this līlā, the theoreticians of bhakti go to great lengths to explain that this is in no sense a case of human love, but that the love of the gopīs for Kṛṣṇa is a salvific love, a love bereft of egotism or egocentrism, in contradistinction to the kāma of this world, which is *laukika*. Bhakti classifies the rasas of the devotee like the poetic rasas, and if the different schools do not always agree on the names and number of these rasas, the parallelism between the two classifications is nonetheless striking. At the same time, we must emphasize that Kṛṣṇa is himself rasa through and through: so we are not surprised in the least—since he is composed of that bliss which already characterized the *Brahman*, and which is Śiva—to find him replacing Viṣṇu as the supreme form of godhead. Conversely, it is Viṣṇu who becomes an avatāra of Kṛṣṇa. But once more, nothing is lost: the bliss of the *Brahman* exists, but it is inferior to bhakti, with the śāntarasa itself becoming the lowest degree of bhakti.

In the meantime, however, a gopī appears on the scene who is prized above all the others: this is the Rādhā whom the *Gīta Govinda* introduces as Kṛṣṇa's mistress, but with whom the *Bhāgavata Purāṇa* seems not to be acquainted. Their loves are stormy: quarrels and reconciliations, separations and reunions, all of which are meant to depict a wholly affective mysticism. Once again, confronted with this character who appears in a poorly defined—though relatively late—period of Hindu mythology, attempts have been made to resolve the riddle she incarnates by explaining her existence historically or geographically. The goddess of some tribe (for is she not a cowherdess?), she must have slipped into the pantheon like so many goddesses before her. This is so much conjecture which, more importantly, throws no light upon the matter, since it does not advance our understanding in the least as far as her unique position with regard to Kṛṣṇa is concerned. In fact, the role of this unique gopī appears to become more and more indispensible as bhakti develops into a cult in which the love of God takes on a more and more intimate dimension. Even if every soul knows that it shares the field with sister souls, this nevertheless does not reduce its demand that God be hers and hers alone. This is part and parcel of the rāsalīlā, and it cannot help but bear extreme consequences: Rādhā is the ideal gopī, she whom all the others seek to imitate. The theoreticians of bhakti clearly distinguish the classical bhakti of the *Bhagavad Gītā* from the versions that they follow. The first centres on the execution of prescribed rites, not only the brahmanic rites discussed by Kṛṣṇa in the *Gītā*, but also the complex rites of the great Śaivite or Vaiṣṇavite temples which, found all over India, constitute the principal expression of bhakti among mainstream worshippers.[18] In contrast, affective bhakti consists of impassioned attachment—*rāga*—to the divinity. Such a love cannot help but project itself into a love that is sexual, the love of a divine pair: God, the Puruṣa, the Male plays the game of love with a privileged soul which has been feminized.

Rādhā, moreover, is a mistress, and not the legitimate wife of Kṛṣṇa. The most common explanation given for this is, at first blush, somewhat disconcerting: she has to be a mistress in order that the couple might be more certain that the love that binds them is not a banal human love, not a case of mere *kāma*. If the woman were his wife, the husband would be more easily carried away by a self-serving desire for her. This line of reasoning, it must be admitted, does not appear to be entirely convincing; but here again, it is necessary that we locate it in the context of bhakti, which is precisely what the Bengali Vaiṣṇavas argue: the soul is to have an immediate relationship with God, a relationship that is not mediated by dharma, by the accomplishment of rites. It places itself before him stripped of both ornament and merit, without caste or family, reduced to its intimate self. A legitimate wife could not symbolize this soul since she, contrariwise, must place between herself and her husband the entire range of dharma, of social rules and requirements. Besides, the husband has a feeling of ownership—of 'mine', *mama*—towards his wife, a sentiment which favours the development of ahaṃkāra rather than its transcendence. The reciprocal love of Rādhā and Kṛṣṇa is entirely divested of this self-centredness. Each is attentive to the happiness of the other and nothing else. Once again, the religion of secular life, dharma, is visualized as kāma, and kāma is the direct expression of ahaṃkāra. This was as it will be recalled, the judgment passed by the renouncer on a world fallen prey to ahaṃkāra—and this condemnation was a still wholly negative way of expressing the universality of salvation: salvation cannot be limited to or by considerations of dharma. Vyāsa, in the *Viṣṇu Purāṇa*, draws his own conclusions from this as he boasts of the benefits of the Kali Yuga, the joy of Śūdras and women. We have seen how bhakti has constantly been torn—due to its rootedness in brahmanic society—between a wish to preserve orthodox values, and a desire to build a broader cosmos. Such an enlarged cosmos would include everything that considerations for dharma would have ruled out as means to salvation. The bhakti of love, such as it presents itself in the 'extra-legal' couple of Rādhā and Kṛṣṇa, is an outcome of this latter perspective.

But in this case, Rādhā is not a goddess like all other goddesses: rather than depicting Nature, she represents the individual soul; and for this reason she cannot bear the same relationship to māyā as do other goddesses. The game of love profoundly affects the masculine divinity, to the point that it is no longer a game that he plays. Kṛṣṇa's lover belongs to the level of absolute reality. She belongs to the god's very being, inasmuch as he is rasa, and inasmuch as this rasa is typologized according to the relationship that obtains between man and woman. The love that Rādhā and Kṛṣṇa feel for each other is called *preman* rather than *kāma*, as a means to distinguishing it more clearly from the human love which it appears to imitate. The goddess, in those forms in which we have seen her to this point, is located on a plane of reality that cannot be the highest plane.

At this juncture, what separates bhakti from tantrism?

Tantrism

The question is in fact a twofold one, and the answers are not easy: in what way is that which we call 'tantrism' to be theoretically distinguished from bhakti, and why does there exist an entire area of religious phenomena in Hinduism which one would hesitate to list under either heading? The very choice of the term 'tantrism' is not as helpful as it might be, even if it follows a usage proper to the Sanskrit texts themselves. It comes from the name *Tantra*, which technically designates a certain category of works, of which there are a great number, and whose dating is at least as variable as that of the *Purāṇas*. At the same time, the *Tantras* themselves refer to certain texts which are considered to be revealed sources: these are the *Āgamas*, a term with Śaivite overtones, and the *Saṃhitās*, which are proper to the Vaiṣṇavites. This Revelation, originating from the divinity, is often placed in opposition to the Vedic Revelation which bhakti continues to claim for itself. And because tantric ideas are in fact as absent from Vedic literature as are those of bhakti, the notion of a popular, non-Aryan, current of thought surfaces once again. So, by virtue of the 'primitive' practices contained in it, tantra is provided with an ancient pedigree; and this in spite of the fact that the texts at our disposal never predate the common era. However, because of its very strong implantation into North Indian Buddhism, one is more inclined, in the search for its roots, to look in the direction of central Asia and its various shamanic cults, than in that of the Dravidians.

To be sure, a definition of tantrism that would limit itself to calling it anti-Vedic—and, by the same token, extra-Vedic—would be most awkward. Such would in fact force one, from the outset, to deny the possibility of coming to terms with the tensions that are as inherent to tantrism as they are to bhakti, tensions that divide it into practices reserved for the lower castes, and other practices with which the higher castes must content themselves in order to remain true to their dharma and not lose their status. By adopting such a perspective one would also fail to see, within the tantric systems themselves, practices which reflect the same fundamental notions as found in the rest of Hinduism. This common structure, which is identical down to its very details, is totally shaken by any other approach.

Bhakti appeared as a new reading of Vedic Revelation and of its most narrow brahmanic interpretation, a reading in which the world of desire came to be rehabilitated in its relationship to salvation. But this was effected at the expense of desire itself: all of the ends of man—including kāma—are good, but all must be subordinated to mokṣa. The king, that man most vulnerable to desire in all its forms, gains the promise of liberation on the condition that he break the bond that binds his acts to his personal interests or proclivities. The happiness of the worlds and the abandonment of self to the god of salvation must replace kāma and all of the egocentrism that flows from it. In fact, when the goddess enters into the life of the god, it is none other than the sensitive and pivotal position of kāma that is altered within the Hindu universe. Even when we take the added precaution of making a special case for the love of Kṛṣṇa for Rādhā, or between Śiva and his Śakti, by designating it with a new term, kāma remains very much present to the union of the pair, since without it the union could not be consummated. It is impossible to filter it out from the creative act itself, since the goddess is the principle to which the Puruṣa is opposed, both for the generation of the cosmos, and for the act of procreation. On the other hand, since the Puruṣa himself remains immobile and withdrawn, it is his feminine 'half' that is the active principle at work in the universe. It is therefore not surprising—whatever its undefinable historical origins—that the same goddess, the maker of creation and consequently of the world of kāma, also came to be considered, at some point in time, as the essential agent for the return to the Puruṣa, for liberation, the expressed end of the work of creation.

We speak of tantrism when this reversal in perspective is formulated in its most rigorous sense, regardless of the shape its realization takes. The world exists, as a given, with its existence tied to kāma; and it is the fate of kāma itself to ultimately return to the Absolute from which it was originally emitted. Rather than placing desire and liberation in opposition to each other, and rather than denying the one to the benefit of the other, the theory holds, quite to the contrary, that desire is the hallmark of each and every individual's initiation into the path of salvation. It is the seal of the divine in man, so long as he is schooled in the proper techniques for its transformation. It is therefore no longer one's acts, ritual or otherwise, that are valorized as such; rather, it is desire itself which is actually positively re-evaluated; and this change occurs, as always, from the starting point of a modified concept of godhead. If, in most cases, the Absolute in its ultimate form continues to be the Puruṣa into which all—including its feminine Energy or Śakti—is reabsorbed, then the god of the manifest cosmos cannot help but be united with this Śakti in a permanent and happy union. The divine takes the form of a couple, the analogue of the human couple and, conversely, no man—or woman—can approach the divine unless he or she seeks to reproduce this primal couple in him or herself.[19] In this way, the divine couple's happiness as well becomes the analogue of human kāma, even if it is bereft of all the limitations of the former. In practical terms, these doctrines are distinguished from one another by the greater or lesser importance that they attribute to the goddess. Śaktism is the extreme form of this process, wherein the goddess becomes the supreme universal principle. Iconographically, she is portrayed as a black, naked goddess, wearing a necklace of skulls, who stands astride the pale corpse of a recumbent Śiva (who is recognizable by his ascetic's tiger skin). This is the Kālī of Ramakrishna, the late nineteenth century Bengali mystic.

If we are to understand the directions in which the tantric ideal was sought, we are obliged, it seems, to take this glorification of amorous love—of that ground for all forms of desire—as our starting point. This is because tantrism offers the seeker a nearly infinite number of paths to follow, in a context in which the symbolic is more triumphant than ever, in which the role of dharma is reduced to a secondary position (with qualifications that will be discussed below), and in which the usual objects of desire become so many paths to realizing true happiness. The tantric universe is an exploded universe, one in which sects hold sway, in which models are skewed by the omnipotence of the guru, and in which the spectrum of possible options strangely corresponds to the caste hierarchy. Here we can do no more than attempt to grasp the broad behavioural categories through which tantrism is defined. We should not be surprised here to find the great themes of Hindu bhakti (with their valences reversed), and behind these, those of brahmanic renunciation. Tantrism innovates nothing—all it does is to appropriate known values in a reverse fashion, by re-reading Tradition through an esoteric lens. We will not stress the properly theoretical aspects of tantrism here, even though it is interesting to note the parallelism that exists between Śaivite and Vaiṣṇavite developments. In every case, the stages of evolution and involution of the real are multiplied with such a baroque proliferation of grades and levels, that one wonders to what they could have corresponded in the minds of their creators. The Purāṇic cosmogonies reappear, but here they are enveloped in several layers of supplementary categories, added from above and from below.

The first direction into which tantric speculation developed, and that which is striking to even the most distant observer, is that of its manifold ritual; for was it not this in particular that the brahmanic renouncer was obliged to abandon when he withdrew himself from human society? For him, ritual belonged to the universe of kāma and rebirth, quite nearly the converse of salvation. Now it appears promoted—as a specifically privileged case of kāma—to the venerable level of an instrument for self-realization in the presence of the divinity. From the outset, this is a private daily ritual in which we find echoes of brahmanic ritual; but here they are infinitely complicated, with external forms equated with mental states. Whether one installs the divinity upon a diagram drawn on the ground with coloured powders or whether one invokes it in an imaginary setting, one always begins with the invocation of the god within. One cannot worship a god unless one is already consubstantial with him or her: in other words, one offers worship to oneself. Temple ritual is by far the most spectacular, and we cannot help but admire the technical knowledge of priests who specialize in worship, especially in those regions where tantrism is most vital (Bengal, the coastal plain to the southwest of the Deccan, etc.), however vertiginous they may be to watch. The meticulousness of the rites and their multiplicity are such that their execution, according to the priests themselves, has to be altered for reasons of time—and this in a country in which everyone, in day to day life, seems to have all the time in the world! Every gesture, every ingredient, every formula, every movement through space bears a symbolic meaning which the initiate alone is capable of perceiving. In spite of the references made by certain temple priests to the Veda, and their claim to use so-called Vedic manuals—even though Vedic worship was never performed in temples—we may summarily say that the cultus of the great Vaiṣṇavite and Śaivite temples is, to varying degrees, and more so than that of the goddess's temples, tantric. The. Hindu collective consciousness is unaware of this because its devotees, as we have said, generally have no connection whatsoever with the particular tantric sects to which their temple priests subscribe. On the other hand, for the specialist in Hinduism, tantrism primarily appears as ritualism gone amok, and this to such a point that he is unable to recognize it once he leaves his own area of research. In fact, the difference between regions is often but one of degree or, currently, one of degeneration due to historical conditions. Nonetheless, to speak of tantrism in the context of the small temples of the village boundary goddess is out of the question; and this is a sign that tantric practice continues to be accompanied by a certain refinement in knowledge, and correlatively by a certain social position, which village shrines cannot offer.

This notion of a level below which we should not speak of tantrism, is made all the more important by the fact that tantric worship includes, nearly of necessity, offerings of sacrificial animals and alcohol to the goddess (both being justified by the *Devī Māhātmya* myth), even when the priests belong to the higher castes. Any number of permutations is possible, from votive sacrifices of water buffalo and goats in front of the temple — together with offerings of blood and alcohol brought into the sanctuary along with the severed head of the victim—to sacrifices, performed at a good distance from the temple, which are offered to those lower forms of the deity who serve as mediators between her and her devotee. If the phenomena are complex, the underlying principle appears to be simple: the consumption of meat and alcohol is strictly prohibited by brahmanic forms of Hinduism, in which the model of the renouncer, together with that of ahimsā, holds sway. Correlatively, worship of the gods is vegetarian for high caste Indians, with only inferior gods receiving blood sacrifices. So, for example, a subordinate god, ranked among the demons, is portrayed together with a dog (the hunter's companion) and a pot of palm wine. Tantrism, on the contrary, theoretically recommends offerings of flesh and alcohol, offerings that are to be ritually consumed by the god's devotees. What happens in practice corresponds quite exactly to the two-tiered situation that obtains across all other forms of Hinduism. For example, in the highly tantric area of Bengal, the Brahmans with the highest status offer vegetarian worship to the goddess, whom they call Vaiṣṇavī. These Brahmans even refuse to consume fish, a practice which is nearly normative in upper caste Bengali society. More specifically, their tantric worship replaces the animal victim by a symbolic vegetable victim—generally a variety of pumpkin or squash—which the Goddess is happy to accept as a substitute for meat. This is due to the social status of her devotees. The problematic remains constant here, save for the extreme case of Śāktism in which the Goddess openly covers herself and her priests with every sort of impurity: but here her followers are located at a relatively low level in the social hierarchy. Finally, it is the membership (or lack thereof) of priests in a tantric sect, and the initiation they would have undergone to this end, which most clearly distinguishes one tantric cult from another. The devotees themselves are not tantrics unless they have received the first degree of initiation into the sect, in which cases their sectarian duties are formulated in accordance with their caste affiliations. This essentially sectarian character of tantrism has undoubtedly played a crucial role in the coexistence of a Buddhist tantrism together with Hindu tantrism.

The same considerations hold, *mutatis mutandis*, for the sexual practices that are integrated into either ritual or yogic exercises; and it is these that have given tantrism its reputation in India as well as abroad. In this sphere too, variety is the order of the day, encompassing private practices, collective rites (as in the Kaula sect of Kashmir), and the use of temple prostitutes which was once current throughout India. All the same, the number of people who continue to observe such practices is very small. This is the case in spite of the comprehensibility of these within the logic of tantrism, where they transgress normative prohibitions and allow for varying degrees of personal aptitude. Sexual intercourse with a woman other than one's wife is considered to be of a higher order (as with Rādhā and Kṛṣṇa) in the hierarchy of practices because it requires a greater degree of self-control. This is accompanied by variant practices which constitute real feats; for example, the reabsorption through the penis of sperm that has been ejaculated into the vagina of one's female partner. The glorification of kāma thus does not exclude rigorous asceticism.

In a general sense, while the tantric yogins emphasize the body and its sexuality, they do so in a wide variety of ways, with the history of their sects being marked by an unending series of schisms, and by the divergences in beliefs and practices. It comes as no surprise to find all-powerful symbolic substitutes being used on a regular basis. It is in this way that an entire spectrum of yoga comes to be based upon the idea of the *kuṇḍalinī*, of the sexual energy that is found in its latent form in every individual, and which is represented by a coiled serpent residing in the area of the sex organs of the human body. Here, the aim of yogic exercises is to bring the animal to an erect position, and to cause it to rise, level by level and in accordance with the physiological symbolism proper to yoga, up to the top of the head or to a predetermined place in the body. Whatever its location, this is the locus in which the encounter with the Absolute, the realization of the perfect union of Śiva and Śakti, occurs. Here too, any number of gradations is possible, with the levels being increased to an infinite degree, and the passage from the visible 'gross' world to the subtle world being ensured by dint of equally innumerable transitions. From the outset, there is a remarkable concern for the correspondence between the human microcosm and the macrocosm, one that reappropriates the idea that the individual ought to reproduce the cosmic Puruṣa within himself. At the height of its complexity, this system renders vain any attempt to establish correspondences. With yoga, just as with ritual, an external observer—one who is necessarily uninformed—is struck by the feeling that the machine has gone out of control. But this should not hinder us in our search for the meaning of the fundamental symbols these systems put to use. These are probably no more gratuitous than the rest. Here we will only pause to observe the famous Kuṇḍalinī, sexual energy in the form of a serpent. As we have said, her name means 'she who is coiled.' Now, in Sanskrit, this term has a direct synonym, the compound *bhoga-vatī*: *bhoga* (a term derived from two different radicals) at once means curvature or coiling (of the serpent, for example), and all that pertains to the sphere of sensory experience, most especially to sexual pleasure—a wonderful ambiguity for lovers of cryptic language of the order of that which we find in the *Tantras*. At the same time, we can see how the Kuṇḍalinī, substituted for the too obvious bhogavatī, might serve as the epitome of kāma—of a kāma elevated to the dignity of human substance itself—and how the form of a coiled female serpent might be applied to it. As an added bonus, we also find, like some distant echo, a supplementary reference to the serpent Śeṣa, the Remainder of the worlds coiled upon the waters of the deluge where he serves as Viṣṇu-Nārāyana's couch. Decidedly, we have never left the Indian world.

Lastly, we should count among the innovations proper to tantrism the importance accorded to monosyllabic formulae and to the symbolism of phonemes. The tantric construction of the universe already accords a privileged status to sound, such that the stages of the evolution and involution of reality are echoed by symbolic acoustic equivalents—equivalents which no one seems to care about justifying. Subsequently, ritual wildly expands the role of these spoken formulae together with the phonemes, which are traced on diagrams: the mental world created by yogic meditation also complements these diagrammatic figures (geometric shapes, lotus flowers, etc.) with letters that are inscribed in them. Each formula, each letter or sound, is a symbol; and the mental microcosm is thus seen to be as twofold in nature as is the macrocosm emitted by the divinity. At the same time, these formulae constitute protective elements, with their phonemic inscriptions serving to make manifest one or another form of the divinity. Are we not to see in all of this acoustic material, which so permeates the entire gamut of tantric beliefs and practices, an echo of brahmanic speculations on the Veda and on the ritual omnipotence of well-pronounced formulae? To be sure, the content of the Veda has disappeared here, shattered into its atomic elements. But when we witness, at the dawn of the emanation of the cosmos, the rising of Sound in the form of a single point (the graphic inscription of the nasalization of the Vedic *Oṃ*), we are strongly tempted to relate this to Śabda *Brahman*, to *Brahman* in the form of Sound—this being the lesser form of the brahmanic Absolute which certain Upaniṣads placed alongside the supreme *Brahman*. On this point as well, tantrism does nothing more than amplify, *ad delirium*, a genuinely brahmanic current of thought. While this is a strange way of saying no to the Veda, it is undoubtedly the most subtle of all of the Indian ways to glorify kāma.

Tantrism and bhakti

It may be that we have come, in this all too short introduction to tantrism, to the elements of an answer, or of the beginnings of an answer, to the question that was posed at the outset. Although tantric theory clearly distinguishes itself in its most general aspects from bhakti, and although it seeks to deepen this cleavage through a reversal of brahmanic values in practice as well as in a broad range of its religious literature, the gap is in fact a very small one. We find tantric themes in the *Purāṇas*, and references to the *Purāṇas* in the *Tantras* as well as authors who write commentaries on both bodies of literature. The great *Purāṇas* are read in temples in which the ritual is said to be tantric, but in which the majority of worshippers are mainstream Hindus who come to the temple with a very vague notion of the meaning of ritual or even of the iconographic representation of the god, and would never dream of taking initiation into a tantric sect. It is this gap in particular which accounts for the refusal by the majority of Hindus to recognize the phallic symbolism of the liṅga. For them, it is merely that form in which they are used to having their *darśan*—their 'vision'—of Siva, and the question of the image's meaning is one they never think to ask. They would reject, with horror, any suggestion of a phallic cult. For them, the liṅga is, on the contrary, the most basic, the most austere representation of Śiva—one in which a Brahman of Śaṅkaran tendencies, for example, might see the symbol of the formless, attributeless *Brahman*. At the level of these great temples, the fact that the Śaivite or Vaiṣṇavite saints found there are pure bhaktas, eclipses tantrism all the more. Tantric iconography itself performs the same task as did bhakti with regard to Vedic Revelation: they incorporate rather than exclude whatever elements they cannot leave untouched. So it is that Śiva's liṅga, when it is not "self-generated" (that is, not constructed, but simply occurring as a natural rock outcropping) includes, beneath its vertical cylindrical portion, a square base which portrays Brahmā and an octogonal medial segment that is Viṣṇu. It is thus the Purāṇic Trimūrti (see p. 100) that is reproduced in the liṅga. Śiva is naturally taken to be superior here, as he who gives benefits in this world as well as liberation from it: Viṣṇu is subordinate to him, but Brahmā, and therefore the Veda, supports the entire structure. At the same time, a goddess as tantric as Tārā, 'the Saviouress', is 'made of *Brahman*', while another, Tripurasundarī was once the object, it is said, of worship by Brahmā, Viṣṇu, Śiva and the thirty-three (Vedic) gods.

We could go on forever in citing examples of this sort.

Lastly, do hymns of praise and accounts that glorify the god belong to the sphere of bhakti or to that of tantrism? Any attempt to delineate the two would be absurd, since both are indifferently used by bhaktas and tāntrikas alike. They merely serve to confirm the idea that temples are the meeting place between bhakti and tantrism. In effect, it is in the temple that these two aspects of Hinduism exhibit the goals that both hold in common: not to sacrifice this world to the ideal of liberation, but somehow to integrate it into the perspective of salvation. For the bhakta, worship born of the heart ought to accompany that of ritual gestures and speech in an attitude of total disinterest. For the tāntrika, the externals of worship are but a first step towards a transformation of the total person, body and soul, one which will lead him to a divine plane of existence. In both cases, the welfare of the worlds is as much in play as is the final salvation of every individual.

At the same time, we are warned against going too far in our fusion of these twin paths in the search for salvation, paths which by all rights ought to be kept separate—and here, we may even return to the couple of Rādhā-Kṛṣṇa who first gave rise to our question. The very emotional bhakti expressed in the *Gīta Govinda* and in a great many texts of the Kṛṣṇa tradition, in both Sanskrit and modern languages, and that form of which Caitanya's successors became the theoreticians, is still very much a form of bhakti. If the latter feel that Caitanya 'realized' the union of Rādhā and Kṛṣṇa in himself, this is primarily because they see him as an incarnation of Kṛṣṇa. But they themselves can only be spectators in the love play of the divine pair. They are the other gopīs who rejoice in Rādhā's ecstasy of love without being able to aspire to take her place. The union of Rādhā and Kṛṣṇa thus depicts, yet again, the mystic union to which every individual should aspire, the mystic union that constitutes salvation. The case of the Sahajiyās of Bengal, perhaps heirs to a tantric Buddhist sect that survived in this marginal Indian state, is altogether different. Each member of the sect, according to its adherents, is called to realize within himself the union of Rādhā and Kṛṣṇa; and since this is a case of a sect in which the tantric ideal has greatly deteriorated, the kāma of the common man is extremely close here to the tāntrika's act of love. The two are considered to be practically identical. Rādhā ends up being more important than Kṛṣṇa: therefore this is in fact a form of Śāktism, in which every woman is Rādhā in person.

From this standpoint, we might even hypothesize on her name, which distinguishes her from Srī or Laksmī as well as from the wives of Kṛṣṇa. It is interesting that this hypothesis originates in that compendium of classical bhakti, the *Mahābhārata.* The epic in fact knows of another Rādhā, who is promised, to be sure, a future less glorious than that of her namesake, but one which is nevertheless significant. This is the wife of the Sūta (a mixed caste born from the union of a Kṣatriya and a Brahman) who adopted the eldest son of Kuntī, the mother of the Pāṇḍavas. Kuntī had in fact—previous to her marriage with Pāṇḍu—a first son, whom she had abandoned in order to escape dishonour, in spite of the fact that the child's father was the god Sūrya, the Sun. Karṇa, this illegitimate son, would become the bitter enemy of the Pāṇḍavas—who remain unaware of his birthright—and especially of Arjuna, the ideal warrior. Now Kuntī, in the epic, is the incarnation of the goddess Siddhi, Success, Completion, the Realization of one's aim. *Rādhā* is almost a synonym of *siddhi.* The text, then, by designating Karṇa as 'the son of Rādhā'—Rādheya—obliquely indicates his kinship with the recognized sons of Kuntī, the Kaunteyas. In this light, Rādhā the lover of Kṛṣṇa may well symbolize the very essence of tantric worship—*sādhana*—or its practitioner, the *sādhaka*, who strives towards that goal that will make him a *siddha*, a 'perfected one' who has realized within himself the union of the god and his Śakti. In her, we again find the twofold stain of illegitimacy—arising both from the birth of Karṇa and from the mixed caste of the epic Rādhā—together with her status as a cowherdess which, analogous to that of the young Kṛṣṇa, symbolizes the care of cows so dear to the Brahman.

CHAPTER 5

Hinduism and the Future

Have we remained true to the wager of sorts that we proposed at the beginning of this study, that it is possible to recover, from beneath the infinite diversity Hinduism has to offer, a first glimpse at a deeper unity? To be sure, we nowhere find any sort of institutionalized unity which, superimposed upon this field of research, orders the whole in some explicit fashion. But we must not confuse the institutional with the structural. The religion that issued out of the Vedic Revelation, having never had a centralized organization, became fragmented into major movements, and then into sects that are today difficult to enumerate. Every 'saint' is a potential founder of a new religious group, but this did not cause us the slightest problem in our effort to generate an overview of the tantric sects. But does this make the task—of bringing to light, out of an extreme superficial diversity, a deeper holistic unity—all the more problematic? Not a single one of these religious movements, and none of these sects, can be made intelligible outside of its Indian, that is, its brahmanic and Hindu, context. It is obvious that the presence of numerous Brahmans, who were both sufficiently disseminated geographically to be different—yet bound closely together by their priestly status and their connection to the Revelation—was determinative. They asserted their ways of seeing, in speculations that quite often led them to integrate into their worldview religious discoveries which they might well have done without. Let it suffice here to say that these Brahmans, even as they retained their theoretical status and functions (could they, any more than any other Hindu group, have done otherwise?), were honest people who shaped their religion themselves. This they did together with others, along a given line or given lines, in order to give it greater depth and universality. At no time do we sense, behind this work, the lower castes exerting their pressure. More often, the case is quite the opposite: the Brahmans generate, from within their own perspective, those means by which the lower castes might assert themselves over and against them, most particularly on a religious plane.

For the speculation was, nearly always, of an essentially religious nature. This is not to say that all of the dimensions of human life were not explored, as I have attempted to show; rather, they were approached from within the sacred universe. The most secular, even the most empirical sides of the human condition were optimally considered by virtue of the simple fact that they were taken to be indissoluble parts of this sacred universe. At no time did an external source of reflection—from a non-religious perspective—come to shake the ideological citadel of the Brahmans. Those that were introduced over the centuries, and which certainly were a stimulant (but we know not to what extent) to brahmanic speculations, were also of a religious order. These were essentially Buddhism, a tradition that Hinduism would come to reabsorb in India; Jainism, which Hinduism confined to 'reservations' of sorts; and Islam, against which brahman orthodoxy would brace itself in a last hurrah. We have seen, however, how scientific thought, contrary to this development in the west, never laid the groundwork for its own emancipation. It is especially striking to see that the same concrete examples are invoked, indefinitely, throughout the entire history—a history nearly two thousand years old, if we are to judge by the texts we possess—of Nyāya, the Indian school of logic, and throughout that of the associated Vaiśeṣika school as well. The same lines of reason are taken up again and again, and are only refined to the end of responding better to the objections to which they give rise. The history of the mathematical sciences has most certainly enshrined powerful intellects capable of innovation, and capable of contributing to the world history of this discipline (they are credited in particular with the invention of the positional zero). However, apart from the fact that the socio-religious context did not encourage scientific research that exceeded applications to immediate needs, the Indian concept of the human mind allowed neither for great theoretical innovation, nor for the reform of reigning perspectives.

In a similar vein, India's history is a history that exists in spite of itself. There is no element of traditional thought that allows for an understanding of things as really occuring in the world. This is because man is, from the outset, conceived as having no other function than that of maintaining the cosmic order. It follows then that human life on earth, taken as a whole, cannot be oriented towards any but a predetermined specified goal, a goal which lies outside of man himself. Under the impact of renunciant ideals, human activity comes to be more and more analysed in religious, and even ritual terms. It is as if the Hindu universe has become more and more sacralized, in such a way as to definitively empty human existence of any meaning other than that of a perfect integration into a transcendant whole. It is the universe that gives human existence its meaning, and not the opposite. The concept of a cyclic time within which all, apart from a few liberated souls, returns perpetually, bears a logical connection with this anthropology. Regardless of what one does, the end of the world cannot help but come; however, this is but a pause which illustrates, at the level of godhead, the superiority of yogic concentration over any externally oriented activity. At the same time, the very perpetuity of the cosmic rhythm implies that he who lives in the world is bound to it, even if there is no good reason for his being there.

We cannot imagine a more total negation of that which constitutes, on the whole, our own modern western ideology. The implicit assumption of the western mind—that its life and acts have meaning, and that the world is possessed of a unique history in which it participates—is one which appears, to Indian eyes, to be myth. And it undoubtedly is one, just as much as is the Hindu perspective, but it is one that engages us, in our worldview, in a quest for solutions to immediate human problems—problems that are, moreover, often of our own making. In this way, we can understand how India has come to be the chosen land for those westerners who, finding themselves ill at ease in a world that places too many demands on them and that diverts them from the care of their ātmans, have rejected their own culture. On the other hand, we can see just as well how much our modern ideology is heir to Christianity: personal 'salvation', even if it is nothing more than giving some meaning to a life limited by birth and death, is effected through the others and through objective works, which the others will integrate in order to further them. This capacity of the brahmanic ideology to provide us with the possibility of stepping back from our own assumptions, even if only as a means to endorsing them on the basis of a more complete knowledge of them, is no small merit.

Yet, conversely, the West thrusts itself upon India, whereas India merely offers its viewpoint to the West. This is, for India, the crucial problem of the hour, one that has lain just beneath the surface of its every historical event since nearly the beginning of the nineteenth century. We are not attempting to prophesy here, but rather to bring together the necessary elements for as lucid a diagnosis as possible. At the same time, we leave for some future time the task of providing a definitive diagnosis—an *a posteriori* one, since such is always the case in history—for we have not yet completed our survey of human resources.

We should first note—since we have emphasized the West's responsibilities in the present situation—that the occupation of India by the Europeans in the eighteenth century, followed by the British triumph, did not put a stop to a growing and vital civilization. The political decomposition of the country in this period, considerably heightened by the presence of Muslim rulers alongside their Hindu counterparts, is not the final word on the conquest of India. For one who has studied Hinduism through the ages, together with the history of ideas to which it gave rise, the ossification that occurs after the disappearance of Buddhism (in about the twelfth century) and following the arrival of the Muslims, is inevitable. Masked for a brief moment by the anti-Islamic brahmanic renaissance that the Vijayanagara empire (from the fourteenth century onwards) patronized, or by the lightning rise of the Maratha empire, this stagnation was woven into the very texture of a culture that had reduced itself to rehearsing its own truisms, and to polemicizing incessantly in the name of an orthodoxy that each school claimed for itself alone. But is not every civilization mortal?

Long before the arrival of the Europeans, and even before the first appearance of the Muslims in the north, India located itself in the Kali Yuga. It continues to do so. It would therefore be vain to imagine the great period of classical Hinduism—corresponding more or less to the Gupta Age, around the fifth century AD—as a kind of golden age in which dharma would have been universally respected, and the social order faultless. The most ancient of the treatises on dharma already provide for all kinds of substitutes for especially burdensome high caste duties. Giving to Brahmans—or to wandering religious mendicants—ends up being the panacea for whatever is lacking. The possession of a cow is the symbol of piety; that is, of respect for the brahmanic order—and here we should specify that the raising of its calf, which implies the sacrifice of at least some part of the mother's milk, is mentioned as a feature of the golden age, which says a lot about practices in the Kali Yuga. Even today, we find innumerable substitutes for the pitfalls of visiting temples, substitutions that destroy sins and produce merit. The Porbandar (birthplace of Gandhi) temple of Sudāma alone—consecrated to the poor Brahman upon whom Kṛṣṇa, as the exemplary Kṣatriya, bestowed great riches,[1] provides us with two examples. The temple courtyard is filled with cows, which seem to be thriving, and with sellers of handfuls of grass that devotees purchase to feed to the cows. In the same courtyard, we find a curious labyrinth, built on a slightly elevated platform and consisting of a continuous double wall just a few inches high. It is moreover impossible to lose one's way in this labyrinth: to arrive at the exit, it suffices to enter at one end and to follow the narrow way that is closed in by the double low wall. Here we see women, preceded or followed by even their youngest children, doing their utmost to patiently follow the path, with eyes fixed on the ground and mouths achatter. What is the meaning of this? This is an exercise in concentration, in attentiveness, an 'equivalent' of yogic concentration! In a more general sense, salvation through bhakti—which has never lost its deep-rooted relationship to renunciation in the Hindu consciousness—has given rise to structures which, while extremely complex in theory, are hardly arduous in practice. These include pilgrimage to the protector god of one's lineage and affiliation with a guru who is the member of a sect but who need not be a renouncer himself. The guru is generally hereditary, and one's choice in gurus is determined by the caste to which one belongs. In theory, he visits the disciple family once a year, and this is an occasion for them to shower him with gifts. To this may be added staying at an ashram as a show of one's individual piety.

So it goes in the Kali Yuga, an age in which salvation, as Vyāsa said long ago, is the easiest to realize. There is a flexibility within dharma, and—so to speak—a certain law of the path of least resistance that allows one to fall back on less onerous practices when such is the order of the day. And this is perhaps the means by which it has managed to stand up nearly indefinitely to all that has directly opposed it: to wit, the invasion of a modern civilization centred on work, production, and profit. The fact that practices proper to dharma appear to be deteriorating does not necessarily imply that mental attitudes are changing. On the contrary, it is through this very reduction in external requirements, and through the search for adequate substitutes for them, that Hindus always find a way to sustain themselves without placing their lives and practices in question.

Obviously, there are many cultivated, high caste Hindus who are preoccupied with the future of their religion, and their analyses are most relevant here. It is said, for example, that the caste system is dying out, but that Hinduism is not bound to the caste system. In theory, the absolute *Brahman* or the supreme Puruṣa is, in effect, beyond caste distinctions; and this is precisely what the revealed texts themselves have tried to teach from the very beginning. It is also true, at least in the urban environment, that the prohibitions concerning social intercourse and intermarriage are less and less strictly observed. Still, we must not exaggerate: circumstances determine that exceptions to the rules are more immediate and visible to the foreigner's eye than are traditional forms of behaviour. And this is the case even before village India, the true India, is brought into the picture. Elsewhere—and this is yet another of Hinduism's eternal truths, one which we have not minimized—the *Bhagavad Gītā*, and even the whole of the *Mahābhārata*, teaches, together with the ideas of svadharma and unselfish activity, something that corresponds quite directly to what we call duty attached to one's social condition. This is a concept of action that lends itself, at first blush, to an analysis not unlike the one developed by Max Weber regarding the Protestant ethic. The term *sevā*, 'service', is one that recurs quite frequently in the names of many political or social reform groups that have come into being since the arrival of the British powers in India. Here we find an echo of the impression produced among the Hindu intelligentsia by the charitable—'unselfish'—activities of the Christian missionaries. But when we recall that Manu explicitly forbids the practice of any act of *sevā* by Brahmans and assigns the duty of service to Śūdras alone—and here too it is the term *sevā* that is used—there is room for doubt. Undoubtedly, the prestige of those in power played a role; and undoubtedly the influence of Vivekananda who had been so impressed in his travels to the West by charitable institutions, and of his Ramakrishna Mission as well, also lent greater credence to the idea of selfless 'service'. It is nevertheless more than likely that all of this took place within pre-existing ideological frames of reference, and that the *Bhagavad Gītā* was its greatest source of inspiration. Interesting statistics might also be generated—but we are lacking in sufficient data for relatively early times—on variations on the number of commentaries written on the *Gītā* in each period of history. It would be a rather safe bet here to say that their numbers have increased markedly over the past decades, and that this renewal of interest is more than a mere effect of advances in publishing techniques. The *Gītā* is the sole widely accessible text that is able to preach to today's Hindu an ideal of action compatible with his deepest held beliefs. India thus possesses, in its most ancient and most authorized tradition, all that it needs to renew its vision of the world and to edify a theology capable of giving spiritual nourishment to a 'modern' society.

We should nevertheless note that the *Gītā*, whose teachings are addressed to a prince, does not speak of service—for how indeed could it do so? It suggests that Arjuna should imitate a god who acts, without having any personal reason for acting, for the 'good of the worlds', but especially for the good of dharma. If there is a question of service here, it can only be one which concerns the impersonal order that keeps the universe in place—and this order is that which the Vedic Revelation promotes. The social hierarchy is thus consecrated, rather than denied, by Kṛṣṇa's teaching. Unselfish action is public duty in the context of dharma alone. Its transposition onto a society built on non-dharmic principles could only be effected if the notion of man itself, or that of society, were to take on some new content; and only if that content were to place man in opposition to an idea of nature, or to an idea of matter placed in the service of man. It is possible to imagine a so-called 'modern' society based on something other than the western 'egalitarian' ideology, or the idea of a class struggle to which that ideology gave rise. But the problem does not lie here: the fact is that India has been spared the universal intrusion of economic structures of western origin, structures that have been, consciously or unconsciously, intimately connected with a certain view of the world, a view characterized by the presence of certain tensions. We are not concerned here with demonstrating the unity of this western vision of man and his objects; rather, our aim has been to delineate the specificity of the Hindu vision. Might this not provide us with an ideological foundation, as secularized as one could wish for, that would be capable of giving meaning to a kind of modern life in which work is inserted into a complex network of *indirect* relationships with other people, in which anonymity goes hand in hand with increased responsibility—or in which, to put it more simply, we are asked to believe that man was brought into the world in order to transform it? When, in the West, we use the term 'socialization', in a more sociological than political sense of the word, we are sensitive to mass phenomena, to the omnipresence of the aggregate. The term—whether it be taken in a positive or negative sense—is in fact the counterpart to a more or less conscious assertion on the part of a certain kind of individual, one who would very much like to abandon his individual prerogatives to a certain extent, or one who would refuse this altogether. Modern Indian life is forcing people to move from a society in which the individual counts for nothing into one in which he must learn no longer to count without others. In fact, it is the individual in the western sense of the word, who runs the risk of never surfacing out of this situation; and his loss is the gain of those and those alone who have been, or are, able to grab some modicum of power for themselves. So, there are those who are discovering the joys of 'consumerism' before the greater group has even learned 'production'.

Still to speak in Hindu terms, modern, urban, industrial life is entering India at the level of kāma and artha, for the greater triumph of ahaṃkāra and a further degradation of dharma. The ideology which might be a vehicle for that enormous material transformation—the necessity of which is not denied—is still to be born. To speculate further and to conclude on an optimistic or a pessimistic note would be to substitute one's personal philosophy for the unpredictability of history. Some think that the new material conditions will create the appropriate ideology; but it may be doubted whether things have ever happened in that way in history. Others, more sensitive to the role of ideas and values, will anxiously wonder how India will equip herself mentally to face the new challenges. Until then, India will live as best she can and will perhaps take on a face that no one could have predicted.

November 1971
(revised March 1980)

Notes

INTRODUCTION

1. I shall not consider here works written in middle-Indian languages—Pali or Prakrit—because they are essentially Buddhist or Jain—rather than Hindu. The Prakrit used in Indian theatre is mixed with Sanskrit and is used to contrast low characters with the high-caste heroes. As for the literature in Dravidian languages, though it has its own literary conventions, its content cannot be said to modify greatly the knowledge which Sanskrit gives of Hindu culture. At most, I shall refer to regional variants, a phenomenon which is peculiar to the Dravidian south.
2. The history of art (architecture and iconography) may have more solid reference points, but the problem then arises of its relationship to the ideas and beliefs of the time. It is impossible to know what is implied in the presence at a particular moment and in a particular region of an iconographic theme which may, in any case, echo other texts that are less well dated and located.
3. This is not to say that one cannot speak of a sub-set constituted by the civilization of south India, but then the ethnic and linguistic oppositions are no longer pertinent. Long before the Muslim invasions in the north, South India had emerged as the great laboratory and conservatory of Hinduism, and a number of the great Sanskrit texts originated there.
4. Neither the critical editions of the two epics, works of this century, nor the editions now being prepared of the main *Purāṇas* will shed light on this aspect of the question. They will be useful to future generations as synopses of the known versions of these texts, which is, after all, justification enough. One has to be more reserved about the publication of 'reconstructed' texts without a critical apparatus and the appendices which preserve important fragments of the traditional versions. The same is true of translations of these 'reconstructed' texts, which are no more than new, 'modernized' versions, in which practically no Hindu recognizes his heritage.

CHAPTER 1
MAN AND THE ABSOLUTE

1. It will be seen subsequently how alongside this neuter *Brahman* there developed in the mythology a 'personified' masculine Brahman, which we shall call Brahmā (nominative masculine form) so as to distinguish it from the former.

2. The *Śvetāśvatara* (VI. 23) would seem to provide the first instance of use of the term *bhakti*—'partaking, devotion'—in a sense which anticipates that of the *Bhagavad Gītā*, although the Lord is here Rudra-Śiva. The *Śvetāśvatara* also provides the formula which was to become the most traditional expression of devotion (VI. 18): 'I take refuge in this God . . .', but still in an Upaniṣadic context, since it continues: 'I who desire liberation (*mumukṣu*)'.

CHAPTER 2

THE FOUR GOALS OF MAN

1. This detail would be sufficient to show the extent of the prince's religious obligations: blindness prevents a king from exercising his rule because it renders him incapable of sacrificing. It is impossible to conceive of a king who is not also a 'sacrificer'.
2. Yudhiṣṭhira's true father is the god Dharma. This is because Pāṇḍu was condemned never to procreate, as punishment for having slain, while hunting, the male of a pair of antelopes at the moment of their coition. Naturally, the two antelopes prove to be a Brahman saint and his wife, who had taken that animal form in order to satisfy their desire. The dying Brahman cursed Pāṇḍu that he would die when he attempted to have sexual union with one of his wives. *Mahābhārata* citations follow the Poona edition (Chitrashala Press).
3. We cannot be certain that the *TirukkuRal* is a Hindu source. It has been suggested that this is a Jaina text; however, nearly every religious tradition in South India refers to it. Its categories are altogether pan-Indian.
4. This may also be interpreted as a transposition of the soma sacrifice, one of the stately sacrifices which included the consumption of the drink of immortality, an inebriating or even toxic beverage.

CHAPTER 3

SALVATION THROUGH DEEDS: THE YOGIN WARRIOR

1. One might as well enter into the gigantic epic that is the *Mahābhārata* here, since it is both the principal—and undoubtedly the most ancient—of all monuments to bhakti. The *Bhagavad Gītā* is but one of its most dramatic, and doctrinally highly charged, passages. Yudhiṣṭhira, the eldest of the five Pāṇḍavas and thereby the heir apparent to the kingdom is, as we have already mentioned, the son of the god Dharma. He is often designated by the title of *Dharmarāja*, the 'king of Dharma' or 'King Dharma' (I personally prefer the latter translation). It is under this name that he is divinized, and continues to be worshipped, down to the present, in Hindu temples.

2. The term *ahiṃsā* is likewise a desiderative form: literally, it means the 'non-desire to kill.'
3. Following their father's curse, the five Pāṇḍavas, or 'sons of Pāṇḍu,' were fathered by gods from whom they inherited their personalities.
4. What we translate here by 'self-revelation' is the Sanskrit term *a-pauruṣeya-tva*, literally 'the case of not having a puruṣa at its origin.' If we recall that *puruṣa* means 'man', but that it is also one of the names used for the Absolute—that name which bhakti would particularly attribute to the highest God—we immediately see that self-revelation implies a rejection of omniscience on the part of both the human yogin and the great divine Yogin.
5. The young Brahman student will in fact have learned from his guru, prior to his marriage, the totality of the revealed texts, including the *Upaniṣads*. The ritualists see in these an appendix to the rites, one which must be recited in the same way as the rest of the Revelation.
6. Let it be understood clearly here that this in no way constitutes a value judgement, and even less a truth judgement.
7. But should we not yield to India on this point and recognize the fact that even our most rational philosophy—a philosophy that appears to be free of any postulate which is not grounded or explicated in the light of reason—is still nothing more than a theology, to the extent that it in fact rests entirely and *unconsciously* upon a western view of man?
8. Vaiśeṣika philosophy, which generates a theory of the categories of being, draws a correspondence between smell and earth, taste and water, sight and fire (which is also light), touch and air (wind), and sound and the ākāśa. Ākāśa is conventionally translated as 'ether,' even though it bears no relation to the ether of the Greeks. Sāṅkhyan thought draws the same correspondences in its cosmogonic schema.
9. *Cāṇḍāla* (more frequently, *caṇḍāla*) and *paulkasa* designate very low untouchable—and therefore very impure—castes resulting from the worst form of miscegenation between the varṇas (mother of higher birth than father). A Caṇḍāla is the child of a Śūdra father and a Brahman mother, a Paulkasa the child of a Śūdra father and a Kṣatriya mother.
10. Etymologically, the word *śramaṇa*, 'ascetic', no doubt designates any renouncer who has recourse to ascetic techniques rather than knowledge. A *tāpasa* (more commonly, *tapasvin*) was, in the Upaniṣadic period, probably a man who practised *tapas*, a warming technique according to etymology. In particular there was an exercise which consisted of sitting in the middle of four fires, under the fifth fire of the sun. But tapas is also probably linked to techniques of autonomous inner warming. In classical literature it refers more generally to any ascetic practice which enhances extraordinary powers. But, to a certain degree, it is regarded as capable of reducing the triple world to ashes.
11. Here we eschew any translation of the term *ātman*, which is often rendered as 'self' or 'the Self'. This is because the self that is treated here is more internal to myself than I (*aham*) am: therefore, it is a self about which I can never say 'I' or 'mine'.
12. We will return to this passage of the *Bṛhadāraṇyaka Upaniṣad*, a passage whose importance for later speculations cannot be overemphasized. Here, we should

simply note that this *Upaniṣad* presents its teaching in the form of a cosmogony in which the *Brahman* constitutes itself as an 'I', begins to desire things, and creates those desired objects.

13. It is nearly impossible to date any of these texts. This is all the more true for the fact that they represent an oral literature which probably took shape progressively, one whose versions would have varied more or less widely. However, the epics appear to be older (from the first centuries before and after the beginning of the common era?) than the whole of the *Purāṇas*. It should nevertheless be recalled that these different textual categories are already enumerated in the *Chāndogya Upaniṣad*, which itself probably goes back to a period several centuries before the common era.
14. It is impossible, within the context of this short book, to go into any depth in our analysis of the historical data, since we have chosen, on the contrary, to introduce the reader to a structural understanding. But if this undertaking is a success, it ought to offer an approach by which to comprehend the historical data; or at least one that offers an adequate historiographic perspective.
15. The mass of the revealed texts is in fact divided into four Vedas: the *Ṛgveda*, the *Yajurveda*, the *Sāmaveda* and the *Atharvaveda*, each containing ritualistic texts and *Upaniṣads*. Only the first three are related to the solemn ritual and correspond respectively to the different functions of the priests of this ritual. The fourth has a lower status and contains many magic formulae. That is why reference is made on the one hand to the Four Vedas but on the other to the 'triple science'. The *Yajurveda* is itself divided into two branches, the *Black Yajurveda* and the *White Yajurveda*, which are in turn sub-divided into several schools. It seems that the Taittirīya school of the *Black Yajurveda* was mainly responsible for the re-reading of the Revelation which bhakti constitutes. At present one can only note this without being able to explain it.
16. The term 'classical myths' is used to denote the fundamental myths contained in the epics and the great *Purāṇas*. They represent a first level of re-reading of the contents of the Revelation (myths, rites, abstract notions and values) which already contains considerable variations.
17. It is impossible here to give a detailed account of the yogic and cosmogonic levels given the number of Sanskrit terms which have no equivalent in either English or French.
18. The schema is in fact slightly more complex. It is especially important here to see that the end of the world is assimilated with a yogic process.
19. It is from this expression that the title of *mahātma(n)*, attributed to holy individuals such as Gandhi, is derived. It at once connotes superhuman knowledge and an active benevolence towards the world.
20. In the vocabulary of Hindu logic, *guṇa* designates quality as opposed to substance. In the perspectives of the epics, *Purāṇas*, and classical Sāṅkhya, which were already known to the *Śvetāśvatara Upaniṣad*, the three *guṇas* are more akin to components which make up all that exists empirically. They are also naturally hierarchized, and by virtue of this fact, they are able to afford a classificatory principle for beings, according to the relative proportions in which the *guṇas* are found within each of them.

21. In reality, it is Nārāyaṇa who, lying upon the ocean of the floodwaters (see p. 110), transforms himself into Brahmā. According to other versions, there emerges from the navel of the sleeping Nārāyaṇa a lotus which, when it blossoms, causes Brahmā to appear.
22. In fact, the question is slightly more complex than this. Moreover, we will soon see another interpretation of this preserving function that is Viṣṇu's, but this does not preclude the one given here.
23. There are variants to this, but these do not carry us far afield of our model: Subhramaṇya (also known as Skanda, Kārttikeya, Kumāra, Ṣaṇmukha and Murukan) and Gaṇapati (or Gaṇeśa, the elephant-headed god) are the sons of Śiva, whereas Aiyanār is the son of Viṣṇu and Śiva. This filiation is a mythic transposing of the divine manifestation which owes nothing to the theory of avatāras, at least not directly. These gods are nonetheless protectors of dharma and the divinities of brahmanic lineages. Naturally, we must add to these a large population of subordinate gods, who are more or less local.
24. It should nevertheless be noted that, in the account of the reabsorption of the world which begins a few chapters later, it is no longer a question of the end of the Kaliyuga, but of the end of a kalpa. This ending is no longer placed in direct relation to an increase in disorder, but rather to a general weakening of the creatures, with the arrival of the end of a day of Brahmā.
25. We still lack an essential structural element for the understanding of the major currents of bhakti and of numerous reform sects (cf. the preceding chapter). But the universality of salvation, and therefore the integration of the Śūdras (but still not yet of all of the lower castes) is one of the important concrete dimensions proper to both Śaivism and Vaiṣṇavism.
26. It has been asked whether the *Bhagavad Gītā* was truly a part of the *Mahābhārata* or whether it was rather an addition. The question is hardly worthy of consideration, since this beautiful text can only take on its full religious value when it is situated in the epic context.
27. It should be recalled that this is a crime according to dharma, but that it may be justified in the context of artha. Cf. pp. 53–8.
28. Book 10 of the *Bhāgavata Purāna*—another monument of Kṛṣna bhakti—again takes up this theme of the mouth of God as containing the universe. This time, however, the terrible element is entirely lacking: when baby Kṛṣna yawns, he allows his mother to see the universe dwelling in him.
29. This is the properly Hindu formulation of what is undoubtedly a more universal tension: that of being in the world as if one were not, and that of wearing down the world as if one were not.
30. In fact, the two terms are already associated in the *Śvetāśvatara Upaniṣad* (6.13), a text which we may qualify, on the basis of its connection to the *Black Yajurveda*, as well as of its contents, as one that leads from the yoga of the *Kaṭha Upaniṣad* to the bhakti of the *Gītā*.
31. Obviously, there is an analogous proliferation to be found in Christian devotion to Jesus: the Infant Jesus, the Sacred Heart, etc. However, these refer to none other than Jesus, God made man. Undoubtedly, it is herein that the essential difference lies, even if imagination plays the same role in both cases.

32. This in no way hinders a strong personality from asserting itself, in a village or elsewhere, even on a civic level.
33. There are, of course, exceptions to this. The mystic literature of Hindu bhakti certainly implies this uniqueness of the deity, but it no more constitutes bhakti than mystic Christian literature constitutes Christianity.

CHAPTER 4
DIVINE LOVES

1. Prior to the Aryan invasions, the Dravidians probably constituted the dominant element of the subcontinent's population. The majority of South Indians, who speak Dravidian languages, are still ethnically Dravidians. However, the cultural meaning of this ethnic distinction is much more problematic.
2. Conceptual system based on the *Tantras.* See p. 148.
3. Is it not significant that the more or less tantric systems of bhakti, rather than employing the neuter term *pradhāna* preferred by Sānkhya, opt for the feminine term *prakṛti*, for which they offer numerous synonyms?
4. We translate the term *vyangya* as 'suggested' or 'suggestive,' as opposed to 'expressed,' as a means of distinguishing between the rasa and the meaning of a word. But it is also with this term, or with other forms of the same radical, that Bhartṛhari designates the essential or internal word, that word which is to be externally 'manifested' by the dhvani.
5. It is impossible to account for every detail of this myth within the scope of this study. It seems obvious to me that the episode of the asuras Madhu and Kaiṭabha is a transformation of a *Mahābhārata* myth regarding Karṇa ('Ear').
6. *Tejas* is an untranslatable term which especially designates, in the context of classical mythology, the most essential principle of such beings as ascetics or warriors—of those people capable of 'burning up' the worlds in a literal or a figurative sense.
7. Fundamentally, the myths of the goddess found in the *Kālikā Purāṇa*, which is said to be a tantric source, follow the same schema.
8. This in spite of her names which end, according to the language in question, in *amma* or *-ambā* or *āi*, 'mother', a respectful form of address. This may help to bring together the seven sisters with the Saptamātṛkā, 'the Seven Mothers', well known from classical iconography.
9. It should be noted that among the seven sisters, whose names have come down to us in forms in which the original Sanskrit is sometimes markedly disfigured, Lakṣmī remains a goddess in good standing. Village India sees no conflict between a goddess who is supposed to be Śaivite and one who is supposed to be Vaiṣṇavite.
10. In reality, the situation is more complex than this. It is possible to have two or three goddesses associated with a god, with each occupying a niche on a hierarchy. In this case, one of these may play the role of the guardian goddess of

a locality. More than this, the goddess is not necessarily the wife of the god: for example, Paraśurāma, an unmarried god from Konkan and an avatāra of Viṣṇu, has his mother Reṇukā associated with his cult, while the Jagannātha of Purī is flanked by his sister Subhadrā (who is, moreover, duly identified with the virgin goddess), who is herself placed between her two brothers.

11. We should at least indicate that Nārāyaṇa—Viṣṇu in his yogic form—is the god of predilection for the Sannyāsin, that is, of the Brahman renouncer. The formula 'Nārāyaṇa' is always present in his salutations; and it is also this form that he uses when he signs his letters.
12. Is it for this reason that the abbot of Śaṅkaran monasteries is daily obliged to offer worship to the Śrī Cakra, the diagram that represents Śrī? We know that, in the classical view of dharmic society, the good sannyāsin also bears a positive role in the world order.
13. Her name is in fact derived from the name of one of the seven tongues of the sacrificial Fire—Agni—in the Veda. The *Devī Māhātmya* myth gives this tongue a purpose, since Kālī's role in it is to lick up the drops of blood that fall from the demon Raktabīja before they touch the ground—for each drop has the potential of producing a new demon.
14. By Śaiva Brahmans, we are referring to a caste of temple priests who consider themselves to be Brahmans even though Brahmans do not consider them to be such. They are more commonly known in Tamil country by the name *gurukkaḷ*, and are priests in temples of Śiva and of the goddess. The gurukkaḷs of Tamil areas maintain that theirs is a tradition based on the Śaivite *Āgamas* rather than on the Veda, and belong to a sect whose doctrine is codified in the texts of the Śaivasiddhānta.
15. It should be recalled that Nārāyaṇa is Viṣṇu withdrawn into a yogic sleep on the floodwaters of a cosmic night, Viṣṇu who has reabsorbed into himself all of the world's creatures. As the divinity of the sannyāsin, he is also explicitly the god of liberation—which, from the 'orthodox' viewpoint, is a prerogative reserved for renouncing Brahmans alone.
16. The *Brahma Sūtras* constitute the basic text of the classic system of Vedānta. Śaṅkara's is the earliest commentary that has survived down to the present; however, his nondualistic gloss perhaps does not respect the original purport of the *sūtras* themselves. It should be recalled that Śaṅkara succeeded in generating an 'orthodox' synthesis of brahmanic renunciation and ritualism.
17. *Gosvāmin*: one of the numerous names, found in Kṛṣṇa bhakti, to conain *go-*, 'cow', as its first term. The god himself receives the name of Govinda, the signification of which is disputed by various traditions: is he the 'discoverer of the cows' or the 'leader of the cowherds'? As Veṇugopāla, he is the 'cowherd with a flute,' a well-known iconographic depiction. Part of his childhood is spent at Gokula, in the 'family of cows', just as other 'twice-born' individuals spend theirs in the gurukula, the family of the guru: here he is surrounded by cowherds (*gopas*) and cowgirls (*gopīs*). The mountain which he lifts with one finger in order to shelter cows and cowherds from the rain unleashed by Indra is called Govardhana ('that which causes cows to grow or prosper'). Finally, when he is considered to be the supreme form of Puruṣa, as a substitute for Viṣṇu, his

paradise is called Goloka, the 'world of cows' (after the same fashion as Brahmaloka, Viṣṇuloka, etc.). Modern interpretation, which clearly betrays an imagination of a different order from that of the Hindus, sees in these constant references to cows a proof for a pastoral origin of the god, or at least for one of the god's aspects (which one is then obliged to consider as the synthesis of several characters between whom no logical connection exists). Yet, given the symbolism of the cow in the brahmanic ideology, it appears that another interpretation, of the particular mythic order proper to Viṣṇu's avatāras, is possible. In this light, we can understand that monks of the Kṛṣṇa tradition would have distinguished themselves from the innumerable multitude of svāmins by adding the *go*-prefix to their general title of svāmin.

18. We will return to this temple cult which, in itself, has more to do with tantrism than with bhakti. However, uninitiated worshippers participate in these in their own way, and bring to them concepts quite other than those of tantrism. Their spiritual nourishment comes more from the *Purāṇas* and epic narratives than it does from the Tantra.
19. This formula is to be taken in a literal sense. This means, among other things, that the sexual union between a man and a woman cannot help but be one of the means employed to reproduce, *within one's self*, this permanent and consubstantial union with the divine.

CHAPTER 5

HINDUISM AND THE FUTURE

1. Porbandar is not far from Dvārkā, the centre of the cult of Kṛṣṇa in his Kṣatriya form, on the Saurāṣṭra coast which still rings with the epic deeds of Kṛṣṇa. The myth of Sudamā is moreover purāṇic rather than epic.

Glossary

This glossary is intended to indicate to the non-Sanskritist reader, the approximate meaning of the Sanskrit words that it has been necessary to use in the course of the argument. It also includes the names of some frequently mentioned authors and doctrines. The page numbers which follow some of the terms refer to passages which deal more explicitly with the notion in question. English equivalents of Sanskrit terms have been used in the text whenever their use would not be misleading; thus some key items of brahmanic terminology do not appear here.

Abhinavagupta, philosopher of tantric Śaivism in Kashmir.

āgamas, 149. Set of texts regarded by their adepts as revealed, to which the Tantras and most of the rituals of the major temples make reference. They sometimes include the Vaiṣṇavite *Saṃhitās*, but sometimes the term applies only to the Śaivite texts.

aham, 'I'.

ahaṃkāra, 38. Term used to designate the empirical ego which says 'I' and 'mine' to distinguish itself from others.

ahiṃsā, 32. 'Absence of the desire to kill', from which the English term 'non-violence' is derived.

ākāśa, 91. The most 'subtle' of the five material elements. It follows earth, water, fire and air. It is the material support for sound and is conventionally translated as 'ether'.

alaukika, 145. 'Not of this world', i.e. not part of the ordinary custom of this world (*loka*). Hence 'extraordinary'.

ānanda, 'beatitude'. The term most often used for the beatitude of the Absolute, which is attained in liberation.

Ānandavardhana, theoretician of Sanskrit poetics in Kashmir, master of the *dhvani* school; ninth century.

āraṇyakas, 31. Literally, 'forest (books)'. The group of revealed texts which belong between the *Brāhmaṇas* and the *Upaniṣads*.

Arjuna, the third of the five Pāṇḍava brothers in the *Mahābhārata*.

The son of the god Indra (the king of the Vedic gods), he is the close friend of Kṛṣṇa. The latter is the incarnation of Viṣṇu-Nārāyaṇa, while Arjuna is the incarnation of Nara (man, a synonym of *puruṣa*) and represents the ideal prince who imitates the avatāra.

artha, 53–8. Designates any goal of an action, hence everything which is useful, any material interest. It is also the object to which a word points (both its meaning and its concrete use). Technically, it is one of the 'goals of man', the pursuit of wealth and material prosperity, for which the king is more particularly responsible on behalf of his subjects.

Arthaśāstra, 'Treatise of artha', attributed to the Brahman Kauṭilya, identified with a minister of the emperor Candragupta Maurya (fourth century BC). Deals with all aspects of royal governance.

ārya, 'noble'. General name for the three higher categories of brahmanic society.

ashram, see *āśrama*.

āśrama, a Hindu renouncer's hermitage, or a community grouped around a spiritual master. A stage of life.

asuras, inhabitants of the infernal regions. They become evil when they try to usurp the place of the gods in heaven or incarnate themselves as princes on earth to oppress the Brahmans. They are then the personification of *a-dharma*, and an avatāra of Viṣṇu must appear in order to rid the world of them.

ātman, 17. Third person reflexive personal pronoun. The name given to the eternal principle which animates the empirical individual.

avatāra, 103, 113–16. A 'descent' of the supreme God, especially Viṣṇu, into the world to re-establish weakened dharma.

avyakta, 93. 'Non-distinct, unmanifest'. In Purāṇic terminology, it is synonymous with *pradhāna* and *prakṛti*.

Bhagavad Gītā, 113–17. The most famous section of Book VI of the *Mahābhārata*: Kṛṣṇa's speech to Arjuna, which is the charter of orthodox bhakti.

Bhāgavata-purāna, the *Purāṇa* in which Kṛṣṇaite devotion begins to be unleashed in its erotic expression (especially Book X). It develops the story of the childhood of Kṛṣṇa, the theme of the *gopīs* and *rāsalīlā*. Rādhā does not appear in it.

bhakta, 'devotee', a follower of the religion of *bhakti*.

bhakti, the dominant form of Hinduism which implies a relationship of grace given by God to his creature and of total devotion given by the creature to God. Bhakti makes it possible to obtain liberation while remaining in society.

Bhartṛhari, 51. The author of aphorisms on the 'goals of man', the *Śatakatraya*. Indeterminate date. 125. A philosopher of grammar. Late fifth century.

Bhīma, 70. The second of the five Pāṇḍavas in the *Mahābhārata*. He is the son of the Vedic god Vāyu (the Wind).

Bhiṣma, 57. The paternal great-uncle of the Pāṇḍavas and of their enemy cousins in the *Mahābhārata*. He renounced marriage and the throne so as to enable the king, his father, to marry the woman he desired and ensure that the kingdom passed to her children.

Brahmā, see *Brahman*.

brahmacārin, 67. The name given to the brahman student during the time he spends with his guru to learn the Veda, which is also a period of celibacy. It is also the title given to a renouncer who moves directly from the first 'stage of life' to the fourth.

Brahman, 17–23. At the lower level, this term, in the neuter form, designates the ritual formula, and then the Brahman's Vedic knowledge, science and power, the Veda itself or its symbol, the syllable *Oṃ*. In the masculine, it is the name of one of the priests of the Vedic sacrifice. At the higher level, it is the Absolute (distinguished here by italics and a capital letter). This (neuter) Absolute also gives a divine personality, designated here in the nominative masculine form: *Brahmā*.

brāhmaṇas, 18. In the neuter, a group of ritual texts forming part of the Vedic or brahmanic Revelation. 19. In the masculine, it is the name of the first *varṇa*, that of the priests and clerics of brahmanic society. Anglicized here as Brahman.

Brahma-sūtra, 143. Basic text of classical Vedānta, on which every Vedāntic school produced commentaries.

Bṛhadāraṇyaka Upaniṣad, one of the great ancient 'Vedāntic' Upaniṣads, and one of the longest. It is connected to the *White Yajurveda*.

Caitanya, fourteenth century mystic of the Kṛṣṇa cult. While he was not an author himself, he gave the original impulse to the Vaiṣṇavite sect led by the *gosvāmins*.

camatkāra, 128–9. 'Instant astonishment'. A notion held in common by Kashmiri poeticists and theoreticians of mysticism.

Caṇḍāla, an untouchable theoretically born of a Brahman mother and a Śūdra father. In Hindu texts, he often symbolizes the lowest castes.

Chāndogya Upaniṣad, 26. One of the oldest and longest of the *Upaniṣads*, the one in which the identity of the ātman and the *Brahman* is taught. Connected to the *Sāmaveda.*

darśana, 'view, way of seeing'. Generic name given to conceptual systems, in particular to the six systems recognized as orthodox and grouped in pairs: Mīmāṃsā-Vedānta, Nyāya-Vaiśeṣika, Sāṅkhya-Yoga.

deva, 'god', particularly the gods of Vedic sacrifice, the inhabitants of *svarga.*

devadāsī, temple prostitute.

Devīmāhātmya, 'Glorification of the goddess'. Part of the *Mārkaṇḍeya-purāṇa.* In it the goddess is essentially the *asura*-slayer.

dharma, 41–6. The socio-cosmic order which keeps the universe in existence. Disorder, *a-dharma*, leads to an end of the world. Care of dharma is particularly entrusted to the Brahmans.

dhvani, 126–7. Material 'sound', especially articulate, uttered, audible sound, as opposed to the inner speech which carries meaning. In poetics, it is the suggested element, the source of emotion, as opposed to the expressed meaning.

dhyāna, a technical term of yoga which connotes the concentration of the mind on a single object.

Durgā, 'she who is difficult—or dangerous—to approach'. One of the 'terrible names' of the goddess, wife of Śiva.

Gaṇapati or *Gaṇeśa*, the elephant-headed son of Śiva and Pārvatī. According to myth, he was born from filth cleansed from Pārvatī's body. His name means 'leader of (Śiva's) hordes', a name which bears no apparent correspondence to his mythology. He is the god of beginnings, because he destroys those obstacles that would prevent one seeing an enterprise through to its end.

Gītagovinda, 128. Erotic and mystic poem composed by Jayadeva in the twelfth century, and which treats of the loves of the cowherd Kṛṣṇa and the cowherdess Rādhā. Their erotic relations are a metaphor for the mystic relationship between Kṛṣṇa, the highest god, and the individual soul.

gopī, 'cowherdess'. A figure in Kṛṣṇa bhakti who represents the individual soul, Kṛṣṇa himself being the divine cowherd, *gopāla*. Rādhā is Kṛṣṇa's favourite gopī.

gosvāmins, 46. Successors to Caitanya, they produced the literature of the Kṛṣṇa sect that was formed around him.

guṇa, 96. Name of the three components of nature—*sattva*, *rajas* and *tamas*—according to which all beings are classified.

guru, 'spiritual master'.

Haṭha Yoga, a school of yoga that emphasizes bodily techniques.

Hitopadeśa, 'Teaching on that which is beneficial'. A collection of Indian tales whose aim is to illustrate maxims of practical behaviour.

Īśvara, 'the Lord', the title commonly given to God in the context of bhakti.

jāti, 'caste' (literally, 'birth').

Jayadeva, twelfth century author of the *Gītagovinda*.

jñāna, 'knowledge', more especially knowledge of ultimate reality.

Kālī, 'The Black Female'. One of the 'terrible names' for the goddess, Śiva's wife.

Kaliyuga, the fourth and last yuga. We live in this, the worst of times. This is the Hindu 'age of iron'.

kalpa, 101. Name of a day of Brahmā, situated between two cosmic reabsorptions, which constitute his nights.

kāma, 46–52. 'Desire', and more particularly 'amorous desire'. One of the 'goals of man'.

Kāmadhenu, 'that (cow) from which one milks all that one desires'. Name of the cow which symbolizes the power of the Brahman.

Kāmaśāstra, *Kāma Sūtra*. The two names used to designate the 'Treatise on Love' attributed to the Brahman Vātsyāyana. Date undetermined.

karman, 23, 60–61. Any act, but particularly ritual acts. Because all acts are performed with a view to future results, karman is also that which condemns one to be reborn so as to reap the fruits that have not yet 'ripened' in this life.

kāruṇya, 94. 'Compassion'. The pity felt by the mystic for those who remain unaware of Reality and therefore suffer.

Kaṭha Upaniṣad, 27. One of the yogic *Upaniṣads*, belonging to the *Black Yajurveda*.

Kauravas, the name of the Pāṇḍavas' enemy cousins in the *Mahābhārata*.

Kṛṣṇa, the most renowned *avatāra* of Viṣṇu-Nārāyaṇa. In the *Mahābhārata* in particular, he appears as a Kṣatriya who, while divested of his royal power, remains a very much heeded advisor to the Pāṇḍavas. He gives his sister in marriage to Arjuna. In later Kṛṣṇa bhakti, he appears especially as the young cowherd of the Mathurā region with whom all the cowherdesses are in love, but whose favourite is Rādhā.

Kṛtayuga, the first and most 'perfect' (*kṛta*) of the four yugas. This is the Hindu 'age of gold'.

kṣatra, a neuter term designating the function of the Kṣatriya.

Kṣatriya, 20. The second varṇa of brahmanic society, that of warriors and princes.

Lakṣmī, one of the names for the goddess when she is associated with Viṣṇu. An expression denoting prosperity produced through Vedic sacrifice.

laukika, 145. 'Worldly, of common usage'.

līlā, 'play, game'.

liṅga, 106, 156. Phallic symbol of Siva, generally represented engaged in the female organ—*yoni*.

Liṅgāyat, a Śaivite sect from central Deccan, distinguished in particular by the individual liṅga which each member wears around his neck.

loka, 'world', a region of the universe distinguished by those who inhabit or rule it.

Madhva, a Vedāntic philosopher, a 'dualist' who maintained the distinction between God and individual ātmans; thirteenth century.

Mahābhārata, the more voluminous of the two brahmanic epics (the other being the *Rāmāyaṇa*). It is attributed to the mythical Vyāsa and deals with the 'lunar dynasty'. Its composition spanned several centuries, and it has different regional versions. Overall, it appears to have already been established by the first centuries AD.

mahākalpa, 101. Name of the period which constitutes a life of Brahmā.

mahān ātmā, 92, 95. 'The Great Ātman' (in the masculine nominative form). The name given to that level of yogic ascension in which empirical finitude is transcended. In the *Purāṇas, mahān* (or the neuter *mahat*) is the corresponding level of cosmogony.

mama, literally/'of myself', 'mine'. Together with *aham*, it circumscribes the sphere of the *ahaṃkāra*.

manas, both an internal organ and the *sensus communis* which relates the ātman to all empirical data.

mānasapratyaksa, 80. 'Mental perception', that is, perception through the manas, without the participation of the external sense organs.

Maṇḍana Miśra, a 'non-dualist' Vedāntic philosopher, more or less contemporary with Śaṅkara.

mantra, a formula which, accompanying a rite, is always characterized by the fact that what counts is not its meaning but rather its utterance at a particular moment. This is also the term for a formula which is given to a new initiate into a sect and which he is expected to repeat as part of his daily ritual.

Manu, the Adam of several brahmanic myths. He is the supposed author of the most orthodox treatise of laws (*The Laws of Manu*), of indeterminate date.

māyā, 75. The power of illusion attributed to various gods or ascetics. In 'non-dualist' Vedānta, it is the cosmos itself, conceived as an illusion. It came to be identified with Nature—*prakṛti.*

Mīmāṃsa, 28–9. One of the six systems of orthodox philosophy, the one built up to generate the rules for interpreting the Vedic texts (essentially those of the *Black Yajurveda*). Vedānta borrows many of its concepts, and works concerned with dharma make use of its rules of textual interpretation.

mokṣa, 23. Liberation from rebirth. The opposite of *saṃsāra*, transmigration. It is one of the goals of man'.

mumukṣu, 'one who desires liberation'.

Nārāyaṇa, 110. One of the names of Viṣṇu, more especially in his form as a god sleeping on the serpent Śeṣa and the primordial ocean, during the cosmic night.

Nāṭyaśāstra, 'Treatise of dramatic art and dance'. Attributed to the mythical sage Bharata. First centuries AD?

nīti, 'conduct', the 'art of conduct' for someone who seeks to achieve a definite material end—*artha*.

Nītiśāstra, 'Treatise of the art of conduct' (to ensure success). A set of large overlapping collections of aphorisms. They complete the *Arthaśāstra*, but apply to any man who seeks artha.

Nyāya, 74. One of the six systems of orthodox philosophy, which was built up around the brahmanic theory of logic. It is associated with Vaiśeṣika.

Pāñcarātra, one of the tantric Vaiṣṇavite sects of South India. Its *Saṃhitās* inspire the ritual that is found in the majority of Vaiṣṇavite temples in the south.

Pārvatī, one of the auspicious names for the goddess when she is married to Śiva. She is the daughter of Parvata, 'the mountain.'

paśu, 'livestock', 'sacrificial victim'. In South Indian Śaivism, the term is also applied to individual souls, distinct from God who is their master.

Patañjali, supposed author of the *Yogasūtras*, the fundamental text of classical yoga. Approximately second or third centuries AD

pati, 'lord, master'. The Vedic Rudra-Śiva, who was already called Paśupati, 'Lord of Livestock' or 'of sacrificial victims', is, in South Indian tantric Śaivism, the *pati* of the *paśus* who are the creatures.

pradhāna, 'primary basis'. One of the names of original Nature in the *Purāṇas* and in Sāṅkhya.

prakṛti, 'primordial form''. One of the names of original Nature in the *Purāṇas* and in Sāṅkhya. Its feminine form allows tantric identification with Śakti.

prasāda, (divine) 'grace', symbolized by a small amount of consecrated food given to the worshipper in a temple in return for the offering he has himself brought.

preman, 'love' and more especially the transcendent love of the divine couple.

Purāṇas, a group of texts belonging to the Tradition. Theoretically, the Purāṇas relate the origins of humanity and of Indian history. In fact they present, in a form accessible to all, the substance of treatises of ritual, codes of laws, the description of holy places, etc.—everything a Hindu needs to know in order to act correctly in all circumstances. Composed at many different times.

Puruṣa, 24. 'Male; man'. One of the names of the Absolute (capitalized in this case).

puruṣārtha, 'goal of man.'

Rādhā, 145–7. Kṛṣṇa's favourite *gopī*, a character who seems to appear quite late in Kṛṣṇa bhakti, and who contributes in a marked way to the eroticization of its mystic expression. In tantric sects, Rādhā, transformed into the Śakti, becomes more important than Kṛṣṇa.

rājan, 'king' (in compounds: *rāja-*).

rajas, 96. One of the three components or *guṇas* of nature, the one which represents activity and causes there to be movement.

Rāmānuja, the Vedāntic philosopher of the 'non-dualism of the qualified'; eleventh century. The originator of the Śrīvaiṣṇava sect.

Rāmāyaṇa, one of the two great brahmanic epics. The saga of the ideal king of the 'solar dynasty', Rāma, who is also an avatāra of Viṣṇu. Attributed to Vālmīki. Composed over several centuries?

rasa, 124–8. 'flavour, relish,' hence 'agreeable emotion', aesthetic, erotic or mystical, or all three at once.

rāsalīlā, 'game (made) of rasa'.

rasāsvāda, 'enjoyment of rasa'.

ṛṣi, mythic 'seers' who, according to some, transmitted the Revelation. According to others, they 'saw' this Revelation and transmitted its contents in a form accessible to the common man. In the epics and *Purāṇas*, they are exemplary characters, half-renouncers, half-householders, who serve as teachers or who are the heroes of didactic myths.

Rudra, 97. 'The Terrible'. The most common name of Śiva in the Vedic literature.

sādhaka, one who devotes himself to the pursuit of the Absolute or, at times, more particularly to supernatural powers connected with this quest (*siddhi*).

sādhana, process leading towards an internal realization of the mode of being of the Absolute, which ultimately amounts to identification with the Absolute.

Śakti, 149–50. Divine 'power, energy'. The feminine aspect of the divinity which ensures its manifestation as the cosmos.

Śakuntalā, a dramatic work by Kālidāsa, whose subject matter is borowed from the *Mahābhārata*.

samādhi, technical yogic term which designates the highest form of mystic contemplation.

Saṃhitās, 18. Collections of versified hymns. The most ancient texts of the Vedic Revelation. 148. Set of texts regarded by some as revealed, to which the Vaiṣṇavite Tantras refer.

saṃsāra, 23. 'Transmigration'. Opposite of *mokṣa*.

Śaṅkara, 74–5. The founder of non-dualist Vedānta. The works of which his authorship is established consist of commentaries on the major *Upaniṣads*, the *Bhagavad Gītā* and the *Brahmasūtras*.

Sāṅkhya, 118. One of the six orthodox philosophical systems. It was associated, at a very early date, with yoga, but probably not in its classical form (that of the *Sāṅkhya-kārikās*), which is relatively late.

Sāṅkhya-kārikās, basic text of the Sāṅkhya system (fourth century?).

sannyāsa, 24. 'Renunciation' and more specifically the orthodox form of renunciation of the world.

sannyāsin, 27. 'Renouncer', in particular a man of high caste who has renounced the world to become a religious ascetic.

śāntarasa, 'rasa of one who is pacified'. The aesthetic and religious emotion arising from a pacified vision of things, that is close to Absolute truth.

śānti, 'peace'. The term has always had a religious connotation. It is the peace known to one who has realized absolute Reality.

śāstra, an authoritative 'treatise', whose author, whether mythic or historical, is always a Brahman.

satī, the perfect wife, faithful to her husband. In a secondary sense, she is the widow who throws herself on the funeral pyre of her husband.

sattva, 96. The first of the three components or *guṇas* of Nature, the one which is luminous, pure and pacified and which predominates in the being which accedes to Knowledge.

sevā, 'service', forbidden to the Brahman, and the only activity permitted to the Śūdra.

Śivā, 97. One of the two great gods of bhakti. His role as a catalyst of impurity in the Vedic sacrifice (under the name Rudra) causes him to be especially connected with those forms of renunciation which are most removed from the orthodox path.

Skanda, the son of Śiva and Pārvatī, although in the various myths of his birth he is born of the seed of Śiva but not from the womb of a woman. He is already known to the *Chāndogya Upaniṣad* (VII. 26.2).

smṛti, lit. 'memory'. This is the Tradition, as opposed to Revelation, a great mass of texts including additions to the ritualistic parts of the Revelation, treatises of socio-religious laws (*Dharma-śāstra*), the two epics (*Rāmāyaṇa* and *Mahābhārata*) and the *Purāṇas*. This Tradition is capitalized to distinguish it from tradition in general.

Śrī, see *Lakṣmī*. The two names are practically synonymous.

Śrīvaiṣṇavas, a sect of Vaiṣṇavite Brahmans of South India, who combine worship of Viṣṇu and Śrī. They have a Pāñcarātra ritual, venerate the twelve Vaiṣṇavite bhaktas whose poetical and mystical works are the origin of the sect's whole literature, and follow the philosophy of Rāmānuja.

śruti, 18. Literally, 'hearing'. Used to designate the set of fundamental texts of brahmanism that are regarded as revealed.

Śūdra, 20. Fourth varṇa of brahmanic society, that of the servant castes. Not admitted to Vedic ritual.

svadharma, 45 ff. Each varṇa's 'own dharma'.

svāmin, title conferred on renouncers and used to address them. *Swami* is the usual form in English.

svarga, 'Heaven', which, in Vedic literature, represents the abode of the gods and that of men of high caste after their death, if they have been faithful to their dharma. In the *Purāṇas*, it is only the upper part of the 'triple world' organized by dharma. It will be destroyed at the time of cosmic reabsorption.

svārtha, 55. Formed from *sva-artha*, 'personal interest'.

Śvetāśvatara Upaniṣad, 28. One of the yogic *Upaniṣads*, probably more recent than the *Kaṭha*, but also related to the *Black Yajurveda*.

swami, see *svāmin*.

Taittirīya, name of a very important school of the *Black Yajurveda*, which, from the *Saṃhitās* to the *Upaniṣads* which it contains, provides the revealed starting point for many myths or epic and purāṇic speculations. Its ritualistic part provides most of the basic text from which Mīmāṃsā built up the rules for interpreting the Veda.

tamas, 'darkness'. One of the three *guṇas* which constitute Nature, the one which predominates in animals. It connotes ignorance and inertia.

Tantras, 148. A set of texts, based on the Āgamas and the Samhitās, which present a teaching sometimes of ritual, sometimes of yogic practices; the common element is a conception of the divine as formed of the union of the god and his *śakti*. In their extreme forms, the Tantras place the śakti above the god.

tāntrika, a member of a tantric sect.

tejas, the burning and shining heat that especially characterizes gods, warriors and ascetics.

trailokya, 41. The 'three-worlds'—earth, heaven and hell—governed by dharma.

Trimūrti, 100. Level of manifestation of the deity in which it makes itself triple in order to preside over the different states of the cosmos.

Umā, one of the auspicious names of the goddess, wife of Śiva.

Upaniṣads, 17. A group of texts belonging to the Vedic Revelation, which preach deliverance from rebirths and show the path to the Absolute. Until recent times, the different sects continued to compose *Upaniṣads*, but these are not attached to a Vedic school and are not part of the Revelation.

Vaiśeṣika, 74. One of the six systems of orthodox philosophy; it provides the theory of the categories of being. Associated with Nyāya.

Vaiṣṇava, worshipper of Viṣṇu (the common English form is Vaiṣṇavite). Name of the Bengali sect begun by Caitanya, which in fact worships Kṛṣṇa as the highest form of the divine.

Vaiśya, 20. The third varṇa of brahmanic society, that of farmers and merchants.

varṇa, 20. 'Class'. Brahmanic society is ideally divided into four varṇas. The term designates simultaneously a social function, a status, and a specific relationship to Vedic ritual.

Veda, 18, 90. Literally, 'knowledge'. This is Knowledge *par excellence*, the Revelation. The texts which constitute it are divided into four major groups which form the four Vedas: *Ṛgveda, Yajurveda, Sāmaveda* and *Atharvaveda*. The first three correspond respectively to three categories of priests in the Vedic sacrifice. The fourth, which contains many magic formulae, is considered inferior.

vedānta, 18. 'Completion of the Veda'. This term is used to refer to the Vedic Upaniṣads, 26. Classical philosophical system which conceptualizes the teaching of the *Upaniṣads* on the Absolute and liberation (a capital letter distinguishes it in this sense). It is sub-divided into numerous schools.

Viṣṇu, 97. One of the two great gods of bhakti, who, because of his original relationship with the Vedic sacrifice, remains most closely connected to the orthodoxy.

Viṣṇu-purāṇa, 104. One of the most important of the principal Vaiṣṇavite Purāṇas. It is perhaps older than the *Bhāgavata-purāṇa*, if their relative ages are to be determined according to the degree of development of an emotional bhakti centred on the cowherd Kṛṣna.

vyaṅgya, 'manifestable', 'that can be suggested'.

Vyāsa. A mythic Brahman who is regarded as the original 'seer' of the Vedas and the author of the *Mahābhārata* (in which he appears as a character) and the *Purāṇas*. He also goes under the name of Kṛṣṇa Dvaipāyana and, like Kṛṣṇa himself is held to be an incarnation of Viṣṇu-Nārāyaṇa. He is the Brahman counterpart to the Kṣatriya Kṛṣṇa.

yoga, 27. Set of psycho-physiological technique which vary greatly from one school to another. In principle, the goal is to achieve experience of the 'liberated' state in this life, but it is also seen as way of attaining supra-natural capacities. The methods include physical exercises to achieve control over the unstriped muscles and mental exercises to empty thought of all empirical content and maintain it in perfect immobility. The classical system (118, distinguished by capital Y) is what orthodox thought has retained from these concrete yogas.

yogin, adept of yoga; feminine *yoginī*. The common English form is *yogi*.

yoni, female symbol, a vulva in which the liṅga is engaged.

Yudhiṣṭhira, 57, 70. The eldest of the five Pāṇḍavas, the descendants of the 'lunar dynasty' and the central figures of the *Mahābhārata*.

yugas, 102. The name of the cosmic periods which come in groups of four and each of which indicates a given state of perfection or degradation of dharma. An avatāra of Viṣṇu generally appears at the time of transition from one yuga to another.